Trajectories of Popular Expression

Forms, Histories, Contexts

Trajectories of Popular Expression

Forms, Histories, Contexts

Edited by
Navneet Sethi
Ananya Saha

AAKAR

Trajectories of Popular Expression: Forms, Histories, Contexts
Edited by Navneet Sethi and Ananya Saha

First Published 2019

ISBN 978-93-5002-575-8

Published by
AAKAR BOOKS
28 E Pocket IV, Mayur Vihar Phase I
Delhi 110 091 India
aakarbooks@gmail.com

Laser Typeset at
Sakshi Computers, Delhi

Cover Illustration by
Omnipresent Art Group

Printed at
D.K. Fine Art Press, Delhi 110052

Contents

PART IV

The Popular and the Narrative Alternative

PART V

The Gender and the Popular

PART VI

The Popular and the Digital Media

Foreword

The recognition of the category of “popular culture” as a subject of serious and creative scholarly study has marked a breakthrough in the ways in which contemporary culture is now conceived and analysed. While anthropology and its poor cousin, Folk Studies, have in practice long been concerned with forms of culture manifesting at the grassroots, they have rarely thought of it them as representing ‘popular culture’, even if, in fact, that is exactly what they were studying and documenting. While there is no one source for the study of popular culture, a great deal of credit can go to the Birmingham School of Cultural Studies, that drew systematic attention to the intersection of cultural production and consumption with class and ethnicity. Much the same period saw in sociologists like Pierre Bourdieu examining the nature of taste and its links to class and to cultural participation (for example in his work on photography as a popular form of creativity), an emerging interest in previously neglected but important areas of popular culture such as sport, and a shift from the *sociology* of everyday life (as in the work of Erving Goffman) to an interest in the *culture* of everyday life.

The emerging concerns formed the basis of what we now call ‘cultural studies’ and have brought into scholarly and activist discourse a whole range of subjects that were previously marginalized in mainstream social science work—feminism and gender studies in general, the media and increasingly the ‘digital world’ in which so many of us now live, technology, critical theory, post-colonialism, ethnic studies, new forms of art history and literary criticism and the democratization of cultural consumption and its increasing globalization. Japanese popular culture in the form of the ubiquitous *anime* and *manga* for example have become world-wide phenomena, as have the Hollywood movie, its Bollywood equivalent and British pop music, certainly beginning with the Beatles. This has had many consequences—the recognition of the authenticity of popular culture, not as a debased form of 'high' culture, but as representing the reality of lived culture for most people, the legitimizing or liberation of new forms of visuality, writing and reading (for example the graphic novel), and the acceptance into social science and cultural studies discourse of significant but neglected themes such as the emotions, the body, the erotic and the bizarre, and links these in turn to the large zone of popular literature and its many manifestations in such forms as comics, crime fiction, science fiction and romance, and through these to areas such as popular music in its many forms, dance, film, sport and the spatial distribution of these activities in clubs, specialized book shops, music and DVD stores, cinemas and other such locations. Some would certainly argue that it is through popular culture that the 're-enchantment' of our over managerial, bureaucratic and technological civilization is happening—think of Harry Potter, *Narnia, The Lord of the Rings* and the many other examples of 'fantasy' films and books that populate our screens, libraries and bookshops.

All this can have significant political implications: the return for example of the communal and the "tribes" which the French sociologist Michel Maffesoli sees as largely replacing class as the ever shifting groupings in which people increasingly locate themselves precisely around cultural consumption—the jazz lovers, football fans, cooking club members, and a myriad other often ephemeral, but real, temporary but sometimes long term 'communities' which defy the individualism of other dimensions of contemporary society. Popular culture is also linked closely to the nature of social movements with which they are closely associated through music, dance forms, visual arts, theatre and other cultural manifestations. It also forms a significant element in the cultural economy of any society, and the development of the "cultural industries" which international agencies such as UNESCO are now promoting usually means in practice the cultivation and marketing of forms of popular culture. But of course, even as popular culture can be implicitly or explicitly critical of mainstream culture and its political interests, it is also necessary to be critical of many forms of popular culture which are all too often themselves trivial, violent, sexist, social conservative and non-socially transformative.

At their best, the forms of popular culture point towards what might be called a "transformative aesthetics"—the recovery of the everyday and its exposure to the light of day and its inclusion within the universe of scholarly discourse. This book shows how this might be done, not only in the choice of themes by entirely younger scholars and those as yet early in their academic careers, but also by thoroughly contextualizing those themes in the Indian context. Here we find insightful essays on caste and its representation in contemporary popular media, including the graphic novel, popular music, gender as it appears in the South Asian context, media and the digital world as it is now manifesting itself in India. By these means the authors take the framework given to them by the notion of popular culture and show not only how it might be applied in places far from its geographical and intellectual origin, but also themselves transform that framing concept, by showing how it means different things in different contexts. The late major art critic, John Berger once rightly said that "Never again will a single story be told as though it were the only one". This book, and the varied and vibrant essays that it contains, show the truth of this statement. Here new stories are told and told in new ways and in a culturally rich context that will be unfamiliar to many international scholars of popular culture. It signals an agenda of studies that point to the recovery and appreciation of many aspects of Indian culture as it is actually lived, and illustrates brilliantly the originality, insight and creativity of the rising generation of young writers and researchers in this country, and beyond that suggests a model for the ways in which the Humanities can be transformed to fit the contemporary age.

John Clammer

Professor

Jindal Schools of Liberal
Arts and Humanities

Preface

It is with tremendous pride and pleasure, shining forth brightly from within a veil of inexpressible sadness, that I present before the reader this priceless volume, comprising articles on different forms, histories and contexts of popular cultural expression—the swansong of my departed colleague Dr. Navneet Sethi. The sadness that I still fell at the most untimely departure of my dear colleague and editor of this volume, Navneet Sethi, is far outshined by its sheer brilliance, the depth of the articles carefully curated in it, the issues they address...a most fitting document to keep Navneet alive in our memories forever.

The articles included in this volume mostly emerge from a National Young Researchers' Conference, organized by the UGC-SAP-DSA-I of the Centre for English Studies, Jawaharlal Nehru University, New Delhi, on February 16-17, 2017. To quote from the CfP of that conference, and thus to understand the original objectives that lay behind what finally turned out to be the current collection:

> Illustrating the form of technique of modern storytelling, Steven had once said, "People have forgotten how to tell a story. Stories don't have a middle or an end any more. They usually have a beginning that never stops beginning." New narrative forms in storytelling have been variegated, ranging from graphic novels to chick lit to digitally produced hypertexts. These often involve open-ended plots, retelling of myths or classic texts and more. [...] The proliferation of these new narrative forms alerts us to the substantial characteristic of the popular being formalized, with an impetus to innovate and reinterpret. [...] Stimulated by such an idea, it might be intriguing to engage with the attempt to delve

into both the genesis and genealogy of these popular and new narrative forms, as academic concepts as well as historical realities. Within the ambit of this question would be encompassed the need to review these popular adaptations and revisions, as structured by a persuasion to stay abreast of the times; a fascination which debunks the inherent historicity of the classified 'popular'.

While these were the original, somewhat abstract, objectives of the conference, it appears that as the contributions started taking shape, they started falling together in place, like pieces of a jigsaw puzzle, with a key theme of marginalization and the dialectics of assertion and mainstreaming or appropriation seeming to tie together these different 'trajectories of the popular' across different forms, histories, and contexts. The articles started pointing towards common issues, common themes, and common concerns for marginality within popular cultural forms, carving out of the contents of the current volume a coherent narrative as it were, as they kept exploring trajectories of diverse popular articulations through diverse forms, histories, and contexts.

So, what are the diverse 'forms' of the popular, and the 'histories' and 'contexts' of diverse registers of marginality and its assertion and appropriation articulated therein that the contributions anthologised in this book choose to examine? There are, as examples of 'popular forms', the graphic narrative, pop music, graffiti, pop art, advertisement, comic strips, web films, and folk and traditional narrative practices like institutionalised art, *dastan*, *qissa*, and *mangalkavya*, and on the side of 'contexts' of marginalization and assertion are caste, tribal identity, the subcultural and its appropriation, nationalism, regional assertions, religion, age, gender, sexuality, and the category of the 'author' itself. As these paradigms of the forms, histories, and contexts of the popular criss-cross their paths, we find one after the other fifteen brilliant essays spread over six sections.

The first section comprises three chapters which look at popular expressions of caste through Rituparna Sengupta's exposition on graphic novels from the publishers Campfire and Navayana, Prerna Trehan's article on the Punjabi pop music phenomenon 'Chamar Pop', and Vandana's contribution specifically on the graphic novel *Bhimayana*. The two chapters in the second section look at the interfaces between the traditional and the popular, taking us through questions of institutionalization and it subversion in art through Sanchita Khurana's study of graffiti and street art, and Samarth Singhal's discussion of the eclectic 'pop' art of Bhupen Khakhar. The three chapters in the third section focus specifically on the graphic narrative, with Shreya Sangai looking at the questioning of nationalism in the graphic novel *Munnu*, Bibiana Ryntathiang exploring the use of folktales from the north-eastern region of India in the graphic narrative *Hotel at the End of the World*, and Ananya Saha probing into the categories of age and religiosity in 'Muslim' Manga. The three chapters in the fourth section of the book look at the appropriation of traditional narrative forms of experimental and hybridizing output through Soumava Maiti's exploration of how Salman Rushdie uses the medieval Islamicate *dastan* mode of narrativization in a couple of his works, Reeti Basu's survey of how the medieval Bengali epic *Chandimangal* gets appropriated into contemporary 'folk' visual art which itself gets further appropriated into a commercial circuit, and Anindita Ghosh's study of how the medieval Islamicate *qissa* mode of storytelling travels down time with special focus on Akbar-Birbal narratives. The two chapters in the fifth section look specifically at gender and sexuality in the popular through Saheli Biswas's article on the handling of queerness in advertisements, and Sourav Chatterjee's survey of the representation of masculinity in Bengali comic strips. And, the two chapters in the sixth and final section of the volume take us into the domain of digital culture and the question of the 'author' in it through Sayanty Chatterjee's exploration of two short web films on mythological subjects, and Naomi Jose's analysis of web appropriations of *Pride and Prejudice* and their implications for the authorial figure of Jane Austen.

The chapter relentlessly demonstrate how forms the popular, working in different contexts and having different histories—at contradistinction as it is form more authoritative and normative modes of cultural articulation, and as fertile as it is as ground for hybridization and challenging purities—becomes an appropriate medium for dealing with questions of marginality beyond potentially sectarian and fundamentalist assertions of identitarianism, leading to resistive and transformative negotiations instead. While all these chapters are written by 'young researchers'—doctoral candidates and early career academics—they are preceded by a most erudite Foreword by the internationally renowned cultural studies scholar and professor John Clammer, who also delivered the Keynote at the aforementioned conference, tracing the terrain of popular cultural studies, and its trajectories that enable a transformative aesthetics.

So, this is in short the book that I have the proud privilege of writing the 'preface' too, knowing fully well that I have not been able to do a fraction of justice to what the original editor of the volume, Navneet Sethi, would have done could she have written the 'Introduction' to the volume herself, something that her readers are now forever robbed of, due to her sudden and tragic demise. However, I am sure this book has Navneet written all over it—the Navneet of multiple marginalities: a differently abled woman from a minority community who specialised in literatures of ethnic minorities of America; and the Navneet of popular cultural assertions: one who loved, studied, and researched on jazz, hip-hop, reggae—and readers will indeed find Navneet coming alive from every page of this book. What a last piece of work this is, what a legacy to leave behind for generations of friends, colleagues, students to remember her by forever, what a way to sign off!

Saugata Bhaduri
Professor
Centre for English Studies
Jawaharlal Nehru University

PART I

Popular Expressions of Caste

CHAPTER 1

Casting Caste in Graphic Narratives

Rituparna Sengupta

The Indian graphic novel, henceforth 'graphic narrative'[1], is in a vibrant, experimental stage, and its best-loved titles are adaptations from mythology (primarily the Ramayana and the Mahabharata), or biographies and social commentaries. Often, these influences can overlap—mythological transcreations can throw considerable light on the past and the present socio-political practices, and graphic biographies can present alternative accounts of mythology and history. Both these strategies are important tools in the contemporary Dalit resistance movements[2]. The theme of 'casteism' significantly informs in three graphic narratives—the Campfire graphic novel *The Offering—The Story of Ekalavya and Dronacharya*, Navayana's *A Gardener in the Wasteland—Jotiba Phule's Fight for Liberty* and Navayana's *Bhimayana—Experiences of Untouchability*. All these titles, incidentally, were published in 2011. Since a detailed exploration of each is outside the scope of this article, I will concentration on specific selective textual analysis of the three, including their aesthetics, towards elucidating their contribution to the discourse of caste in the popular realm.

The Offering—The Story of Ekalavya and Dronacharya

The Campfire 'mythology' series is a revamped Amar Chitra Katha project, self-professedly more sophisticated in both, graphic and textual components. Campfire's 'mission statement' reads: 'To entertain and educate young minds by creating unique illustrated books that recount stories of human values, arouse curiosity in the world around us, and inspire with tales of great deeds of unforgettable people' (Pathak and Kumar, 2011, inside cover). They have consistently won Comic-Con and other comics awards and several of their titles have found a place on the 'recommended reading' lists for pupils in CBSE schools. Keeping pace with the postmodern preference of micronarratives and alternative points-of-view, Campfire's mythological titles present well-known stories from new and 'interesting' perspectives. However, these do not present much of a challenge to the master narratives they seek to re-present[3]. *The Offering*, written by Hansa Pathak and illustrated by Naresh Kumar, is a curious exception. The book's blurb describes the story of Ekalavya (drawn from the *Mahabharata*) as the 'ungraceful shadow' that fell on the traditional reading of the Pandavas as the 'good side'. The frame narrative consists of Vishnu recounting how once Narada Muni in disguise at the Kurukshetra camp, narrated the story of Ekalavya to two incredulous soldiers, while a small boy, Eka, who turns out to be Ekalavya's son, tried to gain admission to Drona's tent[4].

The caste theme finds the most explicit mention in the competition between Arjuna and Ekalavya. They become rivals for the limited resource that is the teacher Drona, and the contemporary debate over 'merit' and 'reservation' is played out in a refreshingly reverse manner. The conventional hero of popular lore, Arjuna, is introduced as a borderline mediocre student, who despite being ambitious and hardworking, never quite overcomes his insecurity and becomes arrogant instead. When Ekalavya comes in search of a teacher, Drona refuses him, asking "How will you understand something for which you have no natural aptitude?" (Pathak and Kumar, 2011, 17). Drona's non-acceptance of Ekalavya is presented to us as heavily ironical as Drona himself, being a Brahmin, 'overcame his caste' by training as an instructor in arms. A turning point in Drona's life was his appeal to his 'old friend' Drupada for financial assistance, when Drupada mocked him and did not 'recognise' him as an equal and a friend. Drona had got infuriated and made revenge his life's mission and yet, he later 'blesses' Ekalavya, saying "May you be content with your lot in this life." (Pathak and Kumar, 2011, 31). An innocent Ekalavya wonders, "Why would a man, who had himself transcended caste, deny me?" (Pathak and Kumar, 2011, 35).

In two parallel narratives set across different time frames, Ekalavya literally fashions his teacher into a statue on the lines of the image in his mind, and his son Eka bursts forth into the tent of the man he believes to have been his father's guru. Ekalavya naively believes 'Between the banyan tree and the river, where Dronacharya's statue stood, was a timeless place. A place where Ekalavya could attract no one's awe. Or jealousy.' (Pathak and Kumar, 2011, 38). But his skill, nurtured in seclusion, becomes an affront to Arjuna's pride. Importantly, Ekalavya is no natural talent. Eager to learn, he fumbles repeatedly, until he draws inspiration from his environment and finds his particular style. His prowess thus derives not from inborn talent, but from consistent dedication and hard work. He needs no guru and significantly, excels when he forgets his hero worship of Drona. Neither in technique nor training, could he call Drona his preceptor; and yet the self-taught boy cannot let go of his compulsive yearning for a teacher from a superior caste. We discern an unresolved conflict between the languages of 'seva' and self-help, a distinction made by Gopal Guru in context of Dalit thought. (Guru, 2011, 41)

The student-teacher relationship is complicated at several levels. In a fit of jealousy after seeing Ekalavya's skill, Arjuna accuses Drona of being a liar and Drona sees an insolent, diffident and unexceptional student before him, 'stammering, stuttering and hungry for success.' (Pathak and Kumar, 2011, 47). Arjuna too panics as he realises that 'one tool could be easily discarded for another...And he was a tool for Dronacharya's own ambition' (Pathak and Kumar, 2011, 50)[5]. Ekalavya, who overhears the exchange between Arjuna and Drona after his self-mutilation, finally realises that his vow of duty to Drona was pointless and his sacrifice entirely unnecessary[6]. Here, we see a disillusioned student, a teacher trapped by his promises and in general, a world where students and teachers share a utilitarian relationship, very different from the romanticised world of the guru-shishya parampara in popular Indian discourse.

Significantly, Ekalavya chooses to remember and recount his story as a happy one. Therefore, the shock awaiting his son

Eka when he discovers the truth in quite considerable. Ekalavya's story is a tragic one, but one which reveals more about a flawed teacher than an obedient student[7]. Narada chooses to tell the story that Ekalavya kept back. "Why should others suffer from it not being told?" asks Narada (67). Who are these 'others', one might ask? Perhaps, those they are descendants of Ekalavya (like Eka) who might be languishing in their fool's paradise, replicating old structures of domination, while dreaming of a new identity. One is reminded of Omprakash Valmiki recounting his father's dignified challenge to his teacher in his autobiography, *Joothan*, "Who is that teacher, that progeny of Dronacharya, who forces my son to sweep?" (Valmiki, 2003, 6). *The Offering* is a story that debunks the popular myth of the 'selflessly obedient' student and refuses to celebrate the self-seeking, flawed teacher, whose name has inspired awards, townships and metro stations alike in contemporary India. Through its challenging of mainstream reading of mythology, it echoes the need for reclaiming Ekalavya as an icon of caste victimhood, as expressed in this poem by Shashikant Hilgoenkar,

> If you had kept your thumb,
>
> History would have happened somewhat differently
>
> But you gave your thumb,
>
> And history also became theirs.
>
> Ekalavya, since that day they have not even given you a glance.
>
> Forgive me, Ekalavya, I won't be fooled now by their sweet words.
>
> My thumb will never be broken. (Shashikant Hilgoenkar)

A Gardener in the Wasteland—Jotiba Phule's Fight for Liberty

A Gardener in the Wasteland is 'the first instance of 'a historical work (that) has been interpreted as a graphic book in India' ("A Gardener", 2012). Jotirao Phule's treatise *Slavery* (*Gulamgiri*, 1873) was a scathing exposé of Brahminical orthodoxy and its shameful enslavement of India's oppressed castes. Inspired by Thomas Paine's *'Rights of Man'* and the enlightenment ideals of the French Revolution, Phule dedicated *Slavery* to "the good people of the United States as a token of admiration for their sublime disinterested and self-sacrificing devotion in the cause of Negro slavery and with an earnest desire that my countrymen will take their noble example as their guide in the emancipation of their Sudra Brethren from the trammels of Brahmin thraldom"[8] ("Slavery by Mahatma Phule: Introduction", 2005). One of his primary aims is to show that 'important chapters from the history-books of India written so far have been deleted' ('Slavery by Mahatma Phule: Introduction', 2005) so that the 'oppressed castes' may realise how they have been duped by the Brahmins for ages. The book is in the form of a Socratic dialogue between Jotiba and his pupil Dhondiba, presented to us by Savitribai Phule, Jotiba's wife and his partner in the struggle against the Brahminical and patriarchal regime. The frame narrative of the graphic text is in the form of a conversation between Srividya Natarajan and Aparajita Ninan, the creators of the book, discussing Phule while working on the book and travelling through the city, coming across continuing instances of caste prejudice. In this way, they say, they 'marked who (they) were, without claiming transparency' (Natarajan and Ninan, 2011: 2016, 126). The graphic narrative presents itself as 'a manifesto of resistance' in 'today's climate of intolerance' (Natarajan and Ninan, 2011: 2016, back cover). The title of the book refers to the attempt at the weeding out of the ugly, overgrowth of caste hierarchy from the wasteland of orthodox Hinduism, and acknowledges the traditional occupation of Phule's ancestors, who belonged to the 'low caste' gardener community.

The visual treatment of the book in sharp black-and-white, is reminiscent of Joe Sacco's *Palestine* and Marjane Satrapi's *Persepolis* and is in keeping with the stark and unforgiving texture of Phule's vigorous arguments. The deliberate lack of colour is suitable not only because it is the trusted medium of sombre graphic journalism, but also because here, it carries no connotations of skin colour, race and caste. Suitably, the book follows a caricature style, where Phule's antagonist, one among the 'Brahmin mob', is depicted as hirsute, potbellied and slothful, sometimes bandit-like, sometimes metonymic, a slobbering mouth, and always bearing the marks of his caste.

The authors in the Afterword express their fascination with Savitribai, about whom they profess to know little; she is nevertheless creatively imagined and foregrounded often by them. Her (and Jotiba's) struggle for the education of unprivileged girls is compared to that of civil rights activists in America. Natarajan and Ninan wonder why history books carry no mention of Savitribai and conclude tersely, 'Non-Brahmin Female Activist and Thinker. Wife of Bad Person who Challenged the Hindu Way of Life. Censored.' (Natarajan and Ninan, 2011: 2016, 17) In the accompanying panels on successive pages, we have a 'prohibited' sign painted across Savitribai's face, which she proceeds to break free out of. The tyranny over women is depicted in several other panels. In an important illustration, a circle of women partly comprising widows with shaven heads form a pyramid, while Savitribai aims a stick at a hanging pot entrapping a young widow, held up strenuously by what appears to be Lord Vishnu and a Brahmin behind him (Natarajan and Ninan, 2011: 2016, 96) a clear revision of the *matki-phod* ritual from Janmashthami. Feminist stalwarts like Pandita Ramabai and Tarabai Shinde who were the Phules' contemporaries, also find mention[9].

Some striking illustrations in the book are worthy of special mention. On one double spread, caste injunctions in *Manusmriti* are transposed into images of horror when literally visualised, like the tongues of Shudras being ripped out and molten lead being poured into their ears. (Natarajan and Ninan, 2011: 2016, 24-25) This set of images is positioned alongside those of the Ku Klux Klan hanging 'negroes' from trees. In the foreground, the Brahmin and Ku Klux Klan villains share the 'strange fruits' of their oppression. In the chapter 'The Weedbed of Myth', which our gardeners, the Phules attack with their sickles, Jotiba systematically questions and rips apart Hindu mythology enshrined in the Vedas as—'false letters of introduction' (Natarajan and Ninan, 2011: 2016, 50)—that the Brahmins have imposed on a visibly hypnotised mass consisting of other castes, to legitimise their supremacy and justify the exploitation of Sudras. With a blasphemously comic touch and somewhat tedious manner, Phule holds up a book 'full of holes' depicting an uneasy Brahma, in between giving birth to the four varnas, menstruating from the mouth and having a sanitary napkin taped across it. (Natarajan and Ninan, 2011: 2016, 32-33). In 'The Roots of Tyranny', an arresting illustration displays the hierarchical caste structure as a multi-level machine carrying people from the different castes arranged according to occupation, and the whole pulled by means of chains, by hordes of labouring outcastes, while the Brahmins throw down their books at the masses (Natarajan and Ninan, 2011: 2016, 72-73). Elsewhere, Hinduism is symbolically transformed into a colossal giant Brahmin body squelching in both hands, lower caste men and women. Arrows marking 'nationalism' and 'freedom' point away, indicating Phule's realisation that Hinduism cannot be the basis of the two (Natarajan and Ninan, 2011: 2016, 103). Instead, since education could be the only instrument of change, the page that follows features a huge statue of the same Brahmin cracking under the assault of feather-pens dipped in ink, launched by Phule (Natarajan and Ninan, 2011: 2016, 104)[10].

Contemporary parallels are also strewn across the book—the story of Vishnu's avatars is eventually followed by a leap forward and the audacious description of Narendra Modi as 'Parasuram, updated for the 21st century, Hindutva-style' (Natarajan and Ninan, 2011: 2016, 63). Modi is depicted as playing the harp, while scenes of brutality from the Gujarat riots play out in the background. The holier-than-thou attitude of Brahmins is commented upon by quoting contemporary beef bans that are excellent proof of conflation of 'Hindu' and 'Indian' and the 'Brahminical' (Natarajan and Ninan, 2011: 2016, 79). Though Phule's book might have been directed at the oppressed castes and the British colonial administration, *A Gardener* is clearly aimed at urban, educated people from privileged castes and classes in India and beyond, with the aim of uncovering an important chapter hidden from the history books of India, in times notorious for the suppression and manipulation of accounts of history[11]. Building on Anthony Appiah, Pramod Nayar reads this in terms of a 'cosmopolitan reading' which is the 'narrative imagination that we build on when we read about the Other...' that makes us understand the stranger not as abstract but real (2016, 30). But how effective is this and does it succeed in prompting the reader to question his caste privilege? As a counter mythology, it is powerful, and as a narrative with global appeal (peppered with recognisable international events and leaders), it is an important contribution to the genre[12]. But as a conscience-provoking tool, its potential is somewhat limited, demanding as it is, in terms of great leaps of the imagination in time and space, and located as it is, in the slippery realm of mythological accounts.

Bhimayana—Experiences of Untouchability

Bhimayana is a critically-acclaimed graphic biography of Ambedkar culled from his incomplete autobiographical notes intriguingly titled 'Waiting for a Visa', interspersed with comments on modern-day incidents of caste atrocities as reported in various Indian newspapers. The artwork is by Gond artists Durgabai and Subhash Vyam and the 'story' is by Srividya Natarajan and S. Anand. The Ramayana traditionally presents folk artists with a well-known repertoire of stories to depict through various mediums. 'Bhimayana', the coinage of Subhash Vyam becomes a radical statement on the nature of stories that really ought to be preserved, transmitted and remembered and "subverts the commonsensical nationalist narrative of what constitutes an epic" (Oza, 2011, 353). The six sections of 'Waiting for a Visa' are here redivided into three, named 'Water', 'Shelter' and 'Travel'. Thus this alternative epic of heroism features the struggle for basic civic dignities (Desai, 2012). *Bhimayana* has been hailed as an important contribution to the growing world of graphic memoirs and one of the most important political comic books of our time[13]. It has subsequently been translated into various languages, Indian and foreign, and become compulsory reading for the BA English Honours students of the University of Delhi. For S. Anand, the publisher of Navayana and also the book's co-author, *Bhimayana* was an attempt to conscientise non-Dalits about Ambedkar, his personal experience of caste discrimination and the continuing oppression of the Dalits. Comparing the discrimination faced by Ambedkar with that of Gandhi, Anand poignantly asserts, "Gandhi had to travel all the way to South Africa to experience discrimination. However, if you are a Dalit, you may face acute discrimination right at your school, or in your immediate surroundings." (Anand and Vellanki, 2015, 272)

The book features the wonderfully evocative Pardhan-Gond art, which uses a combination of free-flowing Digna patterns (traditionally used to decorate walls and floors of homes) and nature imagery in imaginative combinations. This meets the Dalit discourse's need for a new visual language at once ancient and new (Nayar, 'Towards a Postcolonial', 15) and an organic form that negotiates the dialectic between the real and the ideal (Khilnani, 2015, 122). There are several reasons that make Gond art an especially suitable choice for this project. As a motif-centric art form, Gond art follows the logic of traditional storytelling in which each story is 'a nodal point in a vast network of stories, interconnected by recurring motifs' (Chatterji, 2012, 255). Individual stories thus are not discrete items with fixed beginnings and endings. The structural format of *Bhimayana* complements this artistic vision—here too, we have many interconnected stories across time and space, linked by emotional themes of pain, humiliation and empathy, rather than ones ordered by a linear sequence of chronology. Gond art's mythic quality imparts a certain decontextualised element to the narrative that curiously enough, works in its favour, evoking a collective consciousness of shared experiences across time[14]. This prevents the text from being a factual and chronological account of Ambedkar's life in the usual way of biographies[15].

Importantly, figures in Gond art do not express emotion naturalistically, but suggestively. Suitably, in the text, speech balloons are used to differentiate the intentions of its various characters, the scorpion's sting, signifying viciousness of caste sympathisers, and the human eye, to indicate mental ruminations and the bird shape, used for characters who yearn to fly free from bondage. One of the important aesthetic choices the Vyams made, in consonance with their artistic practise was to not force their characters into boxes as 'it stifles them' (Vyam et al, 2011: 2014, 100). Instead their art is 'mounted onto open spaces, where there is room for all to breathe' (Vyam et al, 2011: 2014, 100). This also contrasts starkly with the suffocating atmosphere of the numerous obstacles that its protagonist, B.R. Ambedkar finds in his quest for a life of dignity and freedom.[16].

Here, we will find no photorealism or cinematically inclined frames and perspectives of the conventional graphic novel. Instead, it is brilliantly subtle and allusive, bursting with delightful details and layers laden with meaning. In 'Water', the child Ambedkar is imagined as a fish gasping for water (Vyam et al, 2011: 2014, 21). When Ambedkar addresses the crowd at the Mahad Satyagraha, his words travel through loudspeakers and get transformed into showers sprinkling water into their parched mouths and souls (Vyam et al, 2011: 2014, 48). The animals so central to Gond art and who accompany Ambedkar through his journey, here take on a deeper resonance as a young Ambedkar remarks that animals enjoy more freedom than Mahars. In the scene where Bhimrao and his brothers are shouted at by the station master, the latter begins to morph into a predatory animal, whereas the boys collectively shrink into its prey (Vyam et al, 2011: 2014, 35). In 'Travel', the Daulatabad Fort becomes a menacing lion and the water tank seems to be infested with crocodiles as its self-appointed Muslim custodians come charging at the party of 'low caste' travellers who come to quench their thirst (Vyam et al, 2011: 2014, 86-89). Sticks and shoes become the metonym for the Parsi troublemakers who come chasing Ambedkar out of an inn in Baroda (Vyam et al, 2011: 2014, 67)[17]. In a superb full-page illustration, Ambedkar's face becomes the Kamathi Baug Public Garden where he is forced to spend long homeless hours, as the city carries on, unmindful of his predicament (Vyam et al, 2011: 2014, 72). Thus the human psyche is foregrounded and depicted in the process of absorbing new experiences and witnessing external events.

Bhimayana can indeed be seen as an example of Barthes's 'writerly text', where there is a proliferation of meanings and the reader is actively engaged in the process of meaning-making[18]. Such a text destabilises the readers' expectations. The artwork is a welcome relief from the almost overwhelming 'linear political consciousness' of the newspaper cuttings which form the accompanying parallel narrative, and is definitely more effective than the latter (Chandra, 2011, 22). Nandini Chandra correctly points out that the Gond art de-iconicises Ambedkar (who was against personality cult himself) and shows how the individual is 'inseparable from the collective destiny of his caste people' (Chandra, 2011, 23).

What is one to make of the frame narrative where a bespectacled young woman, gives the exasperated and unemployed privileged young man a dose of caste reality? His ignorance, reflected in his lack of awareness of Dalit atrocities and his argument of 'merit' vs.

quota, marks him out as the 'young urban yuppie' mentioned in *A Gardener* (Natarajan and Ninan, 2011: 2016, 126). To him is allotted the scorpion speech bubble of the venomous caste proponents. It is only at the very end when he professes a grudging respect for Ambedkar without being completely won over, that his scorpion changes into a bird. If *Bhimayana* is meant to sensitise the non-Dalit privileged class and caste-individual, the frame narrative positions the reader along the point of view of this interlocutor.

D.R. Nagaraj, in his exposition on the problem of Dalit 'cultural memory', enumerates three different strategies that have been used over time. The first showed indifference to questions of cultural symbolism and memory and concentrated on materialist objectives instead, falling prey to a deculturation that ignored the existing radical traditions within Indian culture (like Periyar). The second mode, one of radical revival, sought validation for rebellion through the construction of historical memory such that what was seen as a cause and symbol of degradation was converted into a symbol of protest and transcendence (Nagaraj, 2010,154), thus unwittingly lending strength to the status quo (sects and cults). A third mode of 'alternative memory' comprised a total denial of existing tradition and a turn towards modern capitalism as a means of tabula rasa, but this failed to take into account the collusion of capitalist and upper-caste forces (Ambedkar). Against these, he identifies a fourth approach, one embraced by Ambedkar towards the end of his life where he 'had realised the tragedy of a memoryless community and begun rebuilding it through historical research, and so creating a rich Buddhist past for Indian Dalits.' (Nagaraj, 2010, 163) He concludes, 'The responsibility of the Dalit movement today is to develop and build on this enterprise: the task is to explore the strategies that connect the village to the globe' (Nagaraj, 2010, 163). This then, is the mode that *Bhimayana* too upholds, with its fluid, symbolic power that infuses shared history (in terms of narrative or folk art) with great spiritual dignity. The collusion of Dalit and tribal discourse may be read in the light of Ambedkar's call for Dalit and other non-Brahmin alliances, though his attitude towards tribals is known to have been problematic[19]. The affinity between the Adivasi and the Dalit that is recognised in contemporary Dalit discourse is also evidenced by these texts, whether it be Ekalavya's story or the accretion of the two voices in Bhimayana. When the trees, animals and birds that the Gonds revere find their way into the graphic narrative, we are reminded of Kancha Ilaiah's lengthy elucidation of how the sacred beliefs of Hindus and Dalit Bahujan differ and distinguish themselves.

Conclusion

Navayana Publishing is self-avowedly 'India's first and only publishing house to focus on the issue of caste from an anti-caste perspective', opening up Dalit counter-discourses to the non-Dalit public. Navayana's didactic and creative impulses can be seen in tension if one is to contrast just the aesthetic choices of the two books—*A Gardener*, with its black and white images and 'visual grotesque' (Nayar, "*The Indian Graphic Novel*" 2016, 331) foreclosing other possible readings, and *Bhimayana*, refreshingly subtle and layered, lending a spiritual dignity to Ambedkar's biography, that is also the story of his people. To a large extent, the different tones of these two works can be attributed to one being a treatise (virulent, confrontational) and the other, a memoir (personal, painful). Whether these texts, if used as pedagogical tools, will be taught with proper attention to their teeming references and artistic sophistication[20], may be suspect, one cannot but undermine the power of what Pramod Nayar articulates as 'postcolonial critical literacy'. This 'enables us to see texts as situated within unequal social fields of caste, patriarchy, capitalism and demands that the reader become alert to the position he or she takes vis-á-vis not just the text but the social domains represented in it' (Nayar, *The Indian Graphic Novel*, 2016, 8). Rather than as crash courses in Dalit history, one can view these books as introductions to topics that the selectively amnesiac popular imagination conveniently overlooks. Today, when the CBSE (on orders of the Madras High Court) excises the Class IX textbook portion referring to the Channar revolt of Kerala citing 'factual inaccuracies', the need for other texts providing a historical understanding of current realities cannot be exaggerated. If the suicides of Rohit Vemula and legend of Nangeli can stand testimony to the tragic but dignified choice of death over humiliation (Sen, 2017), the enduring legacies of Phule and Ambedkar can attest to the strength of the long-going war for what Ambedkar terms the 'reclamation of human personality'. In the light of repeated instances of caste-based humiliation in universities and institutes of repute around the country, there is a very real need of sensitising the popular sphere. It is being not by graphic narratives to an extent, among other mediums. (For instance, Nagraj Manjule's acclaimed Marathi films *Fandry* and *Sairat* and Stalin K's documentary, *India Untouched—Stories of a People Apart*.)

Across cultures, graphic narratives are being hailed as a suitable medium for the representation of historical trauma. The uneven terrain of the popular is the territory over which new and existing identities are forged and contested, as in these three texts, within the larger framework of global capital. John Berger, in his Foreword to *Bhimayana*, comments that the book is an exemplum of how the market can be outlived. Drawing upon his words, Nandini Chandra asserts that in this bid to outlive the market, 'residual cultural forms (which derive their oppositional value from being part of a different economy, but are fully active and dynamic in the present, rather than mere survivals) are being mined to imagine and produce a truly political content', but alerts us to the very real danger of their 'reification and incorporation... through acknowledgement and appreciation' (Chandra, 2011, 23). The blurring of the popular/non-popular, as well as the accommodation of the popular into the academia, are symptoms of levelling hierarchies the world over, which can greatly benefit the cause of anti-caste struggle by destabilising established canons. The emerging form of the graphic narrative is indeed a fitting vehicle to carry 'manifestoes of resistance', and non-realistic, indigenous aesthetic styles may well be the new idiom for narratives that seek to question, challenge and disturb the status quo, resisting easy interpretation and assimilation into the dominant discourse.

REFERENCES

1. To move beyond the debates of terminology, I am drawing upon Hillary Chute's definition of graphic narrative as "a hybrid word-and-image form in which two narrative tracks, one verbal and one visual, register temporality spatially". (2008, 452)

2. Especially with reference to the latter two texts under study in the essay, the concept of 'Dalit consciousness' is crucial. For an analysis of how 'Dalit Chetna' has become an essential component of the growing Dalit literary critical vocabulary in Hindi literature, see Brueck, Laura R. "Dalit Chetna in Dalit Literary Criticism". Seminar, Web Edition. www.india-seminar.com/2006/558/558%20laura%20r.%20brueck.htm.
3. It is instructive to compare *"The offering"* to the Amar Chitra Katha title on Drona that is named *Drona—Valiant Archer, Supreme Teacher*. The cover of the book fixes our attention on an incident in his life where Drona elicits our strongest sympathy the cruel tricking of his son Ashwathhama by other boys, when they mix flour with water and make him drink it as milk, a cruel reminder of his poverty and defining moment in Drona's career. Ekalavya, whose story is spread over a mere two pages, makes his 'sacrifice' "with a smile on his face" and casually we are told, '...And Arjuna remained unparalleled' (Chandrakant and Kavadi, 1974: 2010, 18).
4. I am deliberately refraining from commenting on the unremarkable artwork in the text, but would like to draw attention to its aesthetic choice to portray Ekalavya and Arjuna in visually similar manners. Apart from Arjuna's crown and Ekalavya's 'tribal necklace', we do not have any other marker of difference that distinguishes their race on the basis of an acquiline/flat nose or skin colour, etc.
5. Later, when an evidently lower-caste Karna bends the rules in the archery contest where he bests Arjuna, the latter is haunted by the memory of the talented Ekalavya and realises that 'no doubt Ekalavya would have been recognised as a great archer if Drona had just shown him a little kindness.' (Pathak and Kumar, 2011, 63).
6. Ekalavya's loss of thumb, which renders him incapable of shooting arrows, may be read as the 'annihilation and disappearance of indigenous technology' that D.R. Nagaraj accuses 'masters of the colonial and modern development regime' of (Nagaraj, 2010, 160).
7. Amruta Patil, the popular graphic novelist, whose *Parva* duology makes significant subversive interventions in the representation of the Mahabharata, is strangely defensive when it comes to caste and gender critique. *Sauptik*, her second book in the series, emphatically voices Ashwathhama's disclaimer that 'egalitarianism

is a beautiful daydream' and the argument that 'Karn and Eklavya should've just rejected elitist lineages' (Patil, 2016, 115). She goes on to narrate how Ekalavya learnt to shoot arrows without a thumb, thus transforming a liability into an empowerment.

8. As Gail Omvedt observes, Jotirao Phule's book as also his work in the Satyashodhak Samaj, strove to demonstrate that a national revolution for self rule and the social revolution in a colonial society often develop in different directions, and the interests of the Indian elite did not represent those of the masses and were in fact opposed to them.
9. The intersections of caste and (female) gender rarely find graphic depiction, with the most recent exception being Orijit Sen's short six-panel adaptation of the story of Nangeli, the legendary nineteenth-century Ezhava woman who cut off her breasts and bled to death to protest against the caste-based breast tax, in 'A Travancore Tale'.
10. For a lengthier analysis of the visual depiction of caste hierarchies and oppression, see Deepali Yadav, (details in 'Works Cited').
11. For an examination of the different strategies that *A Gardener* employs to escape the claim/threat of authenticity in the representation of Dalit persecution, see Nayar, 'The Indian Graphic Novel and Dalit Trauma' (Works Cited).
12. For Nadim Damluji, '*A Gardener in the Wasteland* produces comparisons that feel overly heavy-handed, instead of letting the fascinating tale of the Phule's fight against an established hierarchy subtly speak for itself...those parallels leave the book overly stuffed with asides that weaken the narrative flow for the benefit of readers...' (Damluji, Nadim. 'Can the Subaltern Draw?: Reframing Caste in Indian Graphic Novels'. The *Hooded Utilitarian*. 22 February 2012. www.hoodedutilitarian.com/2012/02/can-the-subaltern-draw-reframing-caste-in-indian-graphic-novels/. Accessed 5 October 2017.)
13. For a discussion of Bhimayana's production of a new vocabulary for articulation of social trauma in the cultural realm, see Nayar, Pramod K. 'Towards a Postcolonial Critical Literacy: *Bhimayana* and the Indian Graphic Novel'. (Works Cited)
14. Durgabai Vyam speaks in the Afterword of their own experience of discrimination in Delhi, which made them keenly identify with Ambedkar's similar experience and hurt.

15. The Amar Chitra Katha title on Ambedkar, *Babasaheb Ambedkar —He Dared to Fight*, a part of its 'Visionaries' series, makes for interesting comparison. Illustrated by a Mahar artist, Dilip Kadam, it does give space to Ambedkar's struggles and triumphs, but also seeks to contain it within the larger framework of approval by non-Dalit sympathisers, as evidenced, among other things, by the Brahmin teacher after whom he supposedly fashions his own surname, as also the glowing tributes by national leaders like Nehru and Rajagopalachari that follow the story.
16. Where other graphic books like *Sita's Ramayana* that feature Patachitra folk art form, *Bhimayana* succeeds in integrating the aesthetic component and making it an indispensable driving force of the larger narrative.
17. Thus the narrative shows the pervasiveness of caste discrimination across religion, and does not take for its antagonist, the stock figure of the Brahmin, as does *A Gardener in the Wasteland*.
18. This is in stark contrast with the abysmally standardised iconography of Ambedkar in calendar art and other forms of token memorialisation, which go hand-in-hand with his co-option into a sanitised popular discourse that ignores his radical contribution to the Dalit cause, in favour of his stature as 'the father of the Indian constitution'.
19. For a clearer exposition on this, see note 64 on page 178 of S. Anand's annotated, critical edition of Ambedkar's *Annihilation of Caste*, published by Verso, 2014.
20. For an exploration of readership and categorisation issues in the book, read Vasvi Oza's 'Questions of Reading and Readership of Pictorial Texts' (Bibliography).

BIBLIOGRAPHY

"A Gardener in the Wasteland". (2012). *Navayana*. Retrieved from www.navayana.org/books/2012/10/10/a-gardener-in-the-wasteland-2/ on 04 October 2017.

"Slavery by Mahatma Phule: Introduction". *Dr B.R. Ambedkar's Caravan*. 23 July 2005. Retrieved from drambedkarbooks.files.wordpress.com/2017/04/slavery-intro.pdf. on 11 January 2017.

Anand S., and Vellanki, V. (2015). "Bhimayana: Caste, Ambedkar, Art, and Pedagogy". *Contemporary Education Dialogue*. Vol. 12, Issue 2. pp. 271–277.

Barthes, R. (1974: 2002). *S/Z*. (Trans.) Richard Miller. Malden: Blackwell.

Chandra, N. (2011). "Ambedkar Out of the Frame". *Biblio: A Review of Books*, Vol. 16, No. 3, pp. 22–23. Retrieved from www.biblio-india.org/tocMA11.asp?mp=MAl. on 10 February 2017.

Chandrakant K. & Kavadi, P.B. (1974: 2010). *Drona—Valiant Archer, Supreme Teacher*. (Ed.) Anant Pai. Mumbai: Amar Chitra Katha.

Chatterji, R. (2012). *Speaking with Pictures: Folk Art and the Narrative Tradition in India*. New Delhi: Routledge.

Chute, H. (2008). "Comics as Literature? Reading Graphic Narrative". *Modern Language Association*. Vol. 123, No. 2, pp. 452–465.

Desai, Prajna. (2012). "Review: Bhimayana—Experiences of Untouchability". *The Comics Journal*. April 2012. Retreived from www.tcj.com/reviews/bhimayana-experiences-of-untouchability/ on 10 February 2017.

Hingonekar, S. (2011). "Ekalavya". (Trans. Gail Omvedt & Bharat Patankar). Quoted in *Understanding Caste—From Buddha to Ambedkar and Beyond*. New Delhi: Orient Blackswan.

Ilaiah, K. (1996: 2002). *Why I am Not a Hindu: A Sudra Critique of Hindu Philosophy, Culture and Political Economy*. Calcutta: Samya.

Khilnani, S. (2015). "The Case of Bhimayana and the Search for a New Dalit Aesthetic". *Lapis Lazuli*. Vol. 5, Issue 2, pp. 111–125. Retrieved from www.pintersociety.com/wp-content/uploads/2016/01/Khilnani-Shweta-9.pdf. On 05 October 2017.

Nagaraj, D.R. (2010). *The Flaming Fleet and Other Essays: The Dalit Movement in India*. (Eds.) Prithvi Datta & Chandra Shobhi. Ranikhet: Permanent Black.

Natarajan, S. & Ninan, A. (2011:2016). *A Gardener in the Wasteland – Jotiba Phule's Fight for Liberty*. New Delhi: Navayana Publishing.

Nayar, P.K. (2016). 'The Indian Graphic Novel and Dalit Trauma: A Gardener in the Wasteland.' *Dalit Literatures in India*. (Eds.) Joshil K. Abraham and Judith Misrahi-Barak. New Delhi: Routledge. pp. 320–338.

Nayar, P.K. (2016). *The Indian Graphic Novel: Nation, History and Critique.* New York: Routledge

Nayar, P.K. 'Towards a Postcolonial Critical Literacy: Bhimayana and the Indian Graphic Novel'. *Studies in South Asian Film and Media*, Vol. 3, Issue 1, 2011, pp. 3–21. doi: 10.1386/safm.3.1.3_1.

Omvedt, G. (1971). 'Jotirao Phule and the Ideology of Social Revolution in India'. *Economic and Political Weekly*, Vol. 6, Issue 37, 1969–1979.

Oza, V. (2011). "Questions of Reading and Readership of Pictorial Texts: The Case of Bhimayana, a Pictorial Biography of Dr. Ambedkar". *Journal of Writing in Creative Practice*, Vol. 4, Issue 3, pp. 351–365.

Pathak, H., Kumar, N. (2011). *The Offering — The Story of Ekalavya and Dronacharya.* New Delhi: Campfire.

Patil, A. (2016). *Sauptik—Blood and Flowers.* Noida: HarperCollins.

Rege, S.S. & Kadam, D. (1979: 2011). *Babasaheb Ambedkar —He Dared to Fight.* (Ed.) Anant Pai. Mumbai: Amar Chitra Katha.

Sen, Orijit. (2017). *A Travancore Tale.* Retrieved from guftugu.in/2017/01/remembering-nangeli-on-rohith-vemulas-shahadat-day/. on 18 January 2017.

Valmiki, O. (2003). *Joothan—A Dalit's Life.* (Trans. Arun Prabha Mukherjee). New York: Columbia University Press.

Vyam, D. Vyam, S. Srividya et al. (2011: 2014). *Bhimayana – Experiences of Untouchability.* New Delhi: Navayana Publishing.

Yadav, D. (2016). 'Visualising Caste: A Gardener in the Wasteland and the Politics of Graphic Adaptation.' *South Asian Popular Culture.* Vol. 14, Issue 1-2. pp. 49-60.

CHAPTER 2

Deconstructing Narratives of '*Chamar* Pop'[1] in Contemporary Punjab

Prerna Trehan

> "Music expresses that which cannot be put into words and that which cannot remain silent."
>
> –Victor Hugo

Culture can never be viewed in isolation. It is a complex interplay of history, psychology, emotions and essentially human in character. It is a contested and multi-layered concept, relying on the way the idea of culture is constructed and deconstructed. What adds to the complexity is the interplay of social learning and inheritance with personal preference and understanding. It is this interaction between the social and the personal that adds 'multi-accentuality' to culture. Often a dichotomy has been drawn between High and Popular culture which requires to be questioned in understanding the various contours of the concept of culture.

Popular culture and art have come to play a significant role in the contemporary world. There has been a switch from treating 'popular' as a cultural pariah to a body of art requiring deconstruction. Stuart Hall played a significant role in breaking through the binaries to High and Low culture to talk about the crucial role of popular culture in post-war Britain of 1950s. In their seminal work, *The Popular Arts* (Hall and Whannel, 1964), Hall and Whannel place 'popular art' as the meeting ground between folk and mass art. Popular culture thereby becomes the intermediary between the overtly community based folk and the stereotyped, consumption driven mass art. Hall in his later works picks up the Gramscian idea of 'Hegemony,' wherein the space of culture requires 'Deconstruction of the Popular' to understand its paradoxical nature (Hall, 1964).

Culturalism becomes significant in studying the 'humanist' side of culture. It tends to emphasise the 'human agency in determining various historical and creative processes.'[2] Thus culture becomes a platform of expression for people, their ideas, histories and varied socio-economic contexts. Their voice percolates down walls and canvases of paints, streams through the strings of instruments, in the notes of screams of rebellion disguised as songs. Thus Hall's artist has a personality of his own which he infuses in his original creation especially in context of folk art, making it stand apart from the de-personalised, almost de-humanised mass art.

The Conundrum of Popular Music

One of the greatest and oldest components of Culture is Music. From the swishing of the wind through trees, the first tap on leather skin, the strum of guitar strings, the seven notes, a hymn, a song to classical, jazz, pop, rap, reggae, music from its ancient to contemporary form is a footprint of the movement of the human civilisation. Music is seen as an expression of human creativity and thought, deeply reflective of not just the being but also what one wants to be. It is also one of the cultural forms most intrinsically linked to community. The form, content, lyrics, composition are often regarded as an autobiography of a social group. Music is thus, linked to identity and thereby inherently political in nature. It becomes a platform of contention between varying identity groups, a dialogue, a debate, a tug of war among competing groups for political assertion and subversion[3].

T. Adorno's work on popular music presents an interesting yet controversial exploration of 'popular music.' According to Adorno, Popular music is centrally located within mass culture and diseased by the standardised cultural industry churning out music based on a stereotypical phenomenon for the purpose of distribution and consumption. Adorno is immensely critical of popular music for three main reasons (Carrabine, 2007, 233). Firstly, Adorno critiques the 'crystallisation of standards' of a range of songs, most of which sound similar and are produced in mass just like cars or any other product geared towards 'mass consumption.' Secondly, he critiques the passive learning fostered by popular music which distracts the listeners towards the glitter of entertainment industry, instead of critical issues confronting the society. Lastly, popular music creates bonds of subordination among the listeners that make two fundamental categories out of all of them, 'the rhythmically obedient type' and the 'emotional type,' thereby alienating the persons and perpetuating pseudo-individualisation. However, theorists like Walter Benjamin provide a different view. Benjamin sees potential for democratisation of art with the advent of mass media (including in the context of popular music) creating space for collective determination rather than an individual (artist) oriented process. (Carrabine, 2007, 233)

Certain crucial inferences are drawn by the above-named theorists in the context of popular music, and they analyse the same from the production point of view. It is also necessary to draw attention towards what popular music does to the listeners of the same. Roland Barthes provides a critical insight into understanding the Popular. Barthes focuses on taking the attention away from the author and the underlying ideology in his work, to the multiple meanings a work of art can have depending on the consumer. Derrida's concept of 'Deconstruction' thereby is of great significance while attempting to uncover the layers of narrative in popular music and understand alternative meanings of the text available through application of critical reading and understanding. Taking on this idea, Jason Toynbee provides a comprehensive analysis of the interplay between the collective and the individual artist (Carrabine, 2007, 238-89). The creation of the content of popular music is not a practice in isolation. Rather, it is intimately connected to the community concerned. He further argues that popular musicians can be regarded as 'mediators who exchange sounds, styles and forms. They do not generate music from within. Rather their materials are located outside in the 'field of the social'.' Thus, the generation of meaning as well as its understanding is in the domain of the Social. Popular Music is therefore located in particular cultural and social contexts.

Music as a Form of Rebellion

Music, especially on the popular front in its various dimensions has been used as an antithesis to the prevailing conditions. Reggae or rap is seen as African-American music and jazz as an icon of the advent of new age. Beatles becoming champions of Woodstock, Aretha Franklin's 'Respect' symbolising American Civil Rights Movement, Dylan giving voice to the raging anti-war sentiments to punk rock and all women band 'Pussy Riot' sending shivers down Putin regime in Russia. Music is seen as a tool for political and social action, 'performers using strategies for negotiating social, historical and political identities (Post, 2014, 10).' Barett Martin (Martin, 2014) writes how music has been the face of many social movements across the world. 'Fela Kuti's 'Zombie'... against Nigeria's military dictators... In Chile, Victor Jara wrote songs about his country's struggles, sparking the Nueva Cancion (New Songs) movement that caused South Americans to rise up against their military dictatorships and replace them with democracies. In Brazil, the Tropicalia movement was created by songwriters like Caetano Veloso, Gilberto Gil, and Rita Lee as a form of protest against the Brazilian military ...'

Critical theorists such as Hall have analysed the categories of class and race in trying to deconstruct the way popular music is perceived by the audience. In the context of India, the same can be extended to the ideas of Caste. Mattern in his influential work (Mattern, 1998, 25-29) tries to differentiate among three kinds of 'community based political action through music-confrontational, deliberative and pragmatic'. India witnessed the importance of music as a cultural and a political asset, giving voice to those often silenced, be it in the Bhakti movement, Tamil devotional music of Alvar and Nayanar saints, the chants of freedom struggle, Marathi Rashtriyakirtan (Schultz), the songs of Naxal movement etc.

The idea of a Dalit culture has been gaining force and according to Prof. Guru, (Guru, 2001, 162-63) is seen predominantly in the context of Dalit literature. Guru analyses the creation of counter culture via music among Mahars and Mangs using their folk art and specially created musical instruments, peculiar to certain communities. Similarly, Badri Narayan takes up the case of

Pasmangata subgroup within the Dalit Pasi caste. These forms of music and oral traditions continue to play a crucial role as a form of identity assertion as well as the means of political mobilisation. Narayan gives the example of 'Cultural Squads' (Jagriti Dasta) by BSP through engaging with Dalit communities and folk artists, seeking to help generate a coherent Dalit consciousness through various songs, ballads etc (Narayan, 2006, 78). These songs transmit certain myths to glorify caste and consolidate Dalit identity.

Cultural domain in the form of popular music thus, helps communities pour their experience of exploitation and caste oppression into these songs. These strands of cultural assertion continued, incorporating new issues and Ambedkar movement till the 1970s after which there has been a general decline. One of the crucial factors responsible for this decline was the indifference of Dalit youth, who Guru contends do not have the 'ability, patience or enthusiasm' for these cultural performances, and instead being enamoured by mainstream cinema. This is intimately related to the fact that these cultural performances and music remained firmly in the domain of folk, dependent on individual performers or groups to engage with the Dalit community. They were located within the cultural traditions of the community to maintain authenticity to avoid pitfalls of mass art.

Despite being labelled as a 'martial society', Punjab enjoys a rich heritage of cultural development. The state, most studied for 'problem of plenty', also has the highest density of Scheduled Caste population (as per Census 2011). Furthermore, Dalits in Punjab are not limited to just Hinduism, or even Sikhism which doctrinally does not associate itself with caste, has not been immune to the phenomenon of 'Homo Heirarchicus' (Dumont, 1981). Punjab has a long tradition of cultural mobilisation starting with the advent of Bhakti traditions. In the 1920s the *Ad-Dharmi* movement led by Mangoo Ram marked the advent of identity assertion via the *Ravidassia* tradition. *Ravidassia* assertion since the 1920s and social action through Music may be categorised under what Mattern regards as 'deliberative' form of acting in concert (Mattern, 1998, 28) wherein members of a community use musical practices to debate identity and commitments and arrive at mutual negotiations. This categorisation applies to Ravidas tradition and its music which

Peter Friedlander believes depict 'a struggle within the Indian society,' that are both inter-communal and inter-religious with an underlying search and desire for social unity.

Caste Complexities in Punjab

Post-independence after the formation of the Punjabi Suba, Green Revolution brought an another set of problems. The caste division in Punjab has a definite class character and this was crucial in the context of an agrarian state like Punjab where the basis of power of the 'dominant caste' was landownership. Dalits have historically occupied and continue to occupy miniscule landholdings (3.02% in Census 2011). As pointed out by Jodhka, absence of 'Brahminism' (Jodhka, 2009, 51-52) the need for labour in agriculture led to the lack of the purity-pollution binary in the state. This lent a peculiar feature to the caste hierarchy in Punjab. The rise of Jatt[4] Sikhs as British Army's dependable 'martial clan' in the post-1857 revolt and the passing of the Punjab Alienation Act of 1901 which favoured agricultural communities such as the Jatt Sikhs led to their emergence as the 'dominant caste.' The economic stronghold of Jatt Sikhs curtailed the influence of Brahmins and aided their control over Dalits in the rural, land dependent economy.

Over time, the economic predominance of Jatts transformed into political paramountcy as well conveniently displacing the Khatri Sikhs in the political heirarchy. Surinder S. Jodhka (Jodhka, 2009, 52) points out that constituting one-fourth of the electorate in Punjab, the political hegemony of Jatts remains virtually unchallenged with Giani Zail Singh being the last non-Jatt to be the chief minister of Punjab. He further points out how the leading parties of the state-both Congress and Akali Dal are Jatt-controlled and dominated. Punjab has also witnessed numerous zealous reform movements targeting caste divisions from Singh Sabha movement, Arya Samaj, *Ad-Dharmi* movement (Jurgensmeyer) etc. The *Ad-Dharmi* movement hoped to generate a Dalit consciousness through various means. However, the various waves of social reforms were unable to remove both vertical and horizontal caste divisions in the state.

SCs in Punjab are internally divided into self-contained groups that are constantly competing for status in the social pecking order.

In broad terms, SCs in Punjab may be categorised into '*Chamars*' and '*Churhas*' which have further internal bifurcations. Within *Chamars* there are the *Ravidassias* and *Ad-dharmis* who since 2010 have had their own *Ravidassia Dharm*[5]. The *Chamars*, considered the most resourceful of SC sub-groups, (Jodhka and Kumar, 2007, 21) are mainly concentrated in the Doaba area. They took major advantage of educational opportunities, government employment etc. thereby forming the ranks of the elite Dalit middle class in Punjab. Further they led the wave of Punjabi emigration, first to the Middle East and then to the western hemisphere from the state, further strengthening their social status among the Dalits as well as their economic foothold. This in turn has caused friction with other Dalit sub-castes in Punjab.

'*Chamar* Pop' Reclaiming Popular Culture

During the course of the Green Revolution, Punjab in the 1960s and 70s witnessed, an enthusiastic Leftist movement. The unequal opportunities perpetuated by the top down model led to sharpening of relative poverty among different caste groups bringing to fore the contradictions of the agricultural development strategy. From Sant Ram Udassi to Lal Singh Dil to Bant Singh, the Naxalite or Communist ideology has had its share of Dalit content. The revolutionary zeal whether in the form of qawwalis or poetry, has also sought to empower the Dalit identity within their cover. This 'militant or Naxalite' music or poetry is seen as reflecting 'deep conviction, authenticity and almost crude realism and they dream utopian dreams' thereby becoming 'completely political while remaining deeply human. (Judge, 1992, 154)'. However, despite the empathy, the Leftist crusaders failed to reconcile the caste-class ideological dilemma. While differing in the content as well as the means of musicality, both the *Ravidassia* tradition and Leftist music stayed away from commercialisation and mass production. This dramatically changed in the contemporary years, especially since the late 1990s, marking the arrival of '*Chamar* Pop.' While taking on the characteristics of mass art to gain commercial success, the *Chamar* Pop utilised the personal experiences of the community to enter the arena of popular culture.

The 1980s marked the beginning of a 'structural crisis' (Chandoke and Priyadarshi, 2006) in agriculture in Punjab. While, agriculture became less lucrative, the Dalits especially *Chamars* who had taken advantage of education opportunities, or moved to the Gulf region in search of better future, began their rapid rise in economic mobility. On the other hand, the dominant elite of Jatt Sikhs had taken advantages of the first phase of Green Revolution and booming land prices. This led to a heightened sense of entitlement which was reflected in the cultural realm in the form of 'Bhangra pop culture,' valorising Jatt culture. However, with the crisis in agriculture, there was a displacement of the work force in the agricultural community. Large scale selling of land for urban and transnational migration led to the inrush of consumerism, with brand names, cars and Jatt Sikh men chasing women becoming the order of the day. The beat culture led to large scale popularisation of the bhangra music, thereby mainstreaming often discriminatory and sexist songs. However, this mass production of Punjabi pop music led to the development of new cultural traditions among Dalit communities as well especially the '*Chamar*' community dominating the Doaba part of Punjab. It led to the development of popular music, amalgamating erstwhile folk traditions and myths with the Jatt pop music, as a sign of arrival by the community. The Jatt-dominated lyrics and songs are being challenged by songs by Dalits who seek to glorify their identity and elevation due to economic success, with the diaspora playing a major role in producing these albums such as '*Bibe put Chamaran de*' or 'Fighter *Chamar*'.

Santosh Singh points to 'mission singing' as a tradition in Dalit Ballads in Punjab (Singh, 2017, 33). Mission singing seeks to foster and promote the feeling of solidarity in a community by preaching through songs values and anecdotes relating to certain revered heroes or mentors. The tradition of eulogising caste heroes has now been incorporated into a broader narrative thereby creating foundations for popular music that connects with the *Chamar* youth rather than folk music of former years. The advent of *Ravidassia* movement in early twentieth century opened up spaces for caste struggle within the realms of Sikhism. The development of Amrit Bani may be regarded under what Mattern calls 'deliberative form of acting in concert' (Mattern). This form of action envisages use musical practices to debate and discuss identity and commitments and arrive at mutual negotiations. In the 1990s the *Chamar* Pop culture was demonstrative of changing ambitions and social values. As economic, social and political competition intensified, these songs were reflective of the initiation of Mattern's confrontational phase of a community acting in concert.

There have been serious attempts at building a strong culture of resistance such as the Sufi singer Hans Raj Hans' 'Boota Mandi Mela' referring to the site of a mega annual mela on Ravidas Jayanti to end all caste divisions. Hans combines the folk elements of Sufi thing with Dalit content. His stint in popular misc including Bollywood lent a broad following to Hans Raj. However, it is by reflecting caste assertion that Hans Raj Hans emerged as a prominent Dalit leader with him being wooed by BJP in the 2017 Punjab elections. Dalit singer Rajni Thakkerwal attempts to subdue both 'caste and gender hegemonic structure' through her songs like 'Dhee Chamaran Dee'. Thakarwal faced the wrath of Jatt men who attacked her for singing songs glorifying *Chamar* identity. Consequently, local protection squads like Begumpura Tiger, Force Punjab, Ambedkar Sena Punjab and Sri Guru Ravidas Force Punjab sprang up so as to ensure safety of these singers, who had now become icons of an invigorated *Chamar* community (Singh, 2017, 36). There have been other commercially successful singers like J.H. Tajpuri, Roop Lal Dhir etc who may be seen as using similar iconography and symbolism as in Jatt songs to underline the growing status of the Dalit community. One of Tajpuri's most popular songs valorising the *Chamar* youth and their caste identity goes:

Putt Chamaran de, Bibe Putt Chamaran de

Lal Safari Jeepan Te Land Cruiser caraan Te,

Vekh Mele nu chale ni,

Putt Chamaran de, Bibe Putt Chamaran de.

(Sons of Chamars, Good Sons of Chamars

In their Red Safari Jeeps and Land Cruisers

Look sons of Chamars are leaving for the fair)

The song echoes the upward economic mobility witnessed by *Chamars* helping them acquire goods usually cornered by dominant caste. The song talks about the increasing wealth, as well as pride in their community with the western cars being driven to attend the fair, referring to the Bootan Mandi Mela, which continues to showcase the strengthening of the *Chamar* community especially in the Doaba area of Punjab. The coming up of *deras*, especially Sachakhand Ballan, has been instrumental in instilling the community with the aspiration to create a unique social space for themselves. This space is self-defined and mirrors the march of the community from marginalisation towards assertion. Roop Lal Dhir, one of the earliest exponents of '*Chamar* pop' who moved away from folk songs, sings in 'Hummer' or 'Putt Chamaran Da' (Son of Chamar),

> *Jadon da liya une Chandigarh dakhla*
> *rakhda bana ke hun saade kolon faasla*
> *Hummer gadi vich aunda nee putt Chamaran da*
> *hun nahin ankh milaanda putt Chamaran da*
> *(Ever since he started studying in Chandigarh he keeps aloof from me*
> *He comes to college in a Hummer car but the Chamar boy refuses to look into my eyes)* (Kumar and Andre).

The migration towards urban centres of westernisation is attractive to open up more opportunities for Dalit communities. It also gives rise to a sense of awareness, and a need for change in their existing circumstances which demands a change in the existing lifestyle and habits. It further indicates the growing importance of education and hence the issue of reservation. While going abroad and earning well ensures economic status, government service and specifically reaching a position of authority guarantees heightened social status as well. State-sponsored mobility is seen as necessary for ensuring recruitment of Dalits to high status groups which also leads to the generation of a class of 'Dalit elite.' The song says:

> Vich pardesan veere karde kamaayi ni,
> Mein vi aithe dil la ke karda padhai ni...;
> D.C. lagan wala putt Chamaran da.
> (My brothers abroad earn money,

And I dedicatedly study here,
For soon the Son of Chamars shall become a D.C.)

Jacobson and Myrvold note how by replacing the term Jatt with '*Chamar*' in songs a term often used as a derogatory word, now offers new avenues of pride to the community (Jacobsen and Myrvold, 2016, 181). However they also point out the contradiction within this new form of assertion. They argue that how these songs call upon Dalits to abandon their former submissive postures and respond to their humiliation by lifting arms against their oppressors. By doing so, they attempt to 'appropriate the same qualities of the warrior that had once been used in constrain them.' Thus, they appropriate certain aggressive, highly masculine Jatt archetypes and continue to glorify 'masculinity' and 'fetishisation of the female'. In their songs the singers comment on how the daughters of their community are their honour and anyone trying to take advantage of them shall be dealt with by the entire community. The women in the community are not given the agency or opportunity to rise against the double oppression of caste and gender borne by them.

There are some voices though, that have broken through the glass ceiling of consumerism and misogyny. One of the most popular and recent faces of *Chamar* pop is Ginni Mahi, a teenage Dalit singer gaining popularity for spreading message of Ambedkar and Ravidass through her songs. Ginni Mahi has especially captured popular imagination with her songs becoming a rage among the Dalit communities. The young singer is responsible for combining '*Chamar* pop' with traditions of 'Ambedkar folk' to not only assert Dalit identity but instil it with a rebellious zeal. In fact, Mahi and her songs mark a new trend in 'mission singing' among Punjab Dalits. The combination of past Dalit heroes like Guru Ravidass with the modern day messiah, Dr. Ambedkar, is reflective of Dalits seeking to make use of constitutional instruments to further their interests. Mahi, or Gurkanwal Bharti, is unlike the commercial pop singers, looking to Punjabi folk tunes as Dalit icons like Guru Ravidas and Ambedkar for inspiration as well as using elements of Punjabi folk music to invoke a sense of regional identity. In one of her most popular songs *Fan Baba Sahib ki*, Mahi proudly refers to herself as "*Main thi Babasaheb di, jine likheya si samvidhaan* (I am the daughter of Babasaheb, who wrote the Constitution)." One of her other songs, 'Danger *Chamar*' says, "*Kurbani deno darrde nahin, rehnde hai tayyar, haige asle to wadd Danger Chamar* (the one who is not scared to sacrifice, the one who is the real thing is *Chamar*)" (Chaba and Jaskiran Kapoor). In an age of declining youth participation in issues of Dalit oppression in Punjab, the popular music of Ginni Mahi removes these topics from under the rug. In fact, she attempts to integrate problems of female foeticide and drugs in her songs as well, two dilemmas confronting the entire Punjabi society across caste and class lines.

The Quandary of '*Chamar* Pop'

Contemporary music while falling into Mattern's 'confrontational' category needs to be explored if it contains certain truly uplifting elements. These songs have moved away from the issues of identity and existential struggle that many Dalits are still forced to face, or trying to deconstruct the upper-caste defined idea of a hierarchical society, towards consumerism and a social mobility based on emulation of practices held in high esteem by the upper castes. While there is valid criticism of these songs, it also raises the debate that the upward mobility of the subaltern need not be sanitised or expected to be devoid of any contradiction. Much like Dalit Capitalism which too, is often criticised for not being a mode of emancipation (Teltumbde), these songs may be symbolic of Dalits in Punjab having 'arrived'. It could be seen as a movement towards the 'Pragmatic' form of action, wherein different Dalit groups have seemingly consolidated a sense of identity. However, it is important to explore if this identity may be a product of 'Cultural Imperialism' (Young) rather than self-definition. Globalisation and streaks of economic liberalisation have had a considerable impact upon the music representing the socio-political dynamism of Dalits in Punjab today. Furthermore, an important observation in Prof. Guru's analysis of Dalit cultural movement in Maharashtra that is of immense consequence to Punjab is whether this cultural/music movement represents one 'homogenous cultural expression.' '*Chamars*' or *Ravidassis* from Doaba area have witnessed immense socio-economic mobilisation and are active in the cultural sphere as well. While confronting Jat Sikh dominance, they tend to create a heroic '*Chamar*' image, not only in context of the dominant caste, but also other castes within the Dalit community, thereby restricting the idea of a united Dalit cultural tradition.

It is of immense interest to discover how music can become a weapon towards Arendt's notion of 'power to' (Penta, 1996, 211) wherein power is not the property of a few or an oppressive instrument but the capacity of a community to truly engage and interact in determining their choices. One may also try to comprehend how popular music can come to be 'power over' when it becomes a tool in the hands of dominant elite. T.K. Oommen (Oomen, 1984, 99) talks of the need to create a Dalit 'power pool.'However, the division within the Dalit groups in Punjab has hindered the formation of any such community power resource. 'Chamar pop' on the one hand has been indispensable in helping Dalit assertion and issues of identity entering the mainstream popular music. Whereas many parts of India have witnessed a form of social Sanskritisation, Punjab, especially *Chamars* have sought to identify with the *Chamar* identity and assert it by continually naming it. Furthermore, the Sikh identity has been a cause of much debate in Punjab. There are sections of Dalit population who identify strongly with the Sikh roots, while there are others who feeling shunned seek alternatives. The springing up of *deras* and coming up of *Ravidassia* as separate religious identity has further sharpened this conflict. The intersection of religious and caste identities therein are revealed by these songs.

Chamar pop has resignified the pivotal role played by culture and counter-cultures in exposing the existing power structures in the society. It has not been relegated to the past movements, but continues to engage and excite the youth population. By taking on the features of 'mass art' of being produced to reach widespread consumers, it has made Dalit idols contemporary. However, most of the music has fallen in the trap of 'standardisation' as well as being restricted to certain communities of a 'divided' Dalit population of Punjab. While many critics point out a streak of 'Neo-Sanskritisation' with Dalit folk traditions being hegemonised by symbols of affluence promoted by Jatt Sikh pop culture, it has helped Dalit cultural assertion remain relevant in Punjabi society creating new avenues for evolving Dalit pride and identity. *Chamar* pop offers a platform for engaging in a debate on the evolution of caste hierarchies and how these cultural developments help construct 'imagined communities' (Anderson) based on certain shared experiences and aspirations.

REFERENCES

1. The terms Dalit is used in this paper to refer to communities considered as Scheduled Castes in contemporary Punjab. They were categorised as 'Untouchables' in the oppressive Hindu-Brahminical social order. Furthermore the use of terms like '*Chamar*,' '*Mazhabi*,' '*Balmiki*' are to point out the various sub-categories within the Dalit community and in no way used in a derogatory or disrespectful manner.
2. For further analysis of the concept of Culturalism, see Procter (2004), especially pages 38-39.
3. This part, as well as some others form part of my research proposal prepared for the purpose of PhD admission. My thesis hopes to look at music as a source of socio-political assertion and resistance among Dalits in Punjab during three main movements of struggle—the *Ad-Dharam* movement, the Leftist phase and finally the contemporary phase of *Chamar* pop.
4. The term 'Jatt' has been used to denote the Sikh Jats and differentiate them from the Hariyanvi Jats in this article. While both are dominant castes with certain similarities, the regional and religious identities have led to much variations between the two.
5. Dera Sachkhand Ballan, one of the most influential *deras* among *Ad-Dharmis* located in Jalandhar, announced the new religion at the temple of Sri Guru Ravidass, Seer Govardhanpur in Varanasi following the murder of their *dera* deputy, Sant Ramanand Dass in Vienna in 2009.

BIBLIOGRAPHY

Anderson, Benedict. (2006). *Imagined Communities—Reflections on the Origin and Spread of Nationlism*. London: Verso.

Carrabine, Eamonn. (2007). 'Popular Music.' Edwards, Tim (ed.). *Cultural Theory—Classical and Contemporary Positions*. London: Sage. pp. 231-254.

Chaba, Anju Agnihotri and Jaskiran Jaskiran Kapoor. *Ginni Mahi, the 17-year-old Dalit voice from Punjab, is making waves*. 10 October 2016. Retrieved from <http://indianexpress.com/article/india/india-news-india/a-17-year-old-dalit-voice-from-punjab-is-making-waves-an-artist-has-no-caste-3003291/> on 2 January 2017.

Chandoke, Neera and Praveen Priyadarshi. (2006). 'Electoral politics in post-conflict states—The Case of Punjab.' *Economic and Political Weekly*. pp. 811-19.

Dumont, Louis. (1981). *Homo Heirarchicus—The Caste system and its implications*. Chicago: University of Chicago Press.

Guru, Gopal. (2001). 'The Interface between Ambedkar and the Dalit Cultural Movement in Maharashtra'. *Dalit Identity and Politics*. (Ed.) Ghanshyam Shah. London: Sage Publications. pp. 160-192.

Hall, Stuart and Paddy Whannel. (1964). *The Popular Arts*. London: Hutchinson.

Hall, Stuart. (1981). 'Notes on deconstructing 'the popular'.' *People's History and Socialist Theory*. (Ed.) Raphael Samuel. London: Routledge. pp. 227-40.

Jacobsen, Knut A. and Kristina Myrvold. (2016). *Young Sikhs in a Global World: Negotiating Traditions, Identities and Authorities*. New York: Routledge.

Jodhka, Surinder S. (2012). *How caste matters and doesn't matter*. Retrieved from <http://www.livemint.com/Opinion/9XT3V5cHcbSFHgQZDglKwO/How-caste-matters-and-doesn8217t-matter.html> on 2 January 2017.

Jodhka, Surinder S. and Avinash Kumar. (2007). 'Internal Classification of Scheduled Castes: The Punjab Story'. *Economic and Political Weekly*. pp. 20-23.

Jodhka, Surinder. (2009). 'Initiating sub-classification of Scheduled Castes: The Punjab Story of Quotas within Quotas.' *Dividing Dalits—Writings on sub-categorization of Scheduled Castes*. (Ed.) C.Y. Rao. Jaipur: Rawat Publications. pp. 51-62.

Judge, Paramjit S. (1992). *Insurrection to Agitation: The Naxalite Movement in Punjab*. Delhi: Popular Prakashan.

Jurgensmeyer, Mark. (1998). *Religious Rebels in the Punjab: The Social Vision of the Untouchable*. Delhi: Ajanta.

Kumar, Abhimanyu and Aletta Andre. *Chartbustin' Chamars*. (2016). Retrieved from <http://www.thehindubusinessline.com/blink/

know/chartbusting-chamar-pop/article9246140.ece> on 20 December 2016.

Martin, Barett. *Music and Politics of Resistance*. (2014). Retrieved from <http://www.huffingtonpost.com/barrett-martin/music-and-the-politics-of_b_4087557.html> on 20 December 2016.

Mattern, Mark. (1998). *Acting in Concert—Music, Community and Political Action*. New Jersey: Rutgers University Press.

Narayan, Badri. (2006). *Women Heroes and Dalit Assertion in North India: Culture, Identity and Politics*. New Delhi: Sage.

Oomen, T.K. (1984). *Social Structure and Politics: Studies in Independent India*. Delhi: Hindustan Publishing Corporation.

Penta, Leo J. (1996). 'Hannah Arendt: On Power'. *The Journal of Speculative Philosophy*, vol. 10, no. 3. pp. 210–229.

Post, Jennifer C. (2014). *Ethnomusicology—A Contemporary Reader*. New York: Routledge.

Procter, James. (2004). *Routledge Critical Thinkers—Stuart Hall*. Oxon: Routledge.

Schultz, Ann. (2013). *Singing a Hindu Nation—Marathi Devotional Performance and Nationalism*. New York: Oxford University Press.

Singh. K, Santosh. (2017). 'The Caste Question and Songs of Protest in Punjab.' *Economic and Political Weekly*. pp. 33-37.

Teltumbde, Anand. (2011). *Dalit Captalism and Pseudo Dalitism, Counter Currents*. Retrieved from <http://www.countercurrents.org/teltumbde070311.htm> on 2 January 2017.

Young, Iris Marion. (2005). 'Five Faces of Oppression.' *Feminist theory: A Philosophical Anthology*. (Ed.) Cudd, Ann E. and Robin Andreasen. Oxford, UK Malden, Massachusetts: Blackwell Publishing. pp. 91-104.

URL sources

http://www.iep.utm.edu/2012/05/

https://issuu.com/yoshitomomorioka/docs/the_one_and_the_many

https://issuu.com/ivanradenkovic/docs/understanding-film_-marxist-perspectives---wayne--

https://www.lse.ac.uk/collections/law/news/news-archive.htm

https://quizlet.com/9912350/unit-6-industrialization-and-economic-development-vocab-flash-cards/

http://www.tandfonline.com/doi/full/10.1080/1358684X.2012.704578

http://www.thisissierraleone.com/sierra-leone-emmersons-kokobeh-song-the-truth-revealed/

http://aceproject.org/ace-en/topics/me/onePage

https://indiankanoon.org/doc/91938676/

https://www.scribd.com/document/326324330/AUG-6

https://issuu.com/thenation/docs/september_13__2011

http://wikivisually.com/wiki/Bhagat_Ravidas

http://alchetron.com/Ravidas-950833-W

https://theprg.co.uk/tag/caste/

https://www.revolvy.com/topic/International%20migration&item_type=topic

http://www.cpim.org/content/resolution-ideological-issues-20th-congress

http://wikivisually.com/wiki/Mauryan_Empire

https://dalitmuslims.wordpress.com/category/casteism-among-muslims/

CHAPTER 3

Appropriation of the Tribal Art Form in *Bhimayana*: Ambedkar Through the Graphic Mode

Vandana

The discourse on caste has for so long been subsumed, substituted, appropriated and at times, replaced amid the grand discourses of orientalism, anti-colonialism, nationalism, and post-colonialism. The Ambedkarite revolution in particular, signifies a history of rebellion that has nothing to do with the nationalistic struggle. However, the mainstream historiographical school in India has had the tradition to belittle or ignore every other movement except the national. The absence of Dalit history (and Dalit literary historiography) from mainstream historiographical accounts in India, in spite of the existence of a vast anti-caste intellectual history as well as literature, hence, evokes the need for an alternative cultural imagination. That has been channelised by *Navayana*—first, through *A Gardener in the Wasteland: Jotirao Phule's Fight for Liberty*, and secondly, through *Bhimayana: Incidents in the Life of Bhimrao Ramji Ambedkar*.

These two biographical graphic novels based on the lives of Phule and Ambedkar respectively, are attempts to escort the subaltern cause and history in India to the mainstream. But *Bhimayana*, in particular, is celebrated for its use of the Pardhan Gond art to illustrate Ambedkar's lifelong struggle to eradicate untouchability and annihilate caste. The spectacular absence of Dalit literature within Indian literary history as well as the theorisation of Indian literature however, instigates Dalit critics/ writers to explore this deficiency on the one hand and to stress the significance of Dalit theorisation of literature on the other. As a consequence, Dalit literary historiography, which stands in blatant contrast to Indian literary historiography, strives for something different from the national literary history. If in the postcolonial era, Indian literary historiography rose to prominence to contest colonialism and solidify nationalism, Dalit literary historiography emerges as the need of the hour to contest age-old Hindu dominance and retrieve the resistant Dalit voices.

As against the mainstream school of historiography, the subaltern school of historiography recaptures the role of the downtrodden, the popular, the oral, the local, the vernacular, and the oppressed in moulding significant historical changes. Aijaz Ahmed also notes that:

> ... the locus of literary production [in India]—certainly for those immense movements which changed the face of India in their own time—was most frequently not the urban elite but the life-process of the artisanate, the peasantry, the women, the shudras, the precariously located clusters of dissent. (Ahmed, 1992, 254).

A Graphic Endeavour at Alternative Historiography

The holistic domains of dominant histories clearly give first-hand preference to the nationalist and anti-colonial histories, while the caste-histories incorporating low-caste protests are considered secondary and often stay in oblivion. The unusually interesting project of Navayana—*Bhimayana*—is an effort to popularise Ambedkar's story. Since the graphic mode holds the potential to attract and influence people's imagination across all age groups, through the sequential storytelling format, *Bhimayana* aims to introduce Ambedkar not to the lower castes or the masses but is rather intended for the consumption of international readers and the privileged Indian metropolitan English-speaking bourgeoisie. While the lower castes (especially the Dalits) inevitably know the deified Ambedkar through personalised, familial histories, it is the global audiences who are targeted herein through the appropriation of Ambedkar's life and politics, using the graphic mode. In the Afterword to the book, S. Anand, the founder-editor of Navayana Publishing House, appropriately notes—'If the lives and experiences of Martin Luther King and Rosa Parks, Nelson Mandela and Malcolm X could resonate universally, Ambedkar's—and those of millions of dalits in India—ought to as well. After this 'unusually beautiful' rendering of Bhim's story by Durgabai Vyam and Subhash Vyam, there can be no reason not to engage.' (Anand, 2011, 103).

The soul-stirring biography of Ambedkar which is presented using the far-fetched tribal art of Gond artists, Durgabai Vyam and Subhash Vyam, re-enlivens Ambedkar's lifelong struggles thereby also raising the Dalit question in a very pertinent manner. The image-making techniques used herein to represent Ambedkar as the foremost Dalit intellectual with spectacles, on the cover-page itself, furthermore, goes in tandem with the thought-provoking narrative that runs throughout the book making use of animal and water imagery. For example, an illustration on page 24 shows cattle drinking water from a tank while Ambedkar-the child stands at a distance wondering why only the Mahars are forbidden from partaking water. Just then, an insight from Ambedkar says—"Animals enjoy more freedom!" (Anand, 2011, 25). In another instance, Ambedkar is pained to realise that while his father is helping build a water tank in Goregaon for the famine-affected people, he has no right to drink water at school.

Another interesting aspect about *Bhimayana* is the use of speech bubbles through which the opinions/statements/insults/assaults from each character within the narrative appear. In the Afterword, S. Anand names these bubbles as—(i) bird bubble: contains soft and gentle words, (ii) sting bubble: contains cruel and callous words, and (iii) thought bubble: contains the perspective of the thinking mind.

The illustration of these speech bubbles, undoubtedly signify narrative sympathy—those who have been at the receiving end of casteism speak through the bird bubble, while the asympathisers speak through the sting bubble. Furthermore, in Book 4, "The Art of Bhimayana", the readers are given a glimpse of the lives of the makers of the book using the narrative voices of the prime artists—Durgabai Vyam and Subhash Vyam—who reveal their tribal background and life-histories and duly accredit Jangarh Singh Shyam to have earned them due recognition of their Gond art through proper channelisation.

Use of a Tribal Art Form to Depict a Dalit's Life-History

Pardhan Gond art, as is practised by one of the several tribal communities in modern-day central India, signifies 'painted stories'. Commonly referred to as *Digna* or *Bhittichitra paintings*, this tribal art form of the Pardhan Gonds, traditionally deals with domestic architecture wherein the Gond dwellings (especially the walls and the floors) are painted with this art form as a symbol of good fortune. Through the use of vibrant imagery and motifs, Gond drawings can weave in rich narratives within a precise space. This traditional art form, however, was given a new expression by Jangarh Singh Shyam (who is represented on the dedication page), as he urged the tribal artists to enter the professional domain for the first time in 1990s. The thenceforth adapted modernised Pardhan Gond style re-enlivened the tribal art on canvas and single-sheet paper using multi-coloured clays, ink and paints. The narrative of *Bhimayana*, in fact, follows no formal box-like structure, such as that of traditional graphic novels, but is done through the use of *digna* patterns which manage to maintain the loose (*khulla*) narrative framework and incorporate wide-ranging aspects on a single page.

In his writings, be it by means of politics, anthropology, sociology or religion, Ambedkar repeatedly attempted to theorise the differences and non-belongingness between Dalits and other castes. Alongside political activism, Ambedkar always stressed the importance of cultural activism for mass mobilisation and radicalisation. For Ambedkar, writing was an insurgent and political activity so much so that he is till date admired for his theoretical activism. His comprehensive understanding of the caste system led him to structurally invade the territory of Hindu orthodoxy. Using writing as a battleground, he made attacks on the adversary texts point by point. Yet it would be highly unfair to discard his aims as only destructive, for when he offers insights into the Western parameters of justice, equality, and class-conflicts, for instance, his approach becomes quite constructive. The reservation policy, for instance, was introduced by him as a means of 'positive discrimination'. Apart from capturing several such intricacies of Ambedkar's life, *Bhimayana* brings to light issues as critical as the significant the Khairlanji massacre, the Mahad Satyagraha, the Dalit everyday struggle for water, the Gandhi-Ambedkar tussle, and last but not least the debate on caste-based reservation which instils soul into the narrative. *Bhimayana*, in fact, carries multiple recent accounts of atrocities against Dalits, cited with due references to the newspaper names and the required spatio-temporal information. The Khairlanji lynching, to begin with, sets off the chain of these news items. Other newspaper reports meant to provide newer historiographical perspective about the still prevailing caste discrimination include:

(i) Tension after Dalits draw water from well (Kolhapur, *Hindustan Times*, 29 Sept 2010) (Anand, 2011, 13)

(ii) Honour Killing shocks the capital (New Delhi, *Mail Today*, 15 June 2010) (Anand, 2011, 13)

(iii) Row over 'untouchable' Indian dog (Morena, Madhya Pradesh, *BBC News*, 24 Sept 2010) (Anand, 2011, 13)

(iv) Dalit killed for demanding wage (New Delhi, *The Times of India*, 3 Aug 2009) (Anand, 2011, 13)

(v) Dalit killed for digging own well (Satara, *Hindustan Times*, 4 May 2008) (Anand, 2011, 47)

(vi) Water Wars: Dalit Woman Torched (Bhopal, *The Times of India*, 6 June 2008) (Anand, 2011, 47)

(vii) Dalit siblings thrashed by landlord (New Delhi, *The Hindu*, 5 May 2008) (Anand, 2011, 73)

(viii) Thrown out of hospital, two Dalit women die (Kanpur, *Times News Network*, 2 Nov 2007) (Anand, 2011, 83)

(ix) When Dalits in Chakwara won the right to use the village pond, caste Hindus turned it into a sewer (Chakwara village, 50kms from Jaipur, *Tehelka*, 26 Jan 2008) (Anand, 2011, 55)

Analysing History of Caste and its Unrelenting Effects in India

The setting of *Bhimayana*'s narrative is laid as a conversation, which springs up at a bus station between an educated, modern young boy from an apparently privileged caste in Chennai, and a girl in the traditional North Indian attire (*kurta-pyjama*). The dialogue begins when the boy expresses his discomfort with the reservation policy in the job sector, and eventually leads to a gradual unfolding of the past and present nuances of caste discrimination in India so much so that while Ambedkar's story acts as a leitmotif throughout the book, its protagonist, however, turns out to be caste. For instance, the girl introduces the boy to Ambedkar's figure saying—"I'd read Ambedkar if I were you. I'd want to understand what happened in Khairlanji, and why two dalits are killed everyday in India." To which, the boy retorts—"Ambed—who? The guy in all those statues?" (Anand, 2011, 14). The 'dialogic imagination', thus channelised, shows how a discussion can help yield a consensus. The boy, for instance, throughout the book, speaks through the "sting bubble" but in the end he is shown to have undergone a 'change of heart' as he bids goodbye to the girl saying "Jai Bhim!". On the last page of Book 3, significantly, the final two statements from the boy are encased using the bird speech bubble where he says—"I'm starting to see why he is such an icon for dalits today."

With a huge corpus of writings to his credit, Ambedkar stands firm as one of the primary theorists of caste whose speeches and texts helped disseminate Dalit consciousness across the country. Taking inspiration from Ambedkar's teachings/writings in general and his incomplete autobiographical notes (compiled and edited as "Waiting for a Visa" in *Babasaheb Ambedkar: Writings and Speeches* by Vasant Moon) in particular, Dalit writers developed the mode of autobiography with the intention to hold a mirror up to social reality. Ambedkar's autobiographical notes exemplify his earliest experiences of untouchability as herein, an intellectually mature Ambedkar reflects on his past experiences of caste discrimination from a very specific subject position. The failure of the traditional religions stands as a guiding metaphor for Ambedkar to be able to conceptualise the various intricacies of this institution of untouchability. He stresses how religions have traditionally failed to offer people help. Rather religion itself has been responsible for their miseries. He offers real life glimpses to show that a person who is an untouchable to a Hindu, is also equally an untouchable to a Parsi or Muslim. He also records how irrespective of being educated and having acquired affluence, he continued to face caste discrimination at many junctures in his life.

Noting the significance of Dalit personal experience, in "Of Many Heroes", G.N. Devy remarks:

> The literary historiography of Dalit literature... focuses on the questions of otherness, difference, marginality, canon and the categories of aesthetics. In order to voice the protest of the marginalised, Dalit literature often follows the subversive historiographic path of personalizing history. It is therefore, perhaps, that autobiography is the most potent and often exercised form of fiction produced in Dalit literature. If long entrenched social discrimination separates history from its original twin, fiction, Dalit literature seeks to revert to the primal unity between fiction and history. (Devy, 2009, 127).

Considered in this light, *Bhimayana* stands firm as a historical narrative, which in the words of John Berger, has;

> [no] proscenium arch. No rectangular framing or unilinear time. No profiled individuals. Instead, a conference of corporeal experience across generations, full of pain and empathy, and nurtured by a complicity and endurance that can outlive the Market. Stories are being told like this all over the world. They are seldom printed and published. This book has now set an example. (Berger, (2010), 9).

In fact, *Bhimayana* challenges mainstream historiography by:

(i) Fictionalising Ambedkar's autobiographical notes through a popular mode—graphic fiction.

(ii) Incorporating news archives using a thread of thumbnails about the still prevailing caste violence in rural as well as urban Indian locales.

A Didactic Narration through a Popular/Visual Means

The fusion of a biography, Gond art, and graphic-journalism yields a multi-layered political document called *Bhimayana*, which is infused with critical insights at a number of places. Following the reference to the Mahad Satyagraha of 1927, for instance, comes the ironic sub-text about the 'purification yagya' conducted by the enraged Brahmins to undo the pollution caused to the Chavadar tank. The critical insight offered herein says—"The Brahmins decided to 'purify' the 'polluted' Chavadar tank by pouring into it 108 pots containing a mixture of cow-dung and cow-piss, milk, ghee, and curds—I kid you not—to a soundtrack of Vedic chanting..." (Anand, 2011, 53). This statement, through its ironic undertones, not only attempts alternative history but also shatters the sanctity associated with the myth of the holy cow in India.

Devoid of literacy, the so-called untouchables in India were confined to the oral tradition for ages. Their experiences, memories, and angst, likewise, could never be retained through 'the written word' for posterity. Ambedkar, however, could clearly comprehend the mobilisational power of the print medium and the written material to provide "a homogenous ideology to those divided by scattered thoughts." (Narayan, 2004, 19). Christophe Jaffrelot, in his profound study of Ambedkar and his struggle for social transformation, establishes that with respect to Ambedkar, what is important is not just what he says but also how he says, i.e., not just the content but the craft. The use of rhetoric, for instance, is easily discernible in his works from the manner in which he structures his arguments. Raising his fight against caste-based injustice to an ethical level, in the autobiographical notes, Ambedkar intimates—"Not that there were no washerman in Satara. Not that there we could not afford to pay the washerman... not that there were no barbers in Satara, not that we could not afford to pay the barber..." (Anand, 2011, 12). Moreover, the choice of the chapter headlines—"Be Inhuman than Touch an Untouchable", "A Tonga ride and Dignity", "Bhangi! You want Us to Address You Talati?"—appears quite intriguing for it does not embody self-pity or the narration of a sad story but a will to struggle, survive and somehow surpass this inhumane institution called untouchability. In the introduction to *Humiliation: Claims and Context*, Gopal Guru compellingly notes that to recognise the experience of humiliation is in itself a manifestation of protest and resistance. Accordingly, Dalit writings display a confrontational approach whereby the personal pain presents itself in the form of collective political assertion.

As Ambedkar actualised the project of fighting Hindu majoritarianism by fabricating anti-establishment myths and fiction, he made sure not to naturalise all lower-caste communities. Having had the political motivation to enable the lower castes to consider themselves as non-Hindus, Ambedkar sought to theorise opposition systematically. He did not want a coalition of the Dalits into the non-Brahmin ideology. Bitterly hostile and strongly relevant in nature, Ambedkar's writings reflect his analytical frame of mind. He not only simply records or states his arguments but also offers meticulous analysis and theorisation to justify his ideas even before receiving contestations. Valerian Rodrigues, while emphasising upon the significance of "the written word" in Ambedkar's political career, brackets out all other dimensions of his personality. *Bhimayana*, however, brings to light a holistic portrayal of Ambedkar's political life, barring his marital life.

Bhimayana, thus, emerges as an attempt in alternative historiography through the appropriation of the tribal Gond art-form. The use of Gond art to illustrate the life and struggles of Ambedkar emerges as an affirmative step to highlight the plural nature of the subaltern question in India—for herein, it constitutes not only the Dalits, but also Shudras, tribals, and Adivasis. While the mainstream history mainly records Ambedkar as the Chairman of the Drafting Committee of free India's Constitution, through meta-textual, illustrated, graphic representations, *Bhimayana* lays bare the so-far hidden facts from Ambedkar's life. Its attempt to retrieve archives, contest historical knowledge, and uncover the intentionally forgotten document of barbarism namely caste Apartheid, thus, makes way for Dalit historiography.

BIBLIOGRAPHY

Ahmed, A. (1992). ' 'Indian Literature': Notes towards the Definition of a Category.' *In Theory: Classes, Nations, Literatures*. Delhi: OUP. pp. 243-285.

Anand, S. (Eds.) (2011). *Bhimayana: Incidents in the Life of Bhimrao Ramji Ambedkar*. New Delhi: Navayana Publishing.

Berger, J., Foreword. (2010). *Bhimayana: Incidents in the Life of Bhimrao Ramji Ambedkar*. New Delhi: Navayana Publishing. 2011 Print.

Kumar, S. (2014). 'Graphic Novels and Bhimayana'. *Dalit Literature and Historiography*. (Ed.) Saroj Kumar Mahananda. New Delhi: Pragati Publications.

Devy, G.N. (2009). 'Of Many Heroes'. *The G.N. Devy Reader*. New Delhi: Orient Blackswan.

Gore, M.S. (1993). *The Social Context of an Ideology: Ambedkar's Political and Social Thought*. New Delhi: Sage Publications.

Guru, G. & Sarukkai, S. (2012). *The Cracked Mirror: An Indian Debate on Experience and Theory*. New Delhi: OUP.

Jaffrelot, C. (2005). *Dr. Ambedkar and Untouchability–Analyzing and Fighting Caste*. London: C Hurst & Co Publishers Ltd.

Narayan, B. & Mishra A.R. (Eds.) (2004). *Multiple Marginalities: An Anthology of Identified Dalit Writings*. New Delhi: Manohar.

PART II

Art Forms: Interfaces Between the Traditional and the Popular

CHAPTER 4

This is not Street Art: 'Post-Graffiti' Practices and the White Cube in Delhi

Sanchita Khurana

The London-based artist and curator, Cedar Lewisohn once famously said "if you had a degree, you did 'street art' as opposed to graffiti" (Lewisohn, 2008, 18). His quote reinforces revelations of my own research, suggesting quite clearly that institutional legitimisation has led urban street graffiti to be 'brought up' to the mainstream. This article discusses this legitimisation in a post-colonial context and proposes that the contemporary street art movement in Delhi is a peculiar case of institutional appropriation of the once subcultural art form into the mainstream art world and commerce of the post-industrial city. It studies in detail an art exhibition titled 'This is not Street Art', part of the annual street art festival St-Art Delhi 2014, to exemplify this.

In referring to itself as 'post-graffiti', contemporary street art forges an interesting relationship with art history. By analysing the simultaneous distance and proximity of street artists in Delhi to the gallery system, this article comments on the ambiguous relationship between the aesthetic popular and institutions of art. Through studying career trajectories of artists that are part of the street art scenario brewing in this city, it traces the class privilege inherent in this relationship and locates the said art movement, consequently, within 'creative city' debates that have emerged only recently in the context of Delhi.

Tracing the 'Post'

It has been widely agreed that there can be traced a major break between the American subcultural graffiti trends and the more globally dispersed street art culture— in fact, it is a break which can be traced back to the 1980s when New York style hip-hop graffiti was first prized for its value. Artists like Jean Michel Basquiat and Keith Haring can undoubtedly be said to be the predecessors of today's street art: when (their) graffiti was transferred from the subways and onto canvas for sale in galleries during the 1980s art boom in Manhattan, it was widely felt to have 'sold out' to the interests of the art establishment and become a 'post-graffiti' art movement.

'Post-graffiti' is now another term for street art, used to denote the resurgence of a kind of illegal (but legitimate) urban art production. Characterised by a number of techniques such as painting murals, wheat-pasting, postering, stencilling etc., post-graffiti distinguishes itself from graffiti mainly through its shift away from letters to visuals. In hip hop graffiti, the artist's name/ pseudonym is paramount; in post-graffiti styles the name is seen replaced with logos. Even though most street artists have adopted 'street names', they do not have a problem revealing their actual names in their art works if need be, unlike in the graffiti movement where the artist would have to be anonymous. Mostly in street art, the artist might well be recognised by the repeated spread of this logo, or a particular painting style.

Importantly, unlike graffiti writing which has been analysed as semiotic defiance by linguists (e.g. Pennycook 2010), today's street art is much less visually cryptic. In an attempt to communicate with the audience and expand its visual base, either by sending out a social message or simply by being aesthetically pleasing, post-graffiti art manages to increase what Kym Pruesse (1999) calls its 'accidental audience.' The very attempt at escalating one's chances of a meaningful public address reflects a motivational shift towards being viewed, understood and of course appreciated, rather than resisting urban spatial structures.

The appellation of the movement is interesting to me; it nevertheless implicates both graffiti and the current street art movement in a chronological progression very much in the style of in the historical order of art forms. Retaining graffiti's interventionist nature, post-graffiti art derives its essence from the subcultural mores of illegality and urban tacticality. At the same time, it posits itself as a necessary stylistic 'evolution' of the said subculture. Julie Reinecke's (2007) analysis of 'post-graffiti' as a (sub)culture between street, art and commerce, seems particularly insightful because it highlights how this art movement stands in distinction from, but also in connection with, these domains that play an important, and sometimes interactive, role in shaping the urban culture. There seems to be therefore a paradox that this new kind of street art lives on invoking a radical 'historical' reference while indicating 'new'-ness through formal, material and visual development.

Fieldwork enquiry illustrates that most street artists in Delhi tend to have academic art backgrounds (although a number of writers practise both graffiti writing and street art styles). With changing perceptions of what counts as art and with the increasing importance given to urban cultures the world over, it is now seen as fashionable, perhaps even desirable, for artists to critique the 'elitist art world' through both the content and form of their art work—that is, by associating themselves with the idea of cultural democracy. 'Post-graffiti' art movements offer room for both—these artists therefore are seen engaging in work that pose a direct attack, or at least a questioning commentary, on the art establishment. Typical to urban community projects, the teams and the artists interviewed as part of the research on the street art festival St-Art India 2014[1] narrativised a 'benevolent' civic engagement with the local citizens of the neighborhood, distancing themselves from the self-absorbed eccentric figure of the Modernist painter and placing the festival in direct opposition to the secluded gallery space. The curator of St-Art India, Giulia Ambrogi said in an interview about the art works being produced in the festival: "This is not selfish art on the part of the artists, this is about engaging with residents" (Betigeri, 2014).

One must however note that an aspect of art worlds is that '(they) frequently incorporate at a later date, works they originally rejected—thus the distinction lies not in the work but in the ability of an art world to accept it and its maker' (Becker, 1982, 227). In the history of art, one stumbles upon many such avant-gardist movements or as Alana Jelinek (2013) would say 'activism and other not-art,' that have built on and incorporated the 'popular' into their practice only to be incorporated themselves within the formerly critiqued gallery system (and at large the capitalist economy). Susan Gablik in her 1984 book *Has Modernism Failed?* dedicates a chapter specifically to analysing graffiti's integration into the institutional framework of the art world, and asks: "Are we confronted with yet another instance where mass-consumption capitalist economy expands into a taboo art in order to transform private behavior into a commodity?" (Gablik, 1984, 106).

It is not the first time that an urban interventionist movement stands the potential to be seen as 'art in the arms of power' (Zukin, 1982). A thorough Marxist reading of art history does reveal the appropriation of alternative and supposedly 'radical' art movements by capitalist enterprises. Martha Rosler (2010) lucidly writes of this phenomenon, implicating the Situationist Movement for their ultimate role in naturalising capitalist spatial systems; 'One may trace the grounding of the mid-century group the Situationist International in the recognition of the growing role of the visual—and its relationship to spatiality—in modern capitalism and thus in the complicity of art with systems of exploitation.' For the reasons of appropriation, street art has also often been compared to the Pop Art movement for having aestheticised zones formerly outside culturally recognised art space: 'OK, the street artist would say ... let's erase the zones and demarcations and acknowledge a continuum between art-institutional space and the public space surrounding everyday life' (Irvine, 2012, 13). The question then arises as to whether in doing so, such artists bring the gallery to the street or ultimately end up bringing the street to the gallery. It must also be asked whether in doing either of these, street art is 'appropriated' to the purposes of capitalism.

Interestingly, however, street art survives not on a simple incorporation into the art world but on the ambiguous relationship it maintains with art and industry; it is, not a simple 'selling out' but a 'do-it-yourself' entrepreneurialism based on the language of urban creativity, which further foregrounds the contradictions of capitalism and its adaptability to subversive cultural forms (Harvey, 2001, 360). Graffiti is therefore not so much devalued by the art world and by aesthetic criteria taking it over as it is given a double valuation. That is the reason for the popularity also of graffiti cultures in the same cities that are the hubs of global street art with Delhi now having been established as one. Always on the edge of illegality, the artists who are part of both graffiti writing and street art in Delhi (famous Indian graffiti writer Daku, for instance), do feel the inconsistencies and ambiguities in their own artistic trajectories, sometimes even using their 'notoriety' as a graffiti writer to build a 'career' as a radical urban artist.

It is this strategic placement of post-graffiti art from where it derives its value within the art world. Being illegal and urban, it claims to democratise art; but it functions as an art world of its own. The street/neighbourhood, studio, and gallery space intersect one another, and contemporary street artists find it convenient and beneficial for their work to move in and out of any of these literal and metaphorical spaces at any given time. This seems quite in sync with what world famous street artist Hendrik ECB, who painted the famous Gandhi Mural on the facade of the Delhi Police Headquarters at ITO as part of the festival being analysed, had to say in an interview about his work in Delhi: 'I personally don't see this difference between the 'White Cube' (a contemporary art gallery first established in London) and also in Delhi and the public space; it makes more sense to mix it' (Sanyal, 2014), which brings me to talk about the peculiar position of this new kind of street artist in Delhi.

This must be understood within the broader context of the shifts in urban aesthetics the world over, where cities are seen as means of economic growth. Over at least the last two decades, there have been concerted efforts by the Indian State to put Delhi on a global aesthetic, and thus economic, map. The ambition to attain this status is clearly expressed in the Master Plan for Delhi 2021: 'Vision-2021 is to make Delhi a global metropolis and a world-class city'.[2] Additionally, in 2013, a report launched by the Martin Prosperity Institute stated that 'Delhi takes the top spot as the most creative state in India with the greatest potential for success in today's creative economy.'[3] This report was based on research on Indian cities, which have become the new centres for cultural planning, now being hailed as essential to the formation of an economically successful city. In 2015, the Delhi Urban Arts Commission, a body that advises the Government of India on the maintenance of aesthetic and environmental quality in the capital, also announced the formulation of a Delhi Art Master Plan, in order to officially incorporate art into city planning.[4]

In general, discourses around the creative city nominate art and culture as drivers of urban change and regeneration. Since the aim of property developers is to increase economic activity by trading on cultural value, this cultural revalorisation of that which was once rejected, seems to ring true to the capital's very strategy of tapping unproductive or now decrepit spaces and attracting investment. In this sense, artists have often been seen as agents of capitalist urban change since their presence 'puts a neighbourhood on the road to gentrification' (Zukin, 1982, 23) as it happened in SoHo and the Lower East Side in New York. Arts and artists thereby are (inadvertently) co-opted into property redevelopment projects. Stevphen Shukaitis and Anna Kanngieser (2010) write eloquently about this process:

> Social and political movements, new artistic developments and quarters, as soon as they arise (or even before they arise sometimes) are seized upon by real estate developers, urban planners and policymakers to create the image of a new 'hip' district that will boost real estate prices, attract 'more desirable' residents and so forth, in a virtuous spiral of capitalist development. This process of gentrification led by or inadvertently spurred by developments in artistic and social creativity is an old one. (Shukaitis & Kanngieser, 2010, 67)

Examples of this are not difficult to cite even in the city of Delhi, which is the geographical focus of this study: a significant example of such transformation of local spatial practices being the case of beautification projects undertaken by resident associations and civic organisations in various neighbourhoods. Such beautification and community projects not only entrench a new urban aesthetics based on class purity but also pave the way for capital investment. This is exactly what we see happening in the urban villages of Delhi that are either already gentrified (Hauz Khas Village) or are well on the way to be (Khirkee Extension). Rikki Kher, a British Indian designer, in an article in *Tehelka*, describes himself as witness to historic times of creative growth in three great cities of the world—East End in London in the late 1990s, Brooklyn in New York City in the past decade and Shahpur Jat in Delhi at present. In comparing the three neighbourhoods, a clear trajectory is suggested for the urban restructuring of Delhi: there is a reason why Devika Singh regards the urban village as 'the metaphor, the host and the canvas of Delhi's art scene' (Singh, 2012).

The concept of urban village explains why despite being 'illegal', wall murals in the urban villages have been evaluated as 'public art' and as such are not subject to removal. That also helps to explain the co-option of the 'illegality', or at least the unacceptability, of graffiti into the aesthetic nature of post-graffiti or street art, which is readily supported by The Central and state governments in the form of urban art projects in Delhi, and welcomed by urban developers for the ameliorating effects it has on property. In fact, it is not just the developers who welcome this. For the most part of the duration of the street art festival St-Art Delhi 2014, street artists painted murals on walls that they selected based on various reasons. Interestingly, these were private walls, or in other terms, walls of houses owned by families, located in Hauz Khas Village, Khirki Extension and Shahpur Jat. The permissions that seemed to matter most here were the house owners', interactions that produced some interesting transactions and viewpoints on art as well as the street.

Looking at behavioural responses of some local residents whose walls the artists had chosen to work on, provided a glimpse into the broader perceptions of public culture and of artistic activity in India. The villagers staying in these areas were most of the times extremely receptive, except for the few who doubted the 'purpose' behind such decorative gestures. On the festival team's insurance that 'the purpose (was) just art', they seemed vaguely satisfied. The legitimacy of the street work thus stood not only in its purposiveness but also it being 'purely art'. An old woman even happily compared Tona's wall to 'modern art'.

Such responses seemed to serve as a reminder of the paradoxical proximity that such an audience feels or wants to feel towards 'art'. When asked, they told me that such 'beautification' would make their locality 'look better'. Various responses indicated that the communities in these villages looked at such art works as something ameliorating for the neighbourhood. This becomes understandable in the face of the stark contrast that these villages and the surrounding posh areas of South Delhi present. All of this helps to create/reinforce the self-confidence of residents and change the perception of the area within and outside the community, while bringing them closer to (the world of) art.

The Outsider, Inside

For those involved in the post-graffiti worlds of street art or more generally contemporary urban art, the 'creative city' has a 'lot to offer' even professionally. Apart from recognition, the creative economy generates jobs which run on investments in creative hubs and districts that need a multi-functional type of knowledge base and creativity. Banking on the 'outsider' nature of street inscription, post-graffiti confuses notions of public space and art space, but to do so, it employs artists who often already are, or at least aim to be, a part of the very art world that they seem to critique. In a complex manner then, post-graffiti rubs participates in the commercial art world. Street art's relationships with commerce are, however, more complex than either 'selling out' on the one hand, or a radical critique of capitalism on the other, in that the members of the street art culture are educated professionals who are very much a part of the 'knowledge' and 'creative' classes that capital relies on for generating a cultural economy of profit.

In order to understand the make-up of this 'creative class' that Richard Florida (2002)[5] famously talks about, one must also keep in mind George Yudice's (2003) claim that the shift to the creative economy favours the professional-managerial class (Yudice, 2003, 20). Thus, this is a section of population cultivated in what could be called 'artistic' modes of thinking. Actually or functionally middle-class, these professionals are very much at ease with the discourses and modes of intellectual practice required in higher education (or in cases, have themselves undergone rigorous academic instruction).

Often quite flexible in the application of their knowledge, these 'creatives' may bring with them not only training in design and branding, but also the ability to work with technological tools in both physical and virtual spaces. This description fits so well with the multi-disciplinary ways of functioning of contemporary street artists, that one is persuaded to equate post-graffiti artists to an emerging pool of creative professionals, rooted in the arts but suited to work in capitalist institutions.

The new kind of street artist thus possesses the ability to move in and out of the art world at her wish—a strategic back and forth between the street and the gallery, between that which is institutional and that which is the 'outsider'. Martine Irvine suggests that 'now working in a continuum of practice, spanning street, studio, gallery, installation spaces, and the Internet, street artists expose how an artwork is a momentary node of relationships, a position in a network of affiliations, configured into a contingent and interdependent order' (Irvine, 2012, 256). Almost as if to instantiate this, Serbian street artist Artez (who also paints in Delhi) spoke of this self-selling strategy that he employs in the gallery, while deriving pleasure from not being a permanent part of it: 'After all, once my exhibition is over, and my pieces are sold or left in some museum basement, the gallery won't matter to me anymore—I will completely forget about it, like so many times before, and I will go out and paint on the streets because that is where I belong and what I truly love!' (Artez, 2014, personal communication).

One need not say anything more about the class distinction this group must possess for such fluidity. Indian artists who are part of the street art movement find themselves, more often than not, in a global network (founded on artistic passion and a self-claimed distancing from mainstream art worlds) of 'creatives'. The global connect of this friendly-cum- professional network has been maintained by geographical mobility between Germany, Serbia, Japan, Italy and India; as well as via the internet, suggestive of a privileged/privileging social mobility and cultural capital. A sifting biographical study of the 'names' involved in the Delhi street art scene demonstrates how their educational experience has been a formative influence in their attitudes and approach not just to street art, but also to the city in general. From a sociological perspective, their personal testimonies present valuable insights into the peculiar ways their street art careers have come to be. Delhi-based artist Anpu Varkey, who maintained in an online conversation with me, that she is only an artist, not a graffiti writer, said in another interview that 'one loses sight of what it means to be an artist now. This is where I feel that street art is burgeoning due to its limitless visibility, strengthened by the openness of the people who live with it and around it' (Varkey, 2014).

Several other street artists I have worked with through the course of this research have been successful in making the transition into the creative sector, whether as designers, professional artists, or as entrepreneurs selling their skills as youth/arts development workers. These artists work across media, doing what would fall under the definition of graffiti, as well as working within gallery environments, making them 'outsiders' that are always already inside. Hanif Kureshi, the creative director of St-Art India Foundation, himself has been an art student at Maharaja Sayajirao University, Vadodara, exhibiting his works at many biennales internationally and has won awards in design and typography. He currently works as a 'senior creative' at Wieden+ Kennedy, an international advertising agency that brings sundry creative professionals together. Kureshi's design and typography initiative 'Handpainted Type' positively informs his identity as a street artist and a graffiti writer across the globe. In pursuing a professionally driven ambitiousness, there seems to be a legitimising narrative in these artists' approach, which serves the belief that talent must be utilised at any cost.

In fact, part of this post-graffiti culture is also the sprouting appearance of private 'creativity' and communication based start-ups/initiatives revolving around street art: for example 'street art' print house Kulture Shop that has been selling posters and T-shirts of the printed version of these artists' works; street art galleries that act as social hubs, for example, Social Offline in Hauz Khas; documentary channels such as Now Delhi TV by Akshat Nauriyal, which was responsible for documenting St-Art Delhi 2014 and even street curatorial facilitators like Delhi Dallying. This suggests that the post-graffiti scene in Delhi is not about the art work or the artists alone, but is enhanced, perhaps even sustained, by various creative intermediaries that operate as apparatuses to collectively generate and produce a post-graffiti aesthetic.

Walls-Within and Without

In February 2014, an exhibition was launched in a small private rental called Social Offline, used as gallery space in Hauz Khas Village, Delhi; this exhibition was called 'This is not Street Art.' As one of the showcasing events of St-Art Delhi 2014, the title of the exhibition seemed to pose itself in contradistinction from and yet in consonance with the street, the popular. The curator Giulia Ambrogi, who is ironically also the project manager of the public art project 'Walls' in Rome, said on the opening night of the exhibition that 'We're in a post-graffiti era'.

Divorced from any sort of community engagement, the exhibition seemed to be a practice given to globalised street art culture, where 'culture' represents not a localised variety of customs but a homogenous global network that operates across borders. The chronological naming of a street aesthetic behind the exhibition: that is, of 'post-graffiti', seemed only as viable as the 'post' in post-modernism in India, for there cannot be found in the case of Delhi, the context of a separate subcultural graffiti movement to be superseded, with graffiti writing here acting as a potential step towards a 'proper' art career.

Hanif Kureshi was careful to suggest that while the two terms, graffiti and post-graffiti, related to slightly different practices, they did share a similar cultural lineage. However, one must keep in mind that this conscious naming of styles and movements in the gallery world occurs mostly as a way of guiding purchases as well as creating contexts of understanding and association. The title of the exhibition 'This is Not Street Art', then, seemed to serve at once as a method of association with as well as of distancing from the street.

The exhibition showcased various 'visual artists' or 'street artists' from across the world and displayed a range of works from multimedia paintings and wall art to installations that brought into use street objects, garbage and other ephemera. It also drew on issues of social importance at times, and from humour at other times.

Neither was there a connective theme nor a common medium. Each art work had a name plate underneath it, and some artists left their visiting cards for the public. In a move towards showcasing those people embracing the urban environment as a creative medium, and not necessarily just graffiti writers, the exhibition appeared compliant in evoking the language of 'creativity' as a way of marking a graffiti/post-graffiti distinction. A clever paradox to be observed was the presence of non-graffiti works by artists like Yantr, PCO and Daku, who are well-known names in 'illegal' graffiti writing throughout Delhi. There was a complete absence of spray paint in the exhibition even though other kinds of works by Daku were all sold out.

While claiming a democratic principle, the setting of the exhibition in a private space in a gentrified neighbourhood like Hauz Khas Village, acted as a 'filter' to who could visit the exhibition (and who definitely could not). Notably, HKV conforms to the model of an increasingly important inner-city new economy precinct, sporting not just leading cultural industries, but also the fanciest of high-consumption outlets of food, art, fashion and design. The area thus supports the post-graffiti scene, with a number of trendy bars that not only serve as informal social hubs, but also may host specialist 'street art' exhibitions. Only recently gentrified, the former industrial area provides an ample supply of urban canvases for murals -- both legal and otherwise. St-Art India coordinator Mridula Garg (2014) commented in an interview to me:

> Hauz Khas Village had an already set base for street art and graffiti before the festival. In its non-orderly fashion of things, many artists, Indian and International had left their mark on its walls. Also, it is one of the city's markets which has a large footfall of college students and relatively younger crowd. The two factors combined made it a perfect place for the exhibition which was like a congregation space and people could know more about the festival and ongoing works in the city. (Garg, 2014, personal communication)

Kureshi also insisted that 'HKV is an area frequented by all kinds of young people—we wanted to shift the art viewing audience—this attracted a different kind of group towards art viewing' (Kureshi,

2014, personal communication). The shift, however, ultimately happened within the gentry that usually is attracted to and benefits from the 'alternative' aesthetic worlds—the young urban middle class aspiring to view, understand and collect art that is 'hip'. The 'exhibition' space both deliberately aped many formal art world conventions and claimed to be open to all, while avoiding the gaze of the street, resulting in the creation of a new type of upcoming gallery space—a White Cube without walls, perhaps.

Conclusion

In an open-ended conclusion, one can juxtapose with the unique aesthetic space discussed above another discursive space that was generated during the course of the same street art festival as part of a one day event: a curated walk in/through the urban village of Shahpur Jat, another upcoming hub for street art. Conducted by St-Art India in collaboration with Delhi Dallying, a private blogging enterprise run by three architecture students, this urban walk seemed to be in direct contrast with the exhibition, at least in its community-orientedness. The 'curators' took the 'visitors' through the mazy bylanes of Shahpur Jat, bringing into deliberate view all the 'walls' that had been painted. They also put together a small kit which consisted of a stencil, a Shahpur Jat art navigation map and a collage of postcards of the artworks packaged.

Considering the controlled experience it brought to street art, one becomes sure that there seems to be no escape from intramural authentication, no 'outside the wall.' Garg (2014, personal communication) remarked that 'given their academic background of art and architecture, they (Delhi Dallying) were able to synthesise the space, art, artists and the local inhabitants of Shahpur Jat quite well. They narrated incidents that occurred during the making of the walls and put them in the context of the time and history of the village.' Interestingly, while the exhibition 'This is Not Street Art' brought the street aesthetic to the gallery, this walk brought institutional ways of understanding aesthetics onto the street, leaving us with the musings that the art world now is not really standing on what Douglas Crimp (1993) calls the 'museum's ruins', but has kept the 'museum without walls' installed in the institution.

REFERENCES

1. A brainchild of street artist/designer Hanif Kureshi, St-Art Delhi (short for Street Art Delhi) was the first international street art festival in Delhi held in the winter months of 2014. The festival, spread over fifty days with various events including a graffiti jam, a Pecha Kucha talk night, workshops, curated walks and an exhibition, was officially launched on 18 January with a documentary screening/opening gala that took place at Max Mueller Bhavan in Delhi on 24 January. Some of the artists who were part of the festival are: Anpu (Delhi), Tofu (Germany), Yantr (Delhi), Tona (Germany), Alias (Germany), Sergio Cordeiro (Brazil), Inkbrushnme (Pune), Harsh Raman (Delhi), PCO (Delhi), Alina Vergnano (Italy), Amitabh Kumar (Bangalore), DAKU (Delhi), Hendrik ECB (Germany), Mattia Lullini (Italy), Ranjit Dahiya (Mumbai), Bond (Germany), M-City (Poland), Ano (Taiwan) among others.
2. https://dda.org.in/ddanew/pdf/Planning/reprint%20mpd2021.pdf.
3. http://competitiveness.in/delhi-takes-top-spot-creativity-index-report-2013/.
4. http://economictimes.indiatimes.com/news/politics-and-nation/street-art-to-be-guided-by-art-master-plan-in-delhi/articleshow/50275132.cms.
5. Florida's 'creative class' thesis is one of the most important and lasting theories on the shift to a creative economic discourse.

BIBLIOGRAPHY

Becker, H.S. (1982). *Art Worlds*. Berkeley: University of California Press.

Betigeri, A. (2014). 'Gandhi, Tihar Jail and Police Headquarters Get Caught up in Delhi's Street Art Festival.' Retrieved from aartibetigeri.com/portfolio/gandhi-tihar-jail-and-police-headquarters-get-caught-up-in-delhis-street-art-festival on 1 February 2017.

Bochner, M. (2009). 'Why Would Anyone Want to Draw on the Wall?'. *MIT Press Journals,* Vol. Fall 29. pp. 35-140.

Chakraborty, A. (2013). 'Shahpur Jat: Capital's Newest Fantasy'. *Tehelka Magazine*. Retrieved from www.tehelka.com/2013/10/

shahpur-jat-from-sleepy-village-to-urban-hotspot/on 30 January 2017.

Crimp, D. (1993). *On the Museum's Ruins.* Massachusetts and London: MIT Press.

DDA Report. Master Plan for Delhi 2021. Retrieved on https://dda.org.in/ddanew/pdf/Planning/reprint%20mpd2021.pdf on 28 January 2017.

Editorial Team, 'Right up Her Street.' Interview with Anpu Varkey. POOL June 2014. issuu.com/poolmagazine/docs/pool 46_for_web.

Florida, R. (2002). *The Rise of the Creative Class: and how it's Transforming Work, Leisure Community and Everyday Life.* New York: Basic Books.

Gablik, S. (1984). *Has Modernism Failed?* New York: Thames and Hudson.

Harvey, D. (2001). *Spaces of Capital: Towards a Critical Geography.* New York: Routledge

Irvine, M. (2012). 'The Work on the Street: Street Art and Visual Culture' in *The Handbook of Visual Culture.* (Eds.) Barry Sandwell and Ian Heywood. London and New York: Berg. pp. 235-278

Jelinek, A. (2013). *This is not Art: Activism and other 'Not-Art'.* New York: Palgrave Macmillan.

Khurana, Sanchita with Hanif Kureshi. 'Interview St-Art India.' 13 February 2014.

Khurana, Sanchita and Artez. 'Artez.' 9 June 2014.

Khurana, Sanchita and Mridula Garg. 'Interview: St-ART Delhi Team.' 5 January 2014.

Lewisohn, C. (2008). *Street Art: The Graffiti Revolution.* California: Tate Publishing.

Martin Prosperity Institute. (2013). 'Delhi takes top spot in the Creativity Index Report' Retrieved from http://competitiveness.in/delhi-takes-top-spot-creativity-index-report-2013/ on 1 March 2014.

Pennycook, A. (2010). 'Spatial Narrations: Graffscapes and City Souls'. *Semiotic Landscapes: Language, Image, Space.* (Eds.) Jaworski, A. & Thurlow, C. London : Continuum Books.

Pruesse, K. (1999). (Ed.) *Accidental audience: Urban interventions by artists.* Toronto: Off/site Collective.

Reinecke, J. (2007). *Post-Graffiti: Between Street, Art and Commerce.* Berkeley: Gingko Press.

Rosler, M. 'Culture Class: (2010). 'Art, Creativity, Urbanism'. *e-flux* Journal #21. Retrieved from http://www.e-flux.com/journal/21/67676/culture-class-art-creativity-urbanism-part-i/on 29 May 2013.

Sanyal, Amitava with Hendrik. (2014). 'INTERVIEW: HENDRIK BEIKIRCH/ECB, KOBLENZ.' Retrieved from st-artdelhi.org/blog/ on 10 June 2014.

Sharma, Nidhi. (2015). 'Street art to be guided by Art Master Plan in Delhi.'//economictimes.indiatimes.com/articleshow/50275132.cms?utm_source=contentofinterest&utm_medium=text&utm_campaign=cppst on 30 January 2017.

Shukaitis, S. and Kanngieser, A. (2010). 'Cultural Workers, Throw Down Your Tools, The Metropolis Is On Strike'. *Critical Cities: Ideas, Knowledge and Agitation from Emerging Urbanists* Vol. 2. (Eds.) Naik, D. and Oldfield, T. London: Myrdle Court Press. pp. 64-75.

Singh, D. and Raqs Media Collective. (2012). 'Delhi'. *Frieze* Issue 148, 1 June, 2012. Retrieved from frieze.com/article/delhi on 20 March 2014.

Snyder, G.J. (2009). *Graffiti Lives: Beyond the Tag in New York's Urban Underground.* New York: New York University Press.

Yudice, G. (2003). *The Expediency of Culture: The Uses of Culture in the Global Era*. Durham, NC: Duke University Press.

Zukin, S. (1995). *The Cultures of Cities*. Cambridge, MA: Blackwell.

Zukin, S. (1982). 'Art in the Arms of Power: Market Relations and Collective Patronage in the Capitalist State'. *Theory and Society,* Vol. 11, No. 4. pp. 423-451.

CHAPTER 5

Limits to Popularity: Adapting to Bhupen Khakhar's Artwork

Samarth Singhal

> The transition to the predominant modern meaning of 'widely favoured' or 'well liked' is interesting in that it contains a strong element of setting out to gain favour, with a sense of calculation that has not quite disappeared...In mC20 popular song and popular art were characteristically shortened to pop, and the familiar range of senses, from unfavourable to favourable gathered around this. The shortening gave the word a lively informality but opened it, more easily, to a sense of the trivial.
>
> (Williams, 1983, 237-238)

Raymond Williams in *Keywords* is able to clarify the ceaselessly transient definitions of the 'popular', and it seems a popular definition of the term 'popular'- numbers- may not be wholly adequate in describing multiple historical accounts of the term. Bhupen Khakhar's oils are helpful in navigating these narratives. The paper attempts to consider popularity as numerous intertextual routes a work may find itself embedded in, in order to conclude with a more nuanced understanding of forms of popular visual art. It begins by elaborating on a relationship between appropriation and pop culture, and discusses the consequences of a Khakhar exhibition at the National Gallery of Modern Art, New Delhi, and finally discusses the space of digital media as posters following in Khakhar's wake are exhibited online.

I find the idea of 'routes' germane to the larger question the paper attempts to answer: Is popularity adaptable? For instance, when Khakhar is museumised, and thus adapted to, does this symbolise a shift in popularity? If Khakhar adapts to 'pop art' to one Indian scenario, does he also adapt it to its popularity? Where does medium/spatial specificity lie along this spectrum of adaptation and reuse? The essay attempts to provide answers to the questions posed above.

Khakhar's paintings traverse more than one space: the studio, the national gallery, and the news media, specifically the internet. The kitschy cheeky 'Adarsh Balak' comics, shared widely on platforms like Facebook, are an example of social media responding to earlier visual art. Khakhar reworks Hockney and Lichtenstein's 'pop art', as we will see in the course of the discussion. I suggest that Khakhar's reappropriation is not innocent, but a responsible response to canon formation within the category of 'pop'. His canvases indigenise the pop movement. It is fascinating that as Khakhar liberally activates the devices of 'fantasy' and 'irony' in his scenes, his own work is ironically appropriated by the gallery system.

It seems that the adaptation of style, content, or canvas to another space and time is the centrepiece of popular fiction: in fact, genre fiction is arguably a response to reader expectations built over centuries. Popular fantasy for instance is variously an amalgam of faerie, folk, myth, fable, and romance. Linda Hutcheon in her notable work *A Theory of Adaptation* (2006) argues for the inevitable change that occurs between a primal text and its medial or intertextual movement. This movement may be understood as central to popular fiction. The adaptation, perhaps reappropriation, of artistic elements is a motor of creativity and at the same time is able to practise a double manoeuvre: pushing the boundary of the unfamiliar, and pulling back to the familiar. The adaptation is hence both recognisable and not, thus subtly transforming the primal text. This transformation enables the 'trajectory' of popular forms.

Khakhar's 1972 work *De Luxe Tailors* is in clear conversation with Lichtenstein's comic reversals. Lichtenstein parodies popular graphic art by remaking it for the gallery. Khakhar uses the same method here: the lurid colours, the neat architecturally mapped spacing, and most notably, the emphasis on a careful refusal to use 'perspective', as defined by E Gombrich in *Art and Illusion* (1960). The joke, however, lies in him being able to indigenise 'pop art' by reviewing Indian forms of popular art with levity i.e. poster art.

Producing a sign system for denoting, thus signifying, kitsch, Khakhar gave his version of pop art a definite local meaning long before the 'local' gained currency as a binary correlate of the global. Further, he historicised the phenomenon of pop as popular, and linked this to stylistic hybrids in the vernacular schools of Indian art. (Kapur, 2000, 3)

It is possible to read this as Khakhar's investment in adaptation of style and method albeit constrained by context. Khakhar then re-appropriates the popular.

Museum

> "...If the plan of a national museum presented itself at this juncture as an obvious culmination of other practices- as the most natural appendage of the new nation-state- it could do so only through an erasure of the complex politics of belonging and location that surrounded the objects, a subtle blotting out of earlier residences and other contending claims that these objects could naturalise their presence in the new national collection." (Guha Thakurta, 2004, 200).

Guha Thakurta diagnoses a transformation in the construction of a national museum. The 'erasure' of politics and 'other contending claims' demands a reorientation of placement of the art object within the national canon. Khakhar's canonisation as a post-1947 artist representing national claims, and as an artist worthy of rememorialisation in 2016 in the National Gallery of Modern Art (NGMA) embodies this movement. As stated above, adaptation of artists and art objects is a given. However, as Guha Thakurta proves in her study of the National Museum in New Delhi, a reorientation of art work is also a given. Arrangement of art in order to create a coherent narrative of the nation erases areas of contention, and reinstates a sense of unity. Adaptation, or reorientation follows a clear political agenda.

Khakhar's disruption of represented visual space through the insertion of homosexuality, metafiction, fantasy, and myth would be blunted according to this reading. His ironic treatment of poster and pop art would be neutralised and the irony transmuted to a pleasurable and leisurely performance of the nation through exhibition of visual art. For instance, his *Two Men in Banaras* (1982) is selectively precluded from exhibition at the NGMA. As implied in *De Luxe Tailors*, the play with perspective and indeed a dramatic awareness of this play is a running strand in his visual art. But the visual shock of this painting lies in its representation of varied forms of male bodily community: the massage, the dip in the river, and the sexual interaction being the most visible. His emphasis on the male sexual body is unmistakable. These men touch each other, excite each other, and seem to be comfortable around other male bodies. The space of the *ghat* becomes fantastic as it transforms from homosocial to homoerotic. The invocation of the homoerotic, which putatively ruptures the heteroerotic, provides the shock for the viewer. This explains the absence of this particular canvas in the NGMA exhibition, thus exemplifying one of the 'erasures' that Guha Thakurta speaks of.

It is also noticeable that the hair style and colour, the sagging body of the white haired man on the left, and an erection that bends as opposed being erect: all point to a physical union between an old man and a younger man. A gerontological insecurity also imbricates itself in the art of Khakhar. The younger body signifies vitality and virility, while the older body seems to desire the younger sexually, but also in nostalgia for lost youth. Therefore, the public space of the *ghat* is disrupted by a performance of sexuality and age, and such a performance is jettisoned by the NGMA. This gestures to a failure of national spaces to assimilate alternative bodies and sexualities. With the NGMA's covert refusal of exhibition, it becomes possible to reclaim Khakhar as an idiosyncratic artist with a uniquely personal, untrained, yet tolerable vision, and hence assimilate him to the national canon.

At this point we are negotiating with three available routes for 'popular' visual narratives: pop art, Khakhar's playful renditions of the same, and the NGMA's museumisation of Khakhar's intervention. Radical metamorphoses mark each stage in this travel. Pop art demonstrates the ironic potential of juxtaposition and incongruity; between form and content on the one hand, and exhibition space on the other. While it attempts to break plastic boundaries between the high and the low, it reproduces them in the recourse to the gallery system. The gallery system, as Pierre Bourdieu explains in *Distinction*, is implicated in a network of cultural capital, thus restricting access and transforming pop into an inside joke shared by a chosen few. Khakhar, on the other hand, uses indigenous pop, but in a gesture of affectionate caricature: thereby cracking the joke that Lichtenstein, Warhol, Hockney begin, but at the same revelling in the opening of visual access that pop reveals, and expanding the scope of the gallery. In the twenty-first century, this scope is proliferated in public installations and social media.

Digital Media

The multiple adaptations that Khakhar's art enables and is informed by can be studied under two conceptual but related categories: media exhibition and popularity. The question of access relates the two categories together. Bourdieu's brilliant study of the accruing of cultural capital provides a reasonable point of entry into the debate about the adaptability of popular visual art. Unlike Benjamin's idea of the aura which systematically diminishes as the art is accommodated by mechanical reproduction, the popularity of an image follows no such logic. Khakhar's prints and paints are prime examples of suspect popularity.

The 'Adarsh Balak' retellings establish themselves as ironic interventions in digital media platforms. It is difficult to state with certainty whether the distribution of their visibility through the 'share' feature on Facebook defines them as 'viral'. But if wide scope is a measure of popularity, then they can considered an integral, albeit ephemeral, part of popular visual culture. The primary reason they can be understood as descendants of Khakhar or inadvertent adaptations of Khakhar's work is the similarity of method. Both Khakhar and Priyesh Trivedi (the creator of the Adarsh Balak comics) parody poster art.

Poster art itself is now being reimagined as a site for affective community-based apprehension. 'Poster art offers auspiciousness without risk; hence even the most aggressive tantric deities metamorphose into the sorts of persons one can welcome into one's parlour and indeed one's greater family.' (Lutgendorf, 2003, 86). Lutgendorf speaks of 'welcoming' the poster into one's intimate space. Lutgendorf is mostly concerned with posters that depict deities but his argument for the intimacy generated by the poster stands valid. Posters that promote film, ideal behaviour, and national integration are didactic pieces that outline in identifiable detail national professions and codes of behaviour incumbent upon the body of a growing child. Thus they are welcomed by the guardians or care givers who make the choice for the child. The typical 'Adarsh' poster divides the space into rectangular blocks, using a simple colour scheme, and portrays a young boy or girl going through her day in a series of panels which depict acceptable activities. The prescriptive tone is emphatic in its address to both children and adults. 'The basic paradox that underlies all discussions about children's literature is, after all, the fact that the literature is written by adults, while the child-consumers have very little to say about the entire process.' (Gupta and Chatterjee, 2009, 4).

The Adarsh retellings on the other hand, retain the tone but transform the text and the image that the older posters use. This ensures familiarity and a play with this familiarity. Thus they are effectively parodying older art forms. "...and take pleasure in seeing him turn against the lessons he once taught. It's the delight of seeing recognised associations in unexpected situations that shocks and amuses, and resonates- here, especially, the good boy gone bad, and the contemporary references..." (Zainab, 2014, np)

This method, common to parody and adaptation is Khakhar's to use in his *De Luxe Tailors*. The garish colour is one aspect that he brings to attention. Film posters usually work with tones that are loud and attention seeking. The blue and the green seems to be in a state of controlled excess as the tones are unusual for a realistic depiction but the colour respects realism in that it does not cross borders. The management of space is another aspect he highlights in his work. Didactic posters sanitise the visible area. The detail available to the viewer is urgently significant to the plot of the panel, and no unnecessary detail impinges upon the viewer. A consequent neatness, almost excessive, becomes a crucial quality of spatial management.

Lastly, the nature of the profession-tailoring- as opposed to a 'respectable' profession like that of doctor, engineer, teacher, bureaucrat, or farmer lends a layer of complexity to his comedy. Poster art attempts to obviously instruct the viewer into consuming a film or making life choices. As Khakhar paints the tailor, the comedy lies in him pedestalising the profession for an audience that largely comprises individuals with requisite cultural capital to visit the museums he exhibits in. While it may partly be a revision of normative professional aspirations, it is probably a tribute to the urban space of a 'small' non-metropolitan town, which apprehends the 'humble' tailor. The distance that Khakhar makes the watchmaker travel in his canvas—Vadodara to the museum—constitutes his reinvention of pop art. It is comic, and a demonstration of the pastiche rupture of the boundary between the high and the low.

A digression into Khakhar's work is necessary to arrive at the core of exhibition space: museum and galleries. Bourdieu has already encouraged us to be wary of statements that valorise the political subversion of works of art.

Those who suppose they are producing a materialist theory of knowledge when they make knowledge a passive recording and abandon the 'active aspect' of knowledge to idealism, as Marx complains in the theses on Feuerbach, forget that all knowledge, and in particular all knowledge of the social world, is an act of construction implementing schemes of thought and expression, and that between conditions of existence and practices or representations there intervenes the structuring activity of the agents, who, far from reacting mechanically to mechanical stimulations, respond to the invitations or threats of a world whose meaning they have helped to produce. (Bourdieu, 1984, 469)

It is exhibition in spaces, and the determination of compromise, in these spaces that must comprise the effect of such art. In which case, the medium of oil on canvas, most notably found in galleries and museums, suggests a nullification of pointed activism, as found in the case of the NGMA. The question arises now: is it possible to find a medium or space which does not proscribe or prohibit?

Digital Media is potentially one such space or medium. The 'sharing' of art work exponentially increases through the internet.

Unlike the museum, which displays only to restrict, the internet may abet the ceaseless remaking of the 'original' thus subjecting the work of art to a state of unending politicisation. The sharing of an image, however, may also be a more precarious venture. The consumption of political cartooning, for instance, is a matter of pleasure and leisure in that there is a perpetual fond pleasure in the reduction of content, and the consumption takes place in a space of leisure time. I suggest that sharing on Facebook may be understood as an activity that is *also* facilitated by pleasure and leisure. What complicates this neat categorisation—of only pleasure and leisure— is the putatively political content of shared posts and the nature of the pleasure afforded in the digital medium.

After Marshall McLuhan's *Understanding Media* (1964), it is difficult to associate new media or digital media with consumers without thinking of medium specificity. For instance[i], Benjamin's idea of auratic diffusion dependent on reproduction might be useful in understanding digital poster reappropriation. It seems that the almost fantastic quality of the internet to share a message or rework it through memes (specialised text image collaborations that invite adapted reproduction) may be a perfectly convenient example of auratic diffusion. The original message in the Willy Wonka meme is continually transformed. It may be argued that with each share, 'note', 'screenshot', or 'dp' shift, the first is being shorn off its originary power.

This would help us identify the Adarsh Balak retelling as an acme of subversive exhibition. The original poster attempts to peremptorily request the viewer to practice life in coded imperatives. It is first changed to a cheeky message that reuses the didacticism, and is then shared widely on social media. By the above logic, each time the poster is memed or distributed, it forces the original pedantic poster to be revaluated.

However, an optimistic reading is compromised when one begins to think about the manner of consumption. As stated earlier, one rubric, however inadequate, would be to read poster art as effects of a composite of pleasure and leisure. Bourdieu cautions us that participation in an activity is clearly indicative of participation in an economy of access. Pleasure and leisure therefore must also be seen through access. The pleasure in this case is the fond familiarity of nostalgia. Consumers remember the posters from their childhood and are consequently pleased to view them and facilitate others' viewing of them who may be peers, colleagues, friends, or acquaintances. The Zainab article brings attention to the nostalgia of Adarsh Balak.

The leisure associated with the internet also needs elaboration. Facebook, Instagram, Twitter, have become parallel selves to daily living. Greenblatt's idea of a 'self fashioning' (1980) is germane to the construction of identities online. The performance of identities in the digital medium in accordance with varied contexts makes possible for a statement like 'you are what you share' to be idiomatic. It is significant that through discussions of 'fake' profiles or news, the value according to social media presence of an individual is perpetually reaffirmed. In such a scenario, thinking of Facebook as leisure suggests a clear break between lived reality and virtual reality. There is no doubt that twentieth century leisure practices like music, film, books, museums are ultimately political, and are informed by relations of production as Adorno conclusively argues in 'Free Time' but in the twenty-first century it is a blurred line between lived reality and virtual reality in many regions of the world, owing to uneven media development.

The implications of online self-fashioning for the exhibition of poster parodies akin to Khakhar's indigenisation of pop art are immense. Given the ceaseless operative traffic online, the digital medium is particularly fruitful to identity formation. The 'habitus' (Bourdieu, 1984) afforded to participants structures the sharing, and allows the structuring of the digital sphere through the sharing of such art.

However, the structured and structuring nature of the medium makes the effect of the art suspect. Already there is a gap in Zainab's interpretation of Trivedi's art: on the one hand, she terms it 'subversive', and on the other, she confirms that part of the delight of such interventions is the pleasurable re-cognition that allows the consumers to relate to the art. The medium forces the individual to share or bring attention to something she has affectively responded to, and if that response is mediated by delightful nostalgia, then the political expectations of the intervention are rendered null and void.

Moreover, as we are what we share, then the sharing of such art becomes an attempt at forging for oneself a persona who wants to be seen as 'rad' or 'cool' in their apparent rebellion for childhood strictures embodied in the 'original' pedagogic posters. The subversion apparently present in the artwork is neutralised in the sharing of this artwork through the medium. If the idea is to rethink child-friendly literature by parodying literature that is explicitly unfriendly to children, then it is overtaken by the almost surreal caricatures presented by Trivedi. Thus, the discussion that digital art enables does not symbolise politically charged auratic diffusion as predicted by Benjamin, but fond bonding within an imagined community.

As we come to the end of the paper, it is important to remember the questions we posed at the beginning: is popularity adaptable? And where is it possible to place medium specificity in the study of adaptations of pop art? The answers that emerge defy intermedial optimism. As the case of the Adarsh Balak proves the popularity of a style cannot be adapted, and that adaptation will have an unpredictable effect over the style. The rationale for the popularity of Adarsh Balak is the invocation of an apparently apolitical distant childhood that finally reinstates the communally determined affective status quo. The digital sphere cannot offset the 'erasures' inherent in the museum.

In the case of NGMA and the non-exhibition of *Two Men in Banaras*, we see that the performativity of national affective belonging disables the disruptive potential of the artistic intervention. His grotesque representation of the inadequacies of the nation post-1947 is blunted. Conversely, his indigenisation of poster parody is tolerated as an 'Indian' response to international art movements and is consequently allowed exhibition at NGMA. The pleasure of parody as the discussion demonstrates may also undermine the acuteness of any critique. In conclusion then, it is imperative to accept the conservative capability of routing popular visual forms given that the answer to the question of access and distribution (or sharing) will be determined by spatial and medium specificity. The implication for our study is that adaptation or popular fiction studies is a complicated manoeuvre. But one must move beyond simply stating that adaptation or reappropriation is complicated. I suggest that a study of popular visual forms rigorously speculate upon the peculiar pleasure and leisure that spaces demand and then attempt to map politics over aesthetics. The essay has been an attempt at doing so.

(**Note:** I would like to thank my friend and colleague Neha Singh, for suggesting to me this line of enquiry. Our discussion in December 2016 fuelled these ideas.)

BIBLIOGRAPHY

Adorno, T. (1991). 'Free Time'. *The Culture Industry: Selected Essays on Mass Culture.* (Ed.) J. Bernstein. London: Routledge.

Althusser, L. (1971). 'Ideology and Ideological State Apparatuses: Notes Towards an Investigation.' (Trans.) Ben Brewster. Retrieved from *Marxists.org*. www.marxists.org/reference/archive/althusser/1970/ideology.htm on 15 September 2017.

Anderson, B. (2006). *Imagined Communities: Reflections on the Origins and Spread of Nationalism.* New York: Verso.

Armstrong, I. (2000). *The Radical Aesthetic*. London: Wiley-Blackwell.

Benjamin, W. (1969). 'The Work of Art in the Age of Mechanical Reproduction'. *Illuminations*, (Ed.) Hannah Arendt. (Trans.) Harry Zohn. New York: Shocken.

Berger, J. (1972). *Ways of Seeing*. London: BBC and Penguin.

Bourdieu, P. (1984: 2010). *Distinctions: A Social Critique of the Judgement of Taste*. (Trans.) Richard Nice. Massachusetts: Routledge.

Bryson, N. (1986). *Vision and Painting: The Logic of the Gaze*. New Haven: Yale University Press.

Chandra, N. (2008). *The Classic Popular Amar Chitra Katha, 1967-2007.* London: Yoda Press.

Gibson, M. (2010). 'Picturebooks, Comics and Graphic Novels'. *The Routledge Companion to Children's Literature.* (Ed.) David Rudd. Oxon: Routledge.

Gombrich, E. (1960). *Art and Illusion: A Study in the Psychology of Pictorial Representation*. London: Phaidon Press.

Guha-Thakurta, T. (2004). *Monuments, Objects, Histories.* New York: CUP.

Greenblatt, S. (1980: 2005). *Rennaisance Self-Fashioning: From More to Shakespeare*. Chicago: University of Chicago Press.

Gupta, N. & Chatterjee, R. (Eds.) (2009). *Reading Children: Essays on Children's Literature*. New Delhi: Orient Blackswan.

Hutcheon, L. (2006). *A Theory of Adaptation*. Oxon: Routledge.

Kapur, Geeta. (2007). 'The Uncommon Universe of Bhupen Khakhar'. *Pop Art and Vernacular Culture*. (Ed.) Kobena Mercer. Massachusetts: MIT Press.

Khakhar, Bhupen. (1982). *Two Men in Banaras.* Oil on Canvas. N. p. Retrieved from www.queer-arts.org/khakhar/twomen_sm.htm on 20 January 2017.

Khakhar, Bhupen. (1972). *De Luxe Tailors.* Oil on Canvas. N. p. Retrieved from www.sothebys.com/en/auctions/ecatalogue/2017/howard-hodgkin-portrait-artist-l17120/lot.110.html on 20 January 2017.

Lutgendorf, Philip. 'Evolving a monkey: Hanuman, Poster Art, and Postcolonial anxiety'. *Beyond Appearances: Visual Practices and Ideologies in Modern India.* (Ed.) Sumathi Ramaswamy. New Delhi: Sage India.

McLuhan, M. (1964). *Understanding Media: The Extensions of Man.* London: McGraw-Hill.

Mirzoeff, N. (Ed.) (2012). *The Visual Culture Reader.* New York: Routledge.

Mitchell, W.J.T. (2006). 'Showing Seeing: A Critique of Visual Culture'. *Journal of Visual Culture.* Vol. 1, No. 2. pp. 165-181.

One of the Original Adarsh Balak strips 'an ideal boy'. N. d. Ink on Paper. N. p. Retrieved from www.comicsandcola.com/2014/06/priyesh-trivedis-adarsh-balak.html on 20 December 2016.

Pawling, C. (Ed.) (1984). *Popular Fiction and Social Change.* London: Macmillan.

Pierce, W. (2004). 'Fabulously Real'. *Agni*, 59, 2004, pp. 212-228. *JSTOR*, www.jstor.org/stable/23010845. Web. 01 June 2016.

Sontag, S. (1979). *On Photography*. New York: Penguin.

Tibbets, S. and Don. (2017). 'Creepy Wonka/Condescending Wonka'. *Knowyourmeme*, Aug 2017. Retrieved from knowyourmeme.com/memes/condescending-wonka-creepy-wonka on 15 September 2017.

Trivedi, Priyesh. (2013). *T for Toke.* Graphic Art Software. Mumbai. Retrieved from www.comicsandcola.com/2014/06/priyesh-trivedis-adarsh-balak.html on 20 December 2016.

Williams, R. (1989). 'Culture is Ordinary'. *Resources of Hope, Culture, Democracy, Socialism.* New York: Verso.

Williams, R. (1983). *Keywords: A Vocabulary of Culture and Society.* Oxon: Oxford University Press.

Zainab. (2014). 'Priyesh Trivedi's Adarsh Balak: Subverting Traditional Iconography for Traditional Amusement'. Retrieved from *Comicsandcola.com*, www.comicsandcola.com/2014/06/priyesh-trivedis-adarsh-balak.html on 20 July 2017.

PART III

The Graphic vis-a-vis the Popular

CHAPTER 6

Munnu: Testimonials of Counteractions Curated in the Graphic Narrative

Shreya Sangai

Comics in India

The comic book scene in India dates back to *Amar Chitra Katha* (ACK) that started in 1967. Anant Pai, the editor-in-chief of the *Indrajal Comics* (1960s) drew his market 'understanding' from the experiences of *Phantom*, conceived by Lee Falk in 1936. Phantom remotely visualised the experiences of the colonised by operating in the African jungles. He also exploited most of the orientalist stereotypes yet Pai felt that compared to *Superman*, the American superhero, *Phantom* would still be able to strike a chord with the local audience. With the coming of ACK, efforts were made to fight back colonisation by developing the majoritarian cultural heritage of the country and mass-circulating it in the comic medium.

Towards the late 1980s, Anupam Sinha in collaboration with Raj Comics came out with a series of Indian superheroes: Super Commando Dhruv, Nagraj, Doga, Chandika that drew their inspiration from American superheroes, yet their problems were local, and often the solutions were also found locally. Therefore, they were a major success in the country. Before Sinha, Pran Kumar Sharma created his own set of comical characters: Chacha Chaudhry, Billu, Pinki, Shrimatiji, starting in 1971. Most of Pran's characters promoted stereotypes in appearances, gender, ability and therefore, did not compel the reader to think beyond the page.

With the market outreach of these comics, finding readers across age groups, the idea of virulence as well got promoted. While ACK marginalised Muslims and low caste people as *asuras,* raiders, Chacha Chaudhary mocked his fat wife who was mostly placed in the kitchen. Super Commando Dhruv would always save the day, while Chandika would crave his romantic his attention. Invariably, the villain would have some physical or mental disability, or will carry the marks of his previous deeds in the public. So, across images, these comics promoted the idea of heroes in different shapes and sizes yet heavily attacked those who looked different, or belonged to different religions or castes.

Hillary Chute subtly distinguishes comics from graphic narratives in 'Comics as Literature? Reading Graphic Narratives' by stating that 'a graphic narrative is a book length work in the medium of comic.' (2008, 453). It mostly caters to an adult audience based on its contents and the prior 'readings' that one is expected to have made to get the full sense of the 'picture'. The graphic narrative, different from the graphic novel, extends itself to other forms like documentary, non-fiction, autobiography, comic journalism, and memoir. These narratives can be the 'serious, imaginative works that explore the social and political realities by stretching the boundaries.' (2008, 6). *River of Stories* (1994) by Orijit Sen is seen as the first graphic narrative in the Indian history. Post—that, a number of artists like Manjula Padmanabhan, Malik Sajad, Amruta Patil, Appupen, Sharad Sharma, Vishwajyoti Ghosh, and Sarnath Banerjee have taken the publishing industry by storm to address different dimensions using the graphic medium. Graphic narration has been used to highlight and showcase micro-histories in the dominant macro-histories; they give visual form to oral tellings, and small publishing houses have vocalised the tales of sexual abuse and trauma. The graphic narrative, in this way, played an additive role by identifying what the mainstream media, news and popular discussions were missing. They supplied information in a concise and interesting manner, challenging the 'normal' and creating a debilitating effect on the reader who might have been a part of the same for long. Yet, as Pramod Nayar points out that in sharp contrast to comics and literature in regional languages, the graphic 'novel' represents a far more sophistically produced and expensive medium, catering to a small percentage of the population—the English speaking, urban community (*The Indian Graphic Novel*). This article looks at *Munnu: A Boy from Kashmir* (2015) by Malik Sajad which abundantly detarts the daily situation in Kashmir; a conflict-fraught region in India. Sajad, the artist and writer of the text, keeps the categories of interpreting the narrative open: memoir, oral telling, micro-histories, nonfiction, autobiographical or all of them. However, the back cover of the book says "...Based on Malik Sajad's own childhood, *Munnu* is an amazing insight into everyday life in Kashmir.[1]"

The Constitution of India ensures equal rights and social, political, legal access to all its citizens irrespective of caste, religion, creed, gender, or ability. Yet, the on-ground reality, particularly in the conflict-ridden areas, is appalling. The Armed Forces Special Protection Act (AFSPA), amended in 1972, has been in force in the areas of North Eastern India, particularly Manipur, since 1958 and in Jammu and Kashmir since 1990. The Act grants extraordinary powers to the Indian Army to function in the 'disturbed areas': to fire upon or otherwise use force, even to the extent of causing death; arrest without warrant, any person who has committed a cognizable offence or against whom a reasonable suspicion exists; enter and search without warrant any premises, and to make any such arrest as aforesaid. It further provides for that no prosecution, suit or other legal proceedings shall be instituted, except with the previous sanction of the Central Government.[2] A generation of youth has been obliterated; they have either been murdered mercilessly at the hands of the Indian army, or killed in clashes, and many have just 'disappeared.' For twenty-seven years now, Association of Parents of Disappeared Persons[3] has been asking the Indian Government, where their sons, husbands, friends, neighbours are. All those who have disappeared were arrested during military crackdowns, and none of them have returned. One wonders about legal proofs of their crimes, and whether they are alive, if at all.

Munnu: Violence in Graphics

Using such daily realities, where violence and mourning lurk in the air of Kashmir, Sajad starts his book by introducing all his family members in a portrait to the reader. It is a family of

Hanguls, a species of deer, found exclusively in Kashmir, but is rapidly approaching extinction[4]. Relying on the tradition started by Art Spiegelman in *Maus*, Malik Sajad elaborates on the theme of violence by depicting Kashmiris as the Hanguls and the Indian Army as the humans wielding guns. These Hanguls are shown in black ink against a white background that unsettles the readers immediately, at least on two levels. First, it may fill one with a comforting feeling that probably the whole family is together, which is a kind of rarity in Kashmir. Yet, there is the lurking fear that it illustrates the demise of the family member(s) and the text is a recollection. This anxiety is soon addressed by Munnu's mother who chides her children not to flock "like a cricket team". The familiarisation with the family is also an uncomfortable process: there are poking fingers that point out who is who in the family and their order of seniority. This order of arrangement is imperative, as I shall go on to discuss. Similar to the family members, regions of Kashmir are also pointed out. These intrusive fingers unsettle the reader by pointing out the regional and individual vulnerability that is always at stake in a volatile region. Across the coming pages, the rupture in the personal space as a consequence of public violence keeps becoming more and more apparent. This family is gradually shown by an aerial view of Srinagar, the capital of Jammu and Kashmir. This view is furthered to the white of Jammu and Kashmir that is locked in by black landmasses: China, Pakistan and India (*Munnu,* 2). This contrast between the black and white is connotative at multiple levels: identity/soms identity, presence/absence, targeting/targeted, authority/powerless, and *bios/zeos*[5]. At the same time, this page opens up the plethora of possibilities in which the interactions are taking place across the entire graphic narrative.

Between the dialogue boxes and the panels, the initial phase of *Munnu* shows the intergenerational gap between Munnu, the seven-year-old boy, and his father, Gulya, an artisan, who earns a living through Kashmiri handicraft and woodblock tradition. Munnu's father used to spend his childhood playing all day, going to cinema, and loafing around with his friends, while Munnu scribbles are AK-47, and sculpts them out of eraser blocks. He scribbles on the images of the dead bodies that frequently appear in the newspaper to master his drawing skills. His school education is absolutely fragmented as there are frequent and long breaks; often the school teachers go 'missing' and then the locations have to be changed. With his friends, Munnu makes placards and actively participates in protests demanding his rights to proper education. At the same time, the family is the place for sanctuary yet Munnu's parents often jump from one argument to another by discussing about children who became militants, or chose the path of violence—"...Don't tempt my children. At least they are safe. Think about the ones who are being used as human shields in gun battles" (Sajad, 2015, 14). Munnu's family has built their house under the cover of trees so that it is missed by the Army officials when they come for crackdown checking. During the crackdowns, the older boys and the men of the house were taken away for identification by military officials. Usually, the details of crime or allegations were not communicated to the families, and many a time the members of the family would not come back for years on end or return as corpses. Mass mournings (35) would be organised; bodies in shrouds would be kept for public viewing. As they asked questions of the bureaucracy and judicial systems, and they showed the helplessness of the families and no methods of further redressal. Different groups of people expressed their grief differently—"... Mamma also disappeared to join the wailing women", "...Munnu shivered and buried his face in Shahnaz's arms."

The psychological impact of these family conversations and participating in mass mournings aggravates when young Munnu decides to experience how 'life' inside the grave must be like—"it must be dark inside the grave" (Sajad, 2015, 42). Negating his curiosity as childish acts, his brother Bilal, and mother scold him and tell him to go to sleep. As adults, they have accepted daily violence as part of reality they have to fight back, but Munnu is still trying to come to terms with concepts like killing, death, burial, and the loss of lives. But a few pages later, readers find the image repeating and curiosity re-emerging—"...but the nights were quiet." (46) This repetition of images takes the reader back and forth in the text, as they try to jostle their thoughts along with Munnu. They too would anticipate similar questions that Munnu is dealing with: what happens when someone meets with untimely death?

How do they find answers to the questions that have been buried? "The idiots sealed it with concrete." (Sajad, 2015, 46). Munnu asks his sister, Shahnaz, about the certainty of death through Mustafa's burial—"What if Mustafa is alive?" These anxieties prompts in odd questions which are difficult for Shahnaz to answer as she dodges them by obvious replies—"... when you are dead you feel nothing." But, the line between the living and the dead is far too unclear for Munnu to take cognisance of. Munnu reappears across several panels, suffocating himself under a white bed sheet, "...hell. I wish I was never born at all" (Sajad, 2015, 47). Across these three panels, his bed sheet, like a cover of the coffin is white, and the panel is black.

At his tender age, Munnu is trying to empathise with the dead by erasing his own living presence. His presence can only be seen by his thought bubbles, but his body has completely merged with the darkness of the dead. Yet, the imperative question across these three panels, that the protagonist is asking, and through him the Kashmiris are asking is that do the dead "really" feel nothing? What happens to the feelings and emotions of the dead before they were killed and what happens to those who are left behind? Munnu's fear of death and the need to speak from under the ground further multiplies when Munnu imagines that his brother, Bilal, who is like a fatherly figure to him, has 'disappeared'. Despite multiple consolations and reassurances, Munnu sees the family, like those around him, breaking up due to violence. At this moment, another family portrait with a lamp is placed next to him.

In contrast to these susceptible Hanguls, military men are depicted as humans who are in a large number. Their cruelty spans across pages as they resort to violence under legal protection: causing deaths, disappearances, harassing locals, physical assaults, mental torture and with many unanswered questions.[6] These attacks have changed the way families and communities understand their relationship with the Army and the State; instead of feeling secure, there are recollections of lost family members, some of them being extremely brutal. Children face frequent emotional breakdowns: Munnu's classmate recalls the pale face of his father as his family received the corpse. On the body, several razor marks could be seen from where the blood was slowly taken out, causing a painful death—"his face was glowing but it was yellow." As the child lamented the loss, the children around him have limited vocabulary for consoling him; they call the father a "martyr", and the Army personnel "blind serial killers". Children's relationships, like the adults are formed on the lines of violence witnessed, deaths experienced and the brutality with which their family members were taken away from them.

From the beginning of the narrative, stretches of panes across the pages show white tombstones. They are a constant reminder that deaths are how people across age groups are remembered in the lives of Kashmiris, and they run into endless numbers. The tombstones mark unnumbered deaths. These tombstones inform about the children who crossed over to Pakistan-occupied Kashmir: "many of them were already dead" (Sajad, 2015, 5). Writing on *Munnu,* Pramod Nayar suggests that the long panel of the tombstone functions like an epitaph, and while the dead were unnamed and unnumbered, they were real nonetheless. But, such is the plight of Kashmiris, that only their communities will remember the bodies under the graves and their stories; for the State, the dead are just numbers sealed under concrete. These tombstones frequently recur across the text, each time signifying a different death. Such panels force the reader to break their mould and think of the political situation that Sajad has been trying to unravel: Kashmir is now the valley of pain, turmoil and death. The nation outside the valley has only been seeing the pervasive impact of the violence; the unfortunate part will be to pick sides between Kashmir and the nation. Yet, what remains out of the public memory is how such a situation came about, and if there was any point in turning it around. Most importantly, when did the Kashmiri lives become so futile?

The concluding pages of *Munnu* provide the answers to the questions about the futility of Kashmiri lives. In the chapter titled 'Footnotes' quite literally Sajad takes a look into the violent occupation of Kashmir from one ruler to another: Afghans, Sikhs, British, Dogras to the Indian State as we know it. From beautiful landscapes, to extremely difficult terrain, the reasons for acquiring and giving up on Kashmir have been many. Yet, the rulers were least sympathetic towards the people. This chapter depicts the history in the typical Kashmiri block print manner, which, like Hangul, is exclusive to the region. Therefore, by engaging in this violent spectacle, and borrowing from the memories of people, Sajad reconstructs and rebuilds the narratives in order to further nuance the voices of counteraction. By spatially creating a grammar of gutter, panel, grid and two colours he creates a participatory conversation with the reader where they do not have a seamless movement. Instead, they have to pause every now and then, enter into the time and situation of Kashmiris to attempt understanding what their situation is like. Hillary Chute, in *Disaster Drawn*, uses the term 'testamentary' (19) which according to me, sums up and yet opens up the way texts from conflict-ridden areas can be read. Chute writes that after a certain point, testimonials also become redundant and that's where comics 'aggregat(e) and accumulat(e) frames of information' (Chute, 2016, 15) to 'express trauma ethically.' (Chute, 2016, 4) They render visible the violence by making an intervention and creating representation in varied forms. So, while Hanguls unsettle the readers at the start, they may also smoothen the process of absorbing the information about the bloodshed in which the reader might have been a silent participant. Using testimonials, the artist creates a set of witnesses within the characters who have not gotten representation previously, or their voices have been left unheard under bureaucratic red-tapism. In this "act of witnessing" (Sajad, 2015, 27) the readers' awareness multiplies as they also participate in listening to the many-dimensional testimonies, their impact and effects on the self.

REFERENCES

1. At an artists' talk in Jadavpur University, 13 January 2017, Malik Sajad was asked if *Munnu* was a political, autographical work that attempted to reach out to the readers explaining the plight of the Kashmiris. Sajad explained that outside Kashmir, it was relatively "easy" to conjecture if the work was political or not, but in a place like Kashmir, politics, violence happens almost seamlessly. Individuals do not have choices. So, when the cover says 'a boy from Kashmir' it contains politics from there.

2. For more information about AFSPA, people's protests, participation of bureaucracy in silencing people's voices, please visit Saheliwomen.org.
3. Apdpkashmir.com is the portal for this association. Furthermore in this context, Warisha Farasat writes that in contrast to the officially quoted number of 10,000, close to 70,000 people have been killed in the conflict. It approximately amounts to 1% of the regional population. Human Rights activists state that even if the credibility of their reports are questioned, the whereabouts of the officially stated 8744 disappearances have not been clarified. Civil Society members place this number over 8000. For further information, refer to *Landscapes of Fear: Understanding Impunity* (2014) by Zubaan.
4. A Hangul is a peace-loving and quiet creature that is facing threat to its life due to excessive tourism and crossfire violence. As a result, the ratio of male Hanguls to females Hanguls is highly skewed, the males being much less. The Hanguls chances of furthering the progeny are also less; the parallels between the Kashmiris and the choice of the cartoonist to depict them as Hanguls is therefore, quite clear.
5. In his seminal work *Homo Sacer*, Giorgio Agamben discusses the idea of sovereign that elaborately fits the situation of Kashimiris. Bios are the active participants in the sovereign, who make their voices heard by politically engaging themselves and therefore, becoming indispensable to the State. On the other end, Zeos are the dispensable members who lack the language skills to articulate their concerns to the State. No matter what they say, their 'killing' is sacrificial. Nonetheless, if Zeos are killed, the State functioning is not hampered. In fact, the State promotes its idea of inclusivity by marking out and stressing the fact that certain sections have been excluded, and wronged. Yet, they must be kept excluded, to keep the otherwise included feel secure about their condition.
6. Warisha Farasat writes that India has deployed close to 500,000 troops since 1989, to quell the armed struggle in the region. For further information, kindly refer to *Landscapes of Fear: Understanding Impunity* (2014) by Zubaan.

BIBLIOGRAPHY

Chanda, N. (2008). *The Classic Popular: Amar Chitra Katha 1967-2007.* (pp. 1-26). New Delhi: Yoda Press.

Chute. H. (2008). 'Comics as Literature? Reading Graphic Narratives.' In *PMLA.* Volume 123. No. 2. (pp. 452-465). Modern Language Association. JSTOR.

Chute. H. (2016). *Disaster Drawn: Visual Witness, Comics and Documentary Form.* (pp. 1-38). United States of America: Harvard University Press.

Nayar, P. (2016). *The Indian Graphic Novel: Nation, History and Critique.* Oxon: Routledge.

Nayar, P. (2016). 'The Post-colonial Gothic: *Munnu,* Graphic Narrative and the Terrors of the Nation.' In *Rupkatha Journal.* Volume 8, No. 1. (pp. 1-12).

Sajad, M. (2015) *Munnu: A Boy from Kashmir.* London: HarperCollins Publishers.

CHAPTER 7

Folktales from India's North-East in Graphic: A Study of Parismita Singh's *Hotel at the End of the World*

Bibiana Ryntathiang

North-East and Storytelling

Folklore and folktales serve as instructions for most communities in India's North-East which are still very new to the written word. The mode of instruction and passing on of knowledge from one generation to the other has been one that has depended largely on the spoken word. The amalgamation of images and the word is not new to the listener of these stories, for when a listener listens to a story being told, the images that arise are the ones seen scratched on walls of caves in ancient days. This creates a new form of narrative that passes on from the storyteller to the listener and from the listener to the image on the walls of a cave. In this region, stories are also found in stone carvings and garments woven to depict legends and mythical creatures.

Graphic Narratives perhaps are the best suited medium for the rendering of tales especially folktales that feature mostly experiences that are not scientifically proven but heard and retold over and over again with a belief that such incidents in the stories did really take place once upon a time. As all folktales from the region start with the phrase 'Once upon a time...' or 'Long long time ago..' an authenticity to the incidents based on true facts is given to the tales and one does listen and tell the stories with some belief that truly it was the way of their forefathers and that the listeners, common though they may be can strive to be legendary one day and they can even become immortal like the gods. A sense of morality and righteousness that is found in the tales becomes the way of life for the people and motifs and symbols of a particular tribe become the identity of a people who still rely on elders for the word and thus allowing for the formation of thoughts, beliefs, obedience and alliance within the community.

On the other hand, while wrought with much realism, most folktales are also works of fantasy especially in their representation of characters that are half-man half-animal, ghosts and evil spirits, as also incidents that are beyond scientific reasoning. The story of half man half animal as found in the tale of *Kabui Keioiba* from Manipur and many others, which tell the story of a man who prides himself on having attained supreme knowledge. Kabui decides to put his knowledge to test only to be defeated by human emotions, fear and shock. Before using his knowledge to turn himself into a tiger, he had instructed his wife to tap him on the head three times after he turns into tiger, at which he would turn into a normal man again. However, when his wife sees him turned into a tiger, she forgets the instructions that her husband had given her and flees the scene along with her son. The Kabui was left to live life as half man half tiger much to his dismay. The thought of man turning into a were-wolf or were-tiger is a common phenomenon amongst tribal folk stories and people who live in close union with nature. A man who turns into such a creature is believed to have been cursed by the gods and therefore must live amongst animals far from people and civilisation. The fantasy in these tales serves as a warning as to what may happen should one have human hubris.

The amalgamation of image and words is therefore one that is best suited to represent the folktales of the region in which descriptions of legends and the fantastical element tend to fall short with words. A characteristic of the folktales presented in graphic narratives is one that is immersive in nature where the reader becomes completely part of the fantastic world. Common people as characters though amazed by the magical phenomenon are neither oblivious to nor shocked by such occurrences and accept such incidents as part of reality of life and truth that are based on reality and fantasy. Reality when conjoined with fantasy results in stories that are at the same time imparting values and knowledge as well as entertainment.

Storytelling as an art form in a society that had for a long time depended on the spoken word to pass information and entertaining the listeners requires the storyteller to also be a performer. This performance which can either make or break any story especially one with fantastical elements is a visual treat. As reiterated the visual-verbal medium or the graphic mode is perhaps the best suited for rendering folktales. Much of this lies also in the fact that the auditory and the visual are the two important senses without which communication and more so the passing on of tribal values, beliefs and histories (which is the purpose of the folktales in the first place) can only be limited to the senses of touch.

The vantage point of the graphic narrative is the same that is applied in gathering information by an onlooker. The auditory function is an important aspect in storytelling as it is carried forward in the graphic mode with onomatopoeic words that shout out from the panels creating an emphasis of sound. The bond created between a storyteller who might be an old relative or a known person in the community and the listener is the same that is created between the creator of the same as folktale in graphic narrative and the reader. It makes the job of the artist and writer of the graphic narrative a slightly difficult one because a storyteller also acts like a historian and chronicler. Once such folktales are rendered as graphic narratives, the graphic artist and writer also become the historian and chronicler. The tale becomes more alive as the artist and writer takes upon themselves the task of playing the role of storytellers, thus becoming collaborators in the age old practice of storytelling. It is a practice that is reminiscent of John Berger's idea of a storyteller in 'Once in a Story':

> Those who first invented and then named the constellations were storytellers. Tracing an imaginary line between a cluster of stars gave them an image and an identity. The stars threaded on that line were like events threaded on a narrative. Imagining the constellations did not of course change the stars, nor did it change

the black emptiness that surrounds them. What it changed was the way people read the night sky. (Berger, 2014, 9)

Parismita Singh's *Hotel at the end of the World* serves as a good example of the oral storytelling and folklore traditions of North-East India in the graphic form rendered with traces of the age-old style of storytelling. There are recurrent temporal shifts, triggered by the present leading to the past, spatio-temporal relations with characters, cycling embedding of temporality, the influence of magical realism on the temporality of the text, and the technical aspects of temporality as used in these graphic narratives—like the vantage point, the position and size of the frames/the panels etc.,—which influence the way the reader is made to look at or be involved in the story and also transcend to a different temporality.

Negotiating Boundaries: *Hotel at the End of the World*

The book which starts at the hotel situated at the end of the world is made complex with not only one story but also several other stories told and retold by different characters in the book. Every character and every person has a story to tell and the characters meet and eat at the hotel, and each narrates a story that is both fantastic and real at the same time. No one character in the book seeks to question the authenticity of the stories. They all listen and accept the stories as truth because the way of life of the characters is a way of life of the tribal folks who have lived and believed in the truth that these stories convey. Histories that only exist for as long as one tells the story and die the moment one stops passing on histories. The representation of characters who live in a fantastic yet real world looking for the floating island is also synonymous with people looking for happiness in a place that may not even exist.

The title of the book is well conceived in that the hotel could either be situated at the end of the world where boundaries end or also a time when the world is at its end. The title reminds one of the science fiction book *The Restaurant at the End of the Universe* by Douglas Adams published in 1980 where the end of the world is also a time when the world did come to an end and characters in the book would watch it from a distance. The hotel in Parismita Singh's

Hotel at the End of the World is taken as a place locally believed to be the end of the world, the setting where all the different characters meet. The hotel is represented as any ordinary eating house much like a traditional kitchen that sells food to travellers as well as the inhabitants of the village. While the hotel is always referred to simply as the hotel, the location is given as the end of the world.

The end of the world could be a time and a place as well. Amongst many tribals, there is a belief that the spirits of the dead wander the world after they die. They visit the world of the living whilst still in search of permanent release. The world that ends is the world of the individual who has died. The end of the world as a location could locally be anywhere and everywhere, a place without boundaries, a resting place where one could find solace for a while. In this context, the end of the world as a point of time could suggest a temporal place of narratives where time comes to a standstill and the past and the present are frequented in the stories told. The temporal place without boundaries is also India's North-East. The remoteness of the region and the troubled past as a result of colonial administrative compulsions known as the North-Eastern Frontier Agency now known as Arunachal Pradesh gives rise to the region's problems with borders within India as well as with the neighbouring countries. The notion of problematic borders as defined by Joy L.K. Pachuau and Willem van Schendel '...borderlands, like the borders that define them, are processes, continually remade, reaffirmed, renegotiated and re-imagined' (Pachuau and van Schendal, 2016, 3) corroborate the existence of a past that was disturbed but seek to align themselves more and more with the passage of time in the stories.

The *Hotel at the End of the World* begins with the arrival of Kona and Kuja at the hotel. They are two travellers stranded on their way looking for the floating island. The setting bears a resemblance to a tribal kitchen where all gatherings take place and stories are told. The mystery behind the sudden arrival of Kona and Kuja is revealed in the story that is narrated by Kuja to the gathering. He tells the story of how he and Kona were lured by a friend to a place where the bridge to China was to be built. The reference of the bridge reminds one of the Stilwell Road which connects India with China via Myanmar. Thus, a historical and geographical reference is seen to have been made here even as the story told is full of fantastical incidents. Kuja and Kona managed to escape from the 'construction gang' (Singh, 2009, 19) who had bought the duo, one without legs and the other partially visually impaired, for the sole purpose of entertainment as circus performers and by chance as they venture back home happen to come across their old friend Sibu dying on the top of a rock in search of the floating island. Floating lakes are a natural occurrence in Manipur known as *phumdis* found in Loktak Lake, Moirang, Manipur. The reference to the land as a land of treasures is also believable as the islands are home to various animal and bird species and vegetation. Thus when Kuja tells the gathering that they are looking for the floating island, no one doubts their story.

Storytelling in the oral folk traditions requires the storyteller to entertain the listener and in doing so, the storyteller tends to give each character in the story a distinct voice and a specific persona. The different characters tell their stories and Singh gives a distinct voice and characteristic to each character and creates a voice and tone that is distinct to each. As Kuja tells the story, his narrative style is one of a happy-go-lucky man with nothing to lose and therefore is ready to embark on another adventure even as he and his friend have just escaped a disappointment and loss of an old friend. The characteristic is portrayed through the words that they use and the emotions on their faces as they tell the stories. As each story ends, the characters disperse to go home to get some rest and the next day till the rain that has brought Kuja and Kona to the hotel stops, another story is recounted.

The next story is the story of Pema, the wife of the hotel's owner. She is shown as a grumpy woman who seems to exist only to help in the business of her husband. She cooks and tends to the customer until she starts reminiscing about her past youthful days when she still had dreams and hopes. Life seems to have taken a toll on her and she no longer is the cheerful girl she used to be and the reason for this lies in the story she tells the gathering. She blames her bad Karma for having landed her in that position and though married there are suggestions of her not being happily married. As a young girl, she had spent most of her days taking care of her ailing father who it would seem was struck by a mysterious ailment. This went on for years until one day she met Keising and fell in love with him.

However, as they decided to get married, on the day when Keising was to come and speak to her father and ask for her hand in marriage, Keising stood in shock at the sight of Pema's father: the reason being the previous night, Keising had seen Pema's father in a truck which met with an accident while he was in sumo on the way to Pema's house. The truck that had met with an accident took away five lives but Pema's father was not part of the dead. It was later revealed by Pema that her father was a nightwalker, a porter of death itself. The ailment that struck him mysteriously turning him delirious was his conscience in the conscious state that taunted him every time he was required to take a soul. Keising never returned after that and Pema was left heart-broken. Heart-broken, she would wander the hills, lonely and sad until one day she slipped and fell down a valley. She was saved by the edge of the tree which leaned forward just in time where she remained till dawn. That same night her father died. It was believed that her father who should have taken her soul to the god of death gave up his life to save his daughter's.

The tone of sadness and regret that is felt in Pema's story is a common story of lost love that is very prominent amongst most love tales of the region. The prospect of love and expected happiness in marriage is shattered and broken on account of either the man or woman belonging to an outcasted family is common. Tales of young women shedding tears for lost love as a result of incompatibility with in-laws renders an in-depth look at the system of marriage amongst the tribal community and also the class divide that exists in tribal society that comes into effect almost immediately when the talk of marriage starts taking place. Pema falls in love with Keising who is educated and has travelled the world and is on a pilgrimage to the holy place depicted as Buddhist monasteries. The story of Pema and Keising could have taken place in Arunachal Pradesh where the Buddhist monastery in Tawang is situated or in Sikkim which is also home to many Buddhist monasteries.

Marriage with Keising would have uplifted Pema to a better social position. However as that failed and Keising was not courageous enough to break the social norms, Pema ended up as a grumpy woman engrossed in cooking and selling food while her husband profits from it. In the pages devoted to the story of Pema, Singh chooses to depict the life of Pema in the Buddhist art form of Mandala. (Singh, 2009, 43). A Mandala has the universe depicted in circles which contains in the centre the image of Buddha or a lotus. The name Pema in many Himalayan dialects means a Lotus. The story of Pema takes centre stage in this context as she is firstly the owner of the hotel at the end of the world around which all the stories are told and retold. Secondly, her choice of a husband who converses with the dead connects deeply to her father who was a night walker and was in close connection with the dead.

Mandala Symbolism

Pema's representation at the centre of the circles in the form of a Mandala adds more insight to her as a character when one looks at the connection that Carl. G. Jung in his *Mandala Symbolism* brings in with regard to the Mandala which has healing effects for the narrator who in this context is Pema helping her to '...put together apparently irreconcilable opposites and bridge over hopeless splits' (Jung, 1972, 5). As the bridge between the outer and the inner world of the restaurant as well as her own outer demeanour and inner thoughts, she becomes the centre of the universe in the 'hotel.' She is the centre around whom all the stories are told and as the universe herself, Pema holds an insight into time and space much like the centre around which the whole solar system and life itself exist. As the centre, all the others are perceived as the periphery. In doing so, the hotel too becomes a centre and as it is set in North-East India, the region becomes the centre and India becomes the periphery.

The following day as the rain still did not stop and, Pema's husband is shown reading Commando comics as to pass time. He enjoys his Commando comics which is also a reference to the popularity of these comics in the region especially in parts of Mizoram, Meghalaya and Manipur. A glimpse of the life of the people in the region is depicted here and the belief in the supernatural and the afterlife is shown when Pema's husband keeps two filled glasses of alcohol untouched for the Soldier. Amongst many tribals, the dead are believed to visit the world of the living people and some tribes do follow the practice of keeping food and drinks for the dead. It is not uncommon and as such while the sceptical may question and mock the system, for a believer like Pema's husband it is not a laughing matter. It is then that he tells the story of the Japanese soldier who travelled to Nagaland during the Second World War as had been told to him by the dead Japanese soldier.

The soldier had been dead for long but had been fighting in all battles until one day he realised that the battles and wars had no longer were the same that he had started with. The British whom he was supposed to fight were no longer seen but yet there were still battles that were being fought around him. The sights seen by the soldier were deplorable, a reference to the turmoil and conflicts that arose after India's independence from the British in Manipur and Nagaland. The conflict and turmoil seen by the soldier masked as a sight seen by a dead person does in many ways also shed light on the delicate relations that the North-East region has within itself as it does with the rest of India. The fantastical element in this particular story is far from believable. It is also present in the questions raised by Kuja and Kona whilst mocking Pema's husband about conversing with the dead soldier in Japanese, yet the historical reference to the incident is not questioned nor is the fact that the soldier had been dead for long.

As another story unfolds, the Prophet's story brings to light the sights of the floating island that Kuja and Kona have been searching for in the travel that led them to the hotel. The Prophet who gets the name by virtue of his ability to predict the weather is an old man shown in a garb very similar to that of an Apatani tribe shaman. He has a bun at the top of his head held together by a stick that acts as a hairpin. He tells the story of how he became blind in the quest to find the floating island which he did find but was attacked by a fellow adventurer who did not want the floating island to be found by anyone else. The story of the Prophet is doubted by the gathering and they all speak amongst themselves about the stories he had told them earlier on how he had lost his eyes and ended up with a compass. The compass that he carries with him at all times was left behind and was given to him by one of the people who had attacked and blinded him. The others do not question the authenticity of the story, but simply expressed their likes and dislikes of the different stories recounted lending a sense of mystery to the whole situation which had led to the Prophet losing his eyes and ending up with a compass.

The last story which is told is by none other than the author herself is that of the girl who helps Pema at the hotel rendered not in words but in images where she sets out to fetch water but ends up encountering a group of dead soldiers running towards a particular location and as she follows them she finds a battle tank. She enters the tank and without thinking fiddles around when the tank starts firing shots in the sky over the hotel. The sky is lit up and everyone from the hotel comes out to watch the sight and sound, at which time Kuja and Kona's mobile starts ringing and a message is displayed. The girl is nowhere to be seen but the floating island is seen by Kuja and Kona and they decide to follow the direction of the message and go eastwards where the island was waiting for them. The incident authenticates the stories narrated and the world of the living and the dead, as also the mysterious and magical are brought together validating the truth that is based on reality and fantasy.

The graphic novel ends with Kuja and Kona setting out for the floating island while the girl returns and all that Pema asked her was the whereabouts when all the fire and the noise took place over the sky to which the girl says nothing. She had lived through the story and was obliged to wait for a few more years before she would tell the story for it is the traditional norm amongst many tribes. It was only the older people who could tell stories as they may have happened or fabricated them for the pleasure of the listener. The narrative rendered in the graphic is more believable to the reader than it may have been than if it were rendered only as written word. The link between the spoken word and the image is is extremely close as the images rendered by the spoken word in a particular setting allows the senses to create a wholly different world altogether. Narratives heard when portrayed in the graphic form have a deeper impact on the mind which eventually leads to motifs and symbols becoming part and parcel of a community's identity. The visual allows for a longer and deeper emphasis making it more prominent in an age where the visual language is gaining more emphasis than the written and spoken language.

The stories told in the same setting by different people used to take place in the past and yet the rendering of those stories through the manipulation of panels and speech bubbles allowed for the stories to be experienced at a certain pace. Space and time play an important role in the rendering of such stories and in the graphic narrative; space and time can be manipulated according to the feel and pace of the storyteller as he or she may deem fit. Though the stories occurred in the past, the feeling experienced is current. Time may be still but within the panels, time moves as per the length and dimension of the panel and also the size of the page itself. The passage of time from one panel to the another moves at the pace of the storyteller thereby conveying the depth of narration and feeling sensed by the storyteller which are also rendered through the use of the circle within a circle, within yet another circle.

The Buddhist cyclic perception of time in Eastern philosophy is central to the cyclic nature of the narrative that Singh has used in the graphic novel. In the case of the Japanese soldier, she has used the single page format without panels to depict him being desolate, lost and alone. At the end as Kuja and Kona leave, life returns to the daily activities and each character continues as they did before the arrival of Kuja and Kona. Life goes on and people continue to come and go to the hotel and the stories get told once again. Nothing changes and nothing much happens except stories getting told and retold and yet time has passed and will continue to do so. The concept of recurring stories and tales are used in *Baital Pachisi* and *The Arabian Nights*. The recurrence of the tales in these two collections is also cyclic in nature thus allowing for time to pass while the essence and nature of being remain the same.

John Berger says, 'Seeing comes before words. The Child looks and recognizes before it can speak.' (Berger, 1972, 1) This saying allows for different perspectives of truth, time and space. The essence of folktale and folklores lies in the realm of understanding the self in the changing world. Perceptions of time, space, truth become essential in the understanding and perception of the self and identity. The centre of time in the universe, the core of survival lies in the telling and retelling of tales and stories. The graphic mode as a post-modern medium of storytelling encompasses all that is initiated in the imagination of first seeing and then telling. The fluidity of the narrative that is found in oral storytelling is the same that is found in the visual-verbal medium where the reader plods through the narrative using his/her imagination to re-imagine the world differently from that of the storyteller.

BIBLIOGRAPHY

Adams, D. (1980). *The Restaurant at the End of the Universe (Vol. II).* London: Pan Books.

Benjamin, W. *The Work of Art in the Age of Mechanical Reproduction.* (1998, 2005) Retrieved from https://www.marxists.org/reference/subject/philosophy/works/ge/benjamin.htm.

Berger, J. *Ways of Seeing*. (1972). London: British Broadcasting Corporation and Penguin Books.

Berger, J. (2014). 'Once in a Story'. *And on Faces, My Heart; Brief as Photos*. London: Bloomsbury.

Dixit, R. & Bhagwagar, Z. (2016). (Dir.) *Spaces Between*. (Performed by) Nikhil Chopra. India: Artist Foundation.

Jung, C.G. (1972). 'Mandala Symbolism'. *The Collected Works of C.G. Jung* Volume 9, Part I, Bollingen Series XX. (Trans.) R.F.C Hull. Bolli U.S.A: Princeton University Press.

McCloud, S. (1994). *Understanding Comics: The Invisible Art*. New York: Harper Perennial.

Negi, R. & Mahanti, A. (2015). (Dir.) *Every Time You tell a Story*. India: India Foundation for the Arts.

Gottschall, J. (2012). *The Storytelling Animal: How Stories Make Us Human*. Boston and New York: Houghton Mifflin Harcourt.

Ong, W.J. (1982). *Orality and Literacy: The Technologizing of the Word*. London and New York: Routledge.

Pachuau, J.L.K. & Schendel, W.V. (2016) 'Borderland Histories, Northeastern India: An Introduction'. *Studies in History*. Vol.32: Issue.1. pp. 1-4. Retrieved from http://journals.sagepub.com/doi/pdf/10.1177/0257643015615989

Pinault, D. (1992). *Story-telling Techniques in the Arabian Nights.* New York: Brill.

Rao, V. (2009). 'Baital Pachisi: An Indian Vampire Meta-Story'. *Ribbon Farm: Experiments in Refactored Perceptions.* Retrieved from https://www.ribbonfarm.com/2009/10/30/baital-pachisi-an-indian-vampire-meta-story/

Singh, P. (2009). *Hotel at the End of the World.* New Delhi: Penguin.

Strauss, C.L. (1962). *Totemism.* (Trans.) Rodney Needham. London: Merlin Press.

Tomba, S. (2015). *Kabui Keioiba: Nanao's Series of Folktales, Children's Lore Game Sons and Lullabies from Manipur.* (Ed.) Dr R.K. Nimai and Translated by Sanatombi Angomcha. Imphal: NE Brothers Entertainment.

CHAPTER 8

Manga and the Impressionable Child: Reinventing Religiosity in *Dōjinshi*

Ananya Saha

The global manga boom in the last few decades has perceivably augmented the cultural hegemonic agency of the medium. Macro-interactions have been amplified through active policy making such as 'Cool Japan' (2012) and multimedial dissemination. Furthermore, with the aid of the cybernetic nexus, the possibility of micro-interactions between fans from around the world has been realised. This has perhaps engendered and crystallised the idea of the invested 'prosumer', a portmanteau term for producer + consumer common to manga discourse. Manga is being refurbished according to the prosumer's conception of the medium, tailored to their objectives of expression. The deluge of dōjinshi(s) that is accessible here and now including OEL (Original English Language) manga, suggests endless possibilities for verbal and visual nuances. Incidentally, the prosumer of a dōjinshi or a fanzine might be an interpellated subject; internalising, subscribing and proliferating a certain set of ideas are reflected in the artwork.

Although manga caters to multifarious readerships stratified by age, it is a common misconception it is entirely meant for a juvenile audience. But this particular misapprehension perhaps trails the comic mode at large, as the comic is often likened to infantilising cartoons. Nevertheless, manga is a popular source of leisure for children in Japan and beyond. Initiated into the practice through *kodomo* (子) manga (漫画), a pre-pubescent child slowly progresses to genres such as *Shōjo*, *Shōnen* and more through their adolescence. As suggested by Ingulsrud and Allen in *Reading Japan Cool: Patterns of Manga Literacy and Discourse*, manga could be instrumental in boosting multiple literacies within a child. Moreover, for the impressionable youngster, engaging in an entertaining medium to inculcate certain notions might result in better reception than rigorous imperatives. How the potentiality of manga is explored in influencing the religious education of a child is the concern of this article.

The proposed dōjinshi texts that are to be explored are published on the website http://nurmanga.com/manga-list, a corollary of the mother site named http://muslimmanga.org. The platform was initiated in 2009 and has grown since then. Their purpose in the 'about' section is outlined as, '[...] a community on social media by providing contests for artists to participate in, in order to encourage the accurate and positive portrayal of Muslims!' The texts are ostensibly created by prosumers to whom their religious affiliation is essential, irrespective of their national identity. The mangaka might be a citizen of Malaysia wherein the Muslim population is prominent; or he could be a Libyan immigrant in Scotland confronting seclusion. In a manner of speaking, the texts are an endeavour to reinstate the image of the Muslim community during the times of extensive Islamophobia. The narratives are consistently featured by child characters to whom the doctrines of Islam are administered in some fashion or the other. The argument proposed would be threefold, as delineated herein,

(i) Why Manga? The 'cool' quotient and the child
(ii) The child figure: Acquiescence and cultural propaganda
(iii) Discursive methods

The Global Cool

The Cool Japan (2012) Policy implemented by the Ministry of Economy, Trade and Industry (METI), Japan was to project the cultural merchandise such as anime, manga, games et al to be the ultimate quotient of coolness. The details of the programme are accessible on the METI website. A report from September 2012 provides these particular guidelines:

> Looking globally, the market for life and culture related industries is expected to expand rapidly, mainly in emerging countries in Asia (the market size will be over 900 trillion yen worldwide in 2020). Under such circumstances, we should promote the Cool Japan strategy to transform the appeal of Japanese culture and lifestyle (food, fashion, lifestyle, and various contents such as animation, dramas, games, films and music; and tourism) into added value (= create a mechanism to convert culture into industry) and create new growth industries, thereby preparing employment and opportunities for SMEs and young people. (METI, 4)

The promise to the receptive child who succumbs to this 'appeal' and acquires 'culture related' merchandise is that they would be automatically included into the fold of 'cool kids'. The Mobius strip mechanism proposes to ensure that the dissemination of cultural merchandise including manga would add to the body of the global cool child who could grow up to be active prosumers and contribute to the ossification of the industry. Perhaps it is not surprising that the creators of these chosen texts have curated the manga form to publicise their epitomes.

While it is conceivable that the fans from South-East Asia have preferred manga, it is curious as to why the prosumers from West Asian nations have done so. With figures such as Marjane Satrapi, the Egyptian artist Andeel, or Lena Merhej to augment the indigenous comic traditions, a West-Asian fan is not sans options. It is apparent that manga has generated a significant influence which has added to the predilection. The popularisation of the medium in the neighbouring European nations in the recent years might also have contributed to their decision. (Bouissou et al, 2010, 253) Besides, as Iwabuchi Koichi argues, Japanese popular culture could be 'mukokuseki' (Iwabuchi, 2002, 33) or culturally odourless. It perceivably suggests that the medium is flexible enough to be adapted to distinct ethno-cultural contexts.

Strategising manga as an interface for ideological diffusion is not unheard of. Ryoichi Yokoyama, the mangaka was sent to the battle front during World War II so that he could create texts which would inspire adolescent boys to conscript. (Aoki, 2016) For instances which are less militant, manga (and anime) has been crucial in the latter half of the twentieth century for the promotion of association football in Japan. Through magnum opus titles such as *Captain Tsubasa*, Japanese children and youth have been motivated to take interest in the game. So much so, Fernando Torres, the professional footballer from Spain revealed in a 2012 interview that Oliver (Tsubasa rechristened in the Spanish dub) was an inspiration for him during his childhood. Incidentally, The JSDF (Japanese Self-Defense Forces), along with the Ministry of Foreign Affairs and Japan Foundation sponsored the airing of which series in Iraq. Peng Er Lam in 'Japan's 'Soft Power': Attraction and Limitation"'informs:

> Japan's 600 non-combat troops in Iraq painted a popular soccer cartoon (Captain Tsubasa in Japanese and Captain Majed in Arab countries) on their water trucks. Apparently, softening its military's image in Iraq via cute cartoons mitigates potential backlash from the public in the Arab world against Japan. [...] A Japanese diplomat who promoted Captain Tsubasa in Iraq noted: "Captain Tsubasa is famous throughout Iraq and the Middle East. The Iraqi people didn't know he was Japanese—they thought Tsubasa was Saudi Arabian [...] Tsubasa became the symbol of our goodwill... (Lam, 2007, 354)

The texts under the purview of this article conspicuously portray child characters, supposedly in the hope that they would speak better to a reader from the same demographic tier. The dōjinshi(s) are primarily OEL. Spelling errors in English are noticeable in certain texts. Either they can be honest mistakes, or a symptomatic strategy for relating oneself to the childish psyche. While referring to the teachings and beliefs of Islam, a multitude of Arabic words transliterated into English are incorporated. Apart from that, depending upon the ethnicity of the creator, words from other native languages have also been included. While the indigenous words, albeit transliterated would attract a local readership, English would aid them with a wider circulation. This imparts the texts with what Mio Bryce would perhaps call a 'glocal' flavour, a characteristic inherent to manga. (Bryce et al., 2012, 323-342) Most of these texts are one-shot pieces, wherein brevity might be attractive to the child reader, the short attention-span notwithstanding. Only a few are ongoing series, which require more patience. But a child who is in the practice of reading manga on the internet hosted by various sites, would be familiar with the interim gap between uploads. If the text is found to be interesting enough, the fan would persevere. For a reader who is slightly older and has access to a smartphone, manga reading apps can provide the user with updates when a new chapter is released. Muslim Manga, like other manga portals also comes with an app.

The texts may or may not feature a plot. While some creators display a proclivity to communicate religious edification through a compact narrative, others are satisfied sermonising with just the aid of a manga setting. In these texts, wherein the predilection for religious inculcation might be distilled, the plot becomes secondary. One such text is *Himawari*, created by Zayn Yusuf and Nisrina Ahmad. The text has altogether six pages, including the front and back cover. The setting is a school for Muslim kids, which is named *Himawari*, implying sunflower. Himawari is a popular name for female manga characters. Also, schools that are devoted to children of the Islamic faith exist in Japan.[1] The creators have not clarified the geographical details of the setting. But given the students are seen eating a *bento* (single portioned boxed meal) with servings of *onigiri* (triangular rice balls) and rolled up omelettes, (Fig. 1) it can be assumed that it is in Japan. The style is distinctly Shōjo mangaesque, where children are seen gathering harmoniously and praying, prior to partaking of their meals during the break. The progression of the panels is non-linear. But unlike traditional manga, it reads from left to right as OELs often do, if not always. But such a progression could be premeditated. For an uninitiated reader, the right to left progression of manga might seem bewildering at first. Especially if the individual is a child whose native script(s) does/do not read from right to left, the idea might be disorienting. Often, when Japanese manga is published for an English-reading audience, the pages are flipped for the convenience of the target audience. Or, the volume covers contain instructions for the reader to pursue an unaccustomed progression. (Goldberg, 2010, 287-88) But with an OEL dōjinshi such as this one, the child would be simultaneously entertained by the manga mode, sans difficulty in comprehension. It would ensure the intended message is disseminated smoothly. The characters portrayed seem to be a multicultural motley, as we see female students with a *hijab* (veil worn by a Muslim woman to prominently cover her head and upper torso in public) and without. (Fig. 2) But given the cover specifically suggests that it is an Islamic institution, it can be assumed that the creators advocate choice when it comes to wearing a hijab. The religious practice of praying before a meal is imparted leniently, without implying fear or punishment demonstrated by certain other dōjinshi(s).

Figs. 1 & 2: *Himawari*, reproduced with permission.

Compatible Discursive Strategies

During a comprehensive perusal of these texts, specific discursive tools which might be conducive to attract child readership could be identified. The tool can be either verbal or visual, thematic or illustrative. Between the texts under consideration, I have discovered four such discursive techniques:

(i) Fictionalising the canon
(ii) Exchange/Transfer student
(iii) *Chibi* figurines
(iv) Competitive Webcomic

Fictionalising the Canon: Fan-fiction writers use canon characters from an existing plot, altering them according to their creative purpose. Dōjinshi or self-published manga succumbs to this affinity quite often. For example, a sprawling collection of *Harry Potter* dōjinshi is available online where the non-canon homoerotic relations between characters are appreciated. On *nurmanga* (NM hereafter), a few texts revise a popular title to enhance religious proliferation. *Naruto* by Masashi Kishimoto is one of the most mainstream manga enjoyed by children and young adults alike. An artist with the nom de plume of Spring Sky revises the characters of this celebrated series into a text titled *An Enlightening Lesson.* Though the original title can be categorised as Shōnen, the author's treatment is remarkably Shōjo.

Figs. 3, 4 & 5: *An Enlightening Lesson*, reproduced with permission.

The artist is presumably female as she draws a chibi (small, de-aged in certain contexts) character to represent herself in a set of meta-textual panels that runs parallel with the narrative. (Fig. 3) The illustration breathes delicacy typical of Shōjo, as represented in the intricate floral patterns with a bird perching on it. (Fig. 4) The panels are non-linear and read from left to right as the characters receive lessons about Islam in a classroom. A school classroom is a recurrent setting that appears in a number of these texts. The final panel of the text expresses a proclivity to proselytisation as the canonical characters are represented in traditional Islamic garb. A trip to the mosque is also suggested, which indicates the possibility of a commitment to the Islamic faith. (Fig. 5)

The other *Naruto* dōjinshi is titled *Izzah's Journey* by Ichi15 wherein Izzah, a non-canonical adolescent female character meets the canonical ones. The figures from the *Naruto* mangaverse are nonplussed by her *hijab*, prayer, mannerisms, and etiquette. Izzah patiently explains the nuances of her belief system to her new friends. She is portrayed as a resilient figure who holds her ground and refuses to be intimidated by this gang of ninjas. The cover art is a traditional *Naruto* manga cover where it seems Izzah has been superimposed in the foreground, given it is her journey the author emphasises upon. (Fig. 6) An idea of a palimpsest is inherent to fan-fiction to which manga contributes to enrich the visual nuance. The trope used in this text is that of a journey wherein the characters hit the road. A child reader who enjoys titles such as *Naruto* ought to appreciate the scent of an adventure. On NM, one committed member seems so enthralled by the text, that she ardently implores the artist to 'make Naruto a Muslim' in the comments section.

Fig. 6: *Izzah's Journey*, reproduced with permission.

Exchange/Transfer Student: A scope of interaction with a stranger from a different culture guides us to the next discursive instrument under consideration, the introduction of the exchange student that unfolds the possibilities in the plot. In *Hana and her Love* by Hamed Nouri and Harihtaroon, a school romance is all set to blossom between Hana, a Japanese girl and Aditya Honda, an Indonesian transfer student who also has Japanese ancestry. (Fig. 7) The text is a work in progress, where the theme of an inter-cultural exchange is as crucial as the Muslim identity of Aditya. The art work is commendable, and conducive to the generic taste of Shōjo.

Figs. 7 & 8: *Hana and her Love*, reproduced with permission.

The panels are fairly linear with what Scott McCloud would call an 'aspect to aspect' transition, making optimum use of the silent spaces within the panels and between. (McCloud, 79) The deliberate colouring of backgrounds is unusual for manga, but nevertheless impactful. The pink cherry blossom petals or a face blushing red creates a contrast against the serene chiaroscuro of the panels. (Fig. 7 & 8) For a pre-pubescent child or an adolescent reader, such a story might be more stimulating than a narrative with a forthright impetus to educate.

Irrespective of how plucky Izzah happens to be, her story takes on a preaching mode which might be monotonous for the target reader. Instead, the subtle presentation of the agenda wrapped within a mantle of romance would generate enough curiosity in the audience to look out for subsequent updates. Also, while Aditya appears to be the male lead, it is Hana and the tale of her love that is accentuated in the title. On NM, another title in progress by Hamed Nouri is featured, namely *The Heart of Fawwaz*. Fawwaz is a Malaysian exchange student in Japan who happens to subscribe to the Islamic faith. Initially, he is alienated by his classmates owing to the culture of paranoia against Muslims. But he earns the regard of his peers by calmly confronting bullies who come to bother them. His poised demeanour is guided by his faith which preaches control and philanthropy, he claims. The characterisation is emphasised rather than the blatant circulation of a religious message.

Figs. 9 & 10: *Best Friends*, reproduced with permission.

The figure of the exchange or transfer student is engaged to combat the classic phobia of 'all Muslims are terrorists' at large. *Best Friends* by Zhar features the bond between Yuki and Fatima, two young female students. Fatima is discriminated against at school as her hijab gives away her religious identity. But Yuki confronts the bullies and helps Fatima settle in an unfamiliar environment. (Fig. 9 & 10) The artwork is coloured but rudimentary. The strokes seem uneven and rough around the edges. But such a style might be appropriate for the message the text tries to diffuse, which is not manifestly religious. It advocates tolerance and sensitivity, dispelling notions of prejudices and phobias. The distinctions of the idea might be better captured by the juvenile mind as the illustration is not convoluted. In the same vein, *United We Stand* by MiSsBeatoChan is a protest against the Boston marathon bombing incident from 2013. The brief five-page text revolves around a Muslim schoolgirl arranging for a silent vigil and prayer for the Boston victims in the schoolyard. Her peers, Muslims and Non-Muslims alike participate in the event. The location of the setting is not specified and neither is it necessary. Irrespective of one's ethnicity, the idea is to stand united against violence and terrorism. The piece incidentally reads from right to left in the spirit of the conventional manga format. (Fig. 11)

Fig. 11: *United We Stand*, reproduced with permission.

Barney Thompson quotes Asia Alfasi, the artist of Libyan origin in his article published on 25 July, 2015 in the *Financial Times*, 'Why Comics and Cartoons are Flourishing in the Middle East'. He writes, 'For Asia Alfasi, the reason politics dominates comics in the Arab world is simple. "Our lives are a lot more politicised than yours," she says.' (Thompson, 2015) Alfasi is the creator of *Beginnings*, an autobiographical tale of her immigration to Scotland as a child. Featured in NM, the text earlier won accolades in a prestigious manga contest. For little Asia who feels ostracised in an unfamiliar space, manga is the sole interface between her and her Scottish friends at school. Her friends call her the 'mango lassie', 'mango' being a clear misnomer for 'manga'. (http://nurmanga.com/manga/beginnings/chapter-one/7 >)The narrative is crisp with a touch of poignancy. In the flashback to the artist's childhood, characters are depicted in the format akin to 'chibi', but not quite so. The panel arrangement seems haphazard, probably reflective of the artist's inner turmoil to find an avenue of self-expression in the formative years. Alfasi's tale backs the argument in favour of manga as the chosen medium for these artists. While a religious memorandum is not apparent, the artist distinctly portrays herself in a hijab; a symptomatic representation of her initial isolation in Scotland where the population is primarily Christian. The vitality of manga as a medium of expression and communication is underlined, an experience which might be relatable for many in the fandom, rendering the text with a hint of ubiquitousness.

Chibi Figurines: Chibi is a format wherein adult characters are often made to impersonate a de-aged, miniature version of themselves, increasing the 'kawaii' (cute) factor in a manga. This is a discursive tool which could be tempting to a juvenile audience. The figurines of popular characters which are commercially produced are also often chibi(s). FullWhiteMoon's *Understanding Islam for Dummies* is a set of imperatives where the narrator is Miss Noor, a chibi female figurine adorned in a hijab. The progression is vertically linear, reminding one of a Korean *manhwa* progression sequence in certain host websites. The series is delivered in a coloured format, which is common to some manhwa texts. The objective of the platform is to portray the Muslims in a positive light. Hence, Miss Noor steps into the shoes of a bespectacled teacher, delivering lectures about ideas such as 'jihad' (Fig. 12) and hijab (Fig. 13), dispelling certain presumptuous misunderstandings. The addresses are more informative than didactic, meant for Muslims and Non-Muslims alike. The concepts propounded can be further problematised, which is the responsibility of the adult readership. But for a juvenile reader, the visuals generated are engrossing for the dictums to be absorbed.

Fig. 12 & 13: *Understanding Islam for Dummies*, reproduced with permission.

Journey of a Muslim by Zhar prominently concentrates on the necessity for a woman to wear a hijab and adheres to certain quotidian rules. The principles might be equally applicable for a Muslim male. But for some reason, female figures are the loci. The text is plausibly of a Filipino origin, as transliterated Tagalog words have been used. The use of the chibi figurines add a tone of light-heartedness to the otherwise dense religious discourse. It evokes humour which might make the narratives more palatable to a child. One particular panel in this dōjinshi is quite titillating, wherein hijab is pronounced as a possible fashion accessory, but perhaps with the hint of a persuasive inclination as the speaker invokes 'Allah' to guide the non-Muslim character. (Fig. 14) In *Huda* by Hafizh and Aiman, the mode of the visual delineation is chibi-like, but without deaged characters. The dramatis personae comprise children in the first chapter, with Huda being a near infant. The art appears to be deliberately rough, as if drawn by a child itself. Young Huda is a pious individual who gets up early to prepare for Ramadhan. Her devotion mortifies her friends who have not been so meticulous. The undertone of instigating the sense of guilt in the juvenile consciousness persists in the narrative. (Fig. 15)

Fig. 14 & 15: *Journey of a Muslim,* reproduced with permission.

Cyprus Beetle's *Why Hijab?* reveals a propensity to conversion as the Shawna claims that she is wearing a hijab for she has subscribed to the Islamic faith, just to ward off the advances of Nile. (Fig. 16) The moral of the story is that hijab is an added protection against unsolicited attention; although it is hardly a solution against public unsafety, as one can argue. While the execution seems a tad exaggerated, the assignation of chibi figures amplifies the hilarity, seeking the child reader.

Fig. 16: *Why Hijab,* reproduced with permission.

Competitive Webcomic: The fourth discursive apparatus under consideration is the competitive impetus of the Webcomic format. Muslim Manga at its inception was about providing a platform to dōjinshi and fan art creators to engage each other in Islamic-themed contests. The Webcomic format allows the possible future prosumers to involve themselves in a series that comprises individual chapters created by various contestants, documented under the same title. The series provides to a plethora of styles and plots which might draw the audience to the vortex of variety. The *Islamic Unity Contest Webcomics* is the product of one such opportunity.

The chapter submitted ranges from a single page of elaborate fan art where a child asks his father about the peace protest for Gaza by Syazwani Hamdan (Fig. 17) to a narrative across a few pages of rustic art about a miscellany of children from different ethnic origins by Akira-Pyon. (Fig. 18) Webcomic encourages colourised formats along with grayscales and monochromes. The panels are regular and apparently unrefined. The progression is linear from left to right. The pre-pubescent child is taught by his father that

Muslims and non-Muslims are encouraged to protest against the atrocities at Gaza as violence is never advisable. The children on the non-coloured panel ostensibly stand together to make their amicable unity apparent.

Fig. 17 & 18: *Islamic Unity Contest Webcomics*, reproduced with permission.

The other series that is accessible on NM is *Short Webcomics*, created by miscellaneous artists. Apart from the regular manga tropes, there are a few texts which are borderline non-mangaesque, adding to the diversity of the title. The first is named *Joseph* who is a ten year old child with Italian ancestry. He pledges loyalty to Islamic faith and his prayer routine (*namāz*) during a school football match confuses his friend. He imagines that Joseph is lying prostrate as he is feeling unwell and tries to assist him. (Fig. 19) The second is titled *Hijab Strip* which is a dialogue between two seemingly pre-teenaged girls about sartorial choices. (Fig. 20) Both have neon colourised pages and heavily lined panel borders. Means of leisure and communal bonding activities such as a football match and sleepover might attract child spectators to these dōjinshi(s). For *Joseph*, the visualisation hearkens the likeness of a *kodomo* manga. Joseph is proud of his ethnic identity. But it comes across in the text that he prefers to keep his religious affiliation hidden, until his friend finds it out accidentally. If we presume the story is set in Europe, the reason behind this secrecy might be Islamophobia. In *Hijab Strip*, it is mentioned that the girl who chooses to wears a hijab can also dress up in haute couture or a 'Pikachu' nightshirt for that matter. The distinction between the public and the private is delineated in the panels, challenging the reader to mature from prejudiced assumptions.

Fig. 19 & 20: *Short Webcomics*, *Joseph* and *Hijab Strip*, reproduced with permission.

With the publication of new chapters and texts, more such discursive tools could be identified on NM. For instance, the wise grandfather-like figure seems emergent. He assumes the role of a wise teacher to inculcate religious values in the grandchild. But it is it yet to be fully realised. NM or Muslim Manga might actually be the portal for initiation of a child into the culture of manga. The reader who is introduced to the medium through these texts could be fascinated by the medium and decide to explore the larger corpus of secular manga at their disposal. Through the practice of religious literacy, the possibility exists that the platform may end up advocating manga literacy to the child reader as well.

Acknowledgement: I am indebted to the *Muslim Manga* website for graciously permitting me the opportunity to reproduce the dōjinshi images used in the article, granted via their Facebook messenger.

REFERENCES

1. https://www.islamcenter.or.jp/history-of-islam-in-japan/

BIBLIOGRAPHY

Aoki, Deb. (2016). 'History of Manga-Manga Goes to War Comics in Pre-War, World War II and Post-War Japan 1920-1949.' Retrieved from http://manga.about.com/od/historyofmanga/a/mangahistory2.htm on 15 March 2016.

Bouissou, Jean-Marie et al. (2010). 'Manga in Europe: A Short Study of Market and Fandom'. *Manga: An Anthology of Global and Critical Perspectives.* (Ed.) Toni Johnson Woods. New York: Continuum Books. pp. 253-265.

Bryce, M. Barber, C. & Plumb, A. (2012). 'Manga and Anime: Fluidity and Hybridity in Global Imagery'. *Researching Twenty-first Century Japan: New Directions and Approaches for the Electronic Age.* (Eds.) T. Iles & P. Matanle. Plymouth: Lexington Books. pp. 323-342.

Cool Japan Strategy (Modified version of the Interim Report submitted to the Cool Japan Advisory Council). (2012) Retrieved from http://www.meti.go.jp/english/policy/mono_info_service/creative_industries/pdf/121016_01a.pdf on 11 July 2017.

Goldberg, Wendy. (2010). 'The Phenomenon of Manga in America'. *Manga: An Anthology of Global and Critical Perspectives.* (Ed.) Toni Johnson Woods. New York: Continuum Books. pp. 281-296.

Ingulsrud, E. John and Kate Allen. (2009). *Japan Cool: Patterns of Manga Literacy and Discourse.* Plymouth: Lexington Books.

Iwabuchi, Koichi. (2002). *Recentering Globalization: Popular Culture and Japanese Transnationalism*. Durham, NC: Duke University Press Books.

Izewar, Serena. (2017). Comment on *Izzah's Journey*. Retrieved from http://nurmanga.com/manga/izzas-journey/chapter-one/1 on 11 July 2017.

Kent, David. (2012). 'Forget Pele, Maradona and Beckenbauer, meet the inspiration behind Torres' career... Japanese cartoon Captain Tsubasa'. Retrieved from http://www.dailymail.co.uk/sport/football/article-2245925/Fernando-Torres-I-took-football-Captain-Tsubasa.html on 15 March 2016.

McCloud, Scott. (1999). *Understanding Comics: The Invisible Art*. New York: Paradox Press.

Peng Er Lam. (2007). 'Japan's 'Soft Power': Attraction and Limitation'. *East Asia: An International Quarterly.* Vol.24, No.4. pp. 349-363.

URL Sources

Akira-Pyon. (2017). *Islamic Unity Contest Webcomics*. Retrieved from http://nurmanga.com/manga/islamic-unity-contest-webcomics on 11 July 2017.

Alfasi, Asia. (2017). *Beginnings.* Retrieved from http://nurmanga.com/manga/beginnings on 15 July 2017.

Cyprus Beetle. (2017). *Why Hijab?* Retrieved from http://nurmanga.com/manga/why-hijab on 5 August 2017.

FullWhiteMoon. (2017) *Understanding Islam for Dummies*. Retrieved from http://nurmanga.com/manga/understanding-islam-for-dummies-with-miss-noor on 11 August 2017.

Hafizh and Aiman. *Huda*. (2017). Retrieved from http://nurmanga.com/manga/huda on 11 July 2017.

Hamdan, Syazwani. (2017). *Islamic Unity Contest Webcomics.* Retrieved from http://nurmanga.com/manga/islamic-unity-contest-webcomics on 12 July 2017.

Ichi15. *Izzah's Journey*. (2017). Retrieved from http://nurmanga.com/manga/izzas-journey on 15 July 2017.

MiSsBeatoChan. (2017). *United We Stand*. Retrieved from http://nurmanga.com/manga/united-we-stand on 11 July 2017.

Nouri, Hamed and Harihtaroon. (2017). *Hana and her Love*. Retrieved from http://nurmanga.com/manga/hana-and-her-love on 11 July 2017.

Nouri. Hamed. (2017). *The Heart of Fawwaz*. Retrieved from http://nurmanga.com/manga/the-heart-of-fawwaz on 12 July 2017.

Short Webcomics. (2017). Retrieved from http://nurmanga.com/manga/short-webcomics on 11 July 2017.

Spring Sky. (2017). *An Enlightening Lesson*. Retrieved from http://nurmanga.com/manga/an-enlightening-lesson on 11 July 2017.

Thompson, Barney. (2015). 'Why Comics and Cartoons are Flourishing in the Middle East' in *Financial Times*. Retrieved from https://www.ft.com/content/26a80334-31fa-11e5-91ac-a5e17d9b4cff on 19 August 2017.

Yusuf, Zayn and Nisrina Ahmad. (2017). *Himawari*. Retrieved from http://nurmanga.com/manga/himawari on 11 July 2017.

Zhar. *Best Friends*. (2017). Retrieved from http://nurmanga.com/manga/best-friends on 11 July 2017.

Zhar. *Journey of a Muslim*. (2017). Retrieved from http://nurmanga.com/manga/journey-of-a-muslim on 15 July 2017.

PART IV

The Popular and the Narrative Alternative

CHAPTER 9

Salman Rushdie and the *Dastan* Tradition

Soumava Maiti

> Man is a storytelling animal. Only a man can weave a story, and stories after stories—one connected with another. Hence complex storylines are created by endless weaving of stories—in many patterns and multiple ways—in words, in music, in lines, sometimes in gestures.
>
> (Sibaji Bandyopadhyay. 'Myth O Itihas' in *Gopal-Rakhal Dwandwa Samas: Upanibeshbad O Bangla Sishusahitya*, 2013, 33. Translation: mine).

> To tell a story about the past is to tell a story about the present.
>
> (Salman Rushdie. *Two Years Eight Months and Twenty Eight Nights*, 2015, 207)

Origin and Features of *Dastan*

The *dastan* originated in the medieval Persia and is believed to have reached South Asia around the eleventh century. The *dastan* was primarily transmitted orally throughout the Islamic world from where it travelled to the Indian subcontinent and flourished in colonial India as *dastangoi*. *The Adventure of Amir Hamza* originated in Arabia in the seventh century to commemorate the brave deeds of Prophet Muhammad's uncle, Amir Hamza. In the course of its travels in the Middle East and Central Asia, this story incorporated many local narratives, local histories and became entirely fictional legends. The story of *Amir Hamza* found its way to India sometime between the eleventh and the fourteenth centuries, and the story was told in the *dastan* genre. Mughal emperor Akbar not only enjoyed its narration, but also in 1562 he commissioned an illustrated album of the legend. In his introduction to Muhammad Husain Jah's *Hoshruba: The Land and the Tilism* (*Tilism-E Hoshruba* Book 1), Musharraf Ali Farooqi informs that:

> In the nineteenth century...it was narrated in the Urdu language in two different *dastan* traditions. The first was a short legend, which recounted all the events preceding Amir Hamza's birth... The second *dastan* tradition was much longer, loosely arranged and of more complex nature... Through telling and retelling, the storytellers enlarged the existing episodes and continuously added new details and adventures. (Farooqi, 2009, x-xi).

Until the first quarter of the twentieth century, a class of professional storytellers in India known as the *dastango*, practised *dastan* narration. The text of the *dastan* was essentially written to be used as cue-notes, or consulted as mnemonical text by the *dastango* before or during *dastan-goi*. But by the close of the first half of this century, the profession of *dastango* disappeared from India, and the tradition of *dastan-goi* came to an end. When the *dastan* as an oral art form gradually became extinct, the Hamza stories became available to the readers largely through the written editions of Ghalib Lakhnavi and Abdullah Bilgrami. Drawing attention to the failure of the written *dastan* to replicate the virtuosity of the *dastangos*, in modifying and adapting the Hamza tales according to their own whims or to the audiences' moods, Musharraf Farooqi in the article 'The Simurgh-Feather Guide to the Poetics of Dastan-e Amir Hamza Sahibqiran' ascribes it to the gap between the orality and literacy:

> In its early days, when the *dastan* 'tradition' was alive, the *dastan* 'genre' had both components—'form' and 'content.' But the form of the *dastan* was imbedded in the tradition of *dastangoi*. And when the tradition ended, so did the form...we are left with nothing to comment on its structure. What remains now is the outlined section; the 'text' of the *dastan*'s contents—a relic of the *dastan* tradition (Farooqi, 2000, 128-30).

In *Haroun*, Rashid fails to respond to the printed text of *The Ocean of the Stream of Stories* in Snooty Buttoo's library (*Haroun*, 1990, 51) which, represents the diminished existence of the written *dastan* that Farooqi has appropriately named as the 'relic' of the *dastan* tradition. Rashid's magical storytelling, inspired by the Sea of Stories in Kahani, which is 'alive' (*Haroun*, 1990, 12), symbolises the old and forgotten stage when 'the *dastan* tradition was alive' as the art of skilful *dastango*.

Walter Benjamin in his essay 'The Storyteller,' says that the art of story-telling is "an artisan form of communication... It does not aim to convey that pure essence of the thing... It sinks in to life of the storyteller, in order to bring it out of him again" (Benjamin, 2007, 1-92). He further says that in the act of storytelling, the relation between a storyteller and his/her listeners is the most important, in reproducing the stories; 'The listener's naive relationship to the storyteller is controlled by this interest in retaining what he is told. The cardinal point for the unaffected listener is to assure himself of the possibility of reproducing the story. Memory is the epic faculty par excellence'. (Benjamin, 2007, 97).

These words greatly resemble the following lines, as uttered by Shamsur Rahman Faruqi, the Urdu poet, novelist and eminent *dastan* studies scholar, in an interview with Mohmood Farooqui:

> In the *dastans*, the most important fact is— the *dastan*-narrator and the audience are together, they interact with each other in fact. The *dastans* can be and is modulated according to the audience. It's an ongoing narrative; it has to be an ongoing, living and dynamic process. Once the story being told, there are layers and layers of the story...each time the *dastango* and the narrator has to prepare themselves for an interaction. (Shamsur Rahman Faruqi, 2014, in interview with Mahmood Farooqui).

Salman Rushdie and Rashid Khalipha, the *Dastangoi(s)*

Salman Rushdie's *Haroun and the Sea of Stories* (1990), *Luka and the Fire of Life* (2010) and *Two Years Eight Months and Twenty Eight Nights* (2015) celebrate the triumph of storytelling and literary imagination over power and dogmatism. The stories of *Haroun*, *Luka* and *Two Years* derive from Indic, Persian, Arabic oral and literary sources. The novelist aims at creating what Timothy Brenan refers to as "written orality" (Brenan, 1989, 139), which involves "digression and juxtaposition of the oral storyteller" and popularisation of tradition, i.e. "epic, holy book, national legend" (Brenan, 1989, 41-42). In *Haroun*, *Luka*, and *Two Years* Rushdie achieves the effect of 'written orality' by introducing the nonlinear mode of storytelling (Indian tradition of cyclical, episodic, and digressive), with the intertwining of multiple storylines as it functions in the *dastans*. The splitting of the name of the caliph of Baghdad, Haroun-al-Rashid, "into the names of father and son," as Meenakhshi Mukherejee observes in her essay "*Haroun and the Sea of Stories*: Fantasy of Fable?" invokes "the cycle of tales that for Rushdie has long been a synecdoche for an inexhaustible storehouse of stories" (Mukherjee, 2013, 153).

The story of the novel *Haroun and the Sea of Stories* (1990) begins in an imaginary 'country of Alifbay,' with 'a sad city, the saddest of cities, a city so ruinously sad that it had forgotten its name' (Rushdie, 1990, 15) and ends happily with a policeman's declaration of "We remembered the city's name"(208). The name of the city is "Kahani" and "It means story" (Rushdie, 1990, 209). The novel tells the story of Haroun Khalifa and his father Rashid Khalifa and their adventure in Gup and Chup in search of Rashid's lost talent of storytelling after Rashid's wife Soraya's disappearance with a clerk who despises stories as useless untruth. While Soraya finds Rashid's impractical storytelling impossible to stand, Haroun on the other hand finds his father's skill fascinating, which implicitly draws our attention to the splendid art of *dastango* tradition. In the practice of storytelling, the talent of the storyteller is celebrated: 'Haroun often thought of his father as a juggler, because his stories were really lots of different tales juggled together, and Rashid kept them going in a sort of dizzy whirl, and never made a mistake' (Rushdie, 1990, 16). On Haroun's insistence Rashid says by way of explanation that his stories come from "the great Story—Sea... I drink the warm Story Water and then I feel full of steam" (Rushdie, 1990, 17). Later on the Water Genie Iff replies to Haroun's question that "Anybody can tell stories... But for stories with that Extra Ingredients, even the best storytellers need the Story Waters... storytelling needs fuel, just like a car..." (Rushdie, 1990, 58). The ocean of the Stream of Story, where Haroun is first taken by his fabulous (mechanical, vegetal, or simply magical) companions in the *palimpsest* story-world of Kahani, is a truly fantastic place, as it combines all forms of stories of the world, those already told, those in the telling, as well as those yet untold. As Iff explains:

> Different parts of the ocean contained different sorts of stories. And as all the stories that had ever been told and many that were still in the process of being invented could be found here, the Ocean of the Stream of Story was in fact the biggest library in the universe. And because the stories were held here in fluid form, they retained the ability to change, to become new versions of themselves, to join up with other stories; so that unlike a library of books, the Ocean of the Stream of Story was much more than a storeroom of yarns. It was *not dead but alive* (*Haroun*, 1990, 72) (emphasis: mine).

The last adjectives for the stream of stories as 'not dead but alive', as explained by Iff, clearly recall eminent Urdu scholar Shamsur Rahaman Faruqi's postulation of *dastangoi* as "an ongoing, living and dynamic process", quoted earlier.

The novel *Luka and the Fire of Life* (Rushdie, 2010) offers another foray into the lives of the now older Khalifa family twenty years after the publication of *Haroun and the Sea of Stories* (Rushdie, 1990).The younger son of Khalifa family, Luka is now ready for an adventure of his own, filled with fantastical creatures, distant lands, and P2C2Es. Luka is a miracle child, born to aging parents with the power to 'turn back Time itself, make it flow the wrong way and make us young again' (Rushdie, 2010, 18). True to his birthright, Luka's mission is not to restore Rashid's voice, but to awake his father from a prolonged sleep, literally restoring him to life. In *Luka*, Rushdie deals with philosophical concepts like *Being and Un-being* (life and death). The spectacular use of the digital media is revolutionary as it opens up a space for independence within the social group that has always been systematically controlled in relation to its access to information, self-expression, and means of social communication. To some extent, this empowerment of young people comes from their creative interactions with popular culture, communal median. Rushdie's use of MMOs—or in his playful pun, "Muu" (Rushdie, 2010, 12)—may be seen as his acknowledgment of their inherent freedom for excursion and digression and to give alternative possibilities. In the story of *Lukas* Rushdie manages to achieve the alternative possibilities through 'an almost infinite number of parallel realities' (Rushdie, 2010, 11) because the 'magical boxes' or 'alternate-reality boxes' (Rushdie, 2010, 12) of Luka offer 'the richest, most complex journeys into other spaces and different-time, into the zone of multi-life and temporary death' (Rushdie, 2010, 12).

Rushdie's constant switching off between the 'pre-lives' and the 'after-lives' in *Two Years* helps the novel to achieve its polyphonic voices that can open up possibilities of many worlds, both fantastic and real. Dunia's constant recalling of the millennium-old past stories 'permits a multiplicity of social voices' and a 'wide variety' of 'links and interrelationship' (Bakhtin, 1981, 63). The novel is narrated by an unidentified voice in a remote future, a millennium from now. The story told is that of a period lasting two years, eight months and twenty-eight nights, during which a war of the worlds is waged. This is heralded by a cataclysmic storm that brings with it certain 'strangenesses', signalling that the boundaries between the human and fairy worlds—the latter being the home of the jinn, the whimsical and wanton creatures—have been breached. Eschatological lightning strikes, oracular infants and local failures of gravity become the norm, as the Dark Ifrits, the mischievous forces of disorder, begin to take advantage of the weakening of the fabric of the everyday. It turns out that four evil jinn, Zabardast, Zumurrud, Ra'im Blood-Drinker and Shining Ruby, have broken through the wormholes separating the world from Fairyland and are bent on causing havoc in the twenty-first century. And so the queen of fairyland, Ibn Rushd's jinn-lover, returns to earth after an absence of 800 years to rally her tribe. The origin of these characters' magical 'strangenesses' lies in their lineage. In twelfth-Century Andalucía, Dunia, a grand princess of the *jiniri* with a penchant uncommon in her kind for human experience, falls in love with the philosopher Ibn Rushd, known in the west as 'Averroes' and has been banished from the court on account of his liberal views. In the generations to come, Dunia's descendants, the Duniazát, spread across continents, oblivious to their magical heritage, until the day they are called upon to rise up in defence of everything their great-great-great-etc-grandfather stood for, the battle of rhetoric between the two now-long-dead philosophers. One hundred and one days after the great storm Ibn Rushd, 'lying forgotten in his family tomb in Cordoba' began to 'communicate with his equally deceased opponent, Ghazali, in a humble grave in the town of Tush' (55) and the narrator then tells us that, it is in that "context of the time of the strangenesses that the dialogue between the dead philosophers should be understood" (Two Years, 2015, 55). In the darkness of the tomb, Ibn Rushd heard with a 'sweet nostalgia' the 'familiar voice' of Dunia and they immediately began to converse (Rushdie, 2015, 15). Hence, the essential elements of *dastans* such as constant warfare, trickery, enchantment and magic fully abound in the latest novel of Salman Rushdie.

Dastan Elements

Madhumita Roy and Anjali Gera Roy in their essay '*Haroun* and *Luka*: A study of Salman Rushdie's talismanic stories' trace the influences of the *dastan* tradition in *Haroun* and *Luka* to establish Rushdie's Indo-Islamic cultural heritage. The *dastan*, translated as 'tales' or 'legends' is primarily an oral art form of epic proportions weaving together loose, episodic tales of magic and adventure about the exploits of larger-than-life heroes. The legendary *dastango* is recalled in the figure of Rashid Khalifa, who is a professional storyteller known as 'The Ocean of Notion'. Like the *dastan*, his stories are a 'never-ending stream of tall, short and winding tales' (Rushdie, 1989, 15) about 'sorcery, love-interest, princess... fantastic locations, cowards, heroes, fights, and half a dozen catchy hummable tunes' (Rushdie, 1989, 17). *Razm* (war), *bazm* (court), *husnoishq* (love for a beautiful woman), and *ayyari* (magic and trickery), four pillars of the *dastan* along with *tilism*, (Khan, 2000, 4-5), are also present in these three novels. *Razm* or war is the key strategy used to resolve conflict in both novels; be it the fight between Gup city and Chup city in *Haroun* or Luka's battle with the Old Man of the River and fight with Time in *Luka*, or Dunia's battle with four black jinn in *Two Years*. Both the oral narrative tradition and the simulacrum of the video games may be viewed as actualising the potential of an open-ended text. In this manner, "the video game setting in *Luka*," as Madhumita Roy and Anjali Gera Roy aptly say, "although similar to Rashid Khalifa's storytelling in being subjected to the logic of textuality, becomes a useful trope for Rushdie for repeating the *dastan's* oral aesthetics with a difference for Milan and children of his age" (Roy, 2014, 178). The incident about the nasty Rats of the Respectorate of We scratching themselves to death or dragon breath burning Captain Aag to ashes in *Luka* resonates with the violence common in video games, but the *dastan*, which also chronicles endless warfare treats death and violence with similar nonchalance. The reference to the legend Titan Prometheus, whom Zeus imprisoned with an eagle munching at his liver in *Luka*, also significantly refers to Hind's devouring of Hamza's liver and heart in the battle of Uhud.

There are several thematic similarities between *Dastan-e-Amir Hamza* and Rushdie's three fictions, under discussion. Like the trinity of the Hamza story that comprise the hero Hamza and his two loyal and faithful friends Amar and Muqbil, Haroun's friends include Iff the Water Genie and Butt the Hoopoe, and in Luka's adventure Dog the bear and Bear the dog are his trusted friends. Another strong similarity between Rushdie's select novels and *Dastan-e-Hamza* is evident in the Qaf episode of Hamza tales. Qaf is the magic land ruled by the king of the Peri clan—Shahpal. Hamza travels to Qaf land with Abdur Rahman, Shahpal's vazir, to rescue the magic kingdom from the monsters called *Devs*, especially the brutal Ifrit. Hamza's encounters with magical creatures such as Peris, Perizads, Devs, and Jinns take place in Qaf. Similarly, Haroun and Luka's travels involve movements from the real worlds to the magical worlds where they encounter numerous fantastical creatures. The story world of *Haroun* is abound in several fantastical creatures like Iff the water Genie, Butt the Mechanical Hoopoe, the Floating Gardener Mali, the plentimaw fishes Goopy and Bhagha. Luka's magic world is even more densely populated with magical creatures such as—talking pets, spectre of his father named Nobodaddy, memory birds with elephant heads, Rats with inflated egos, flying Otters and their queen Soraya, Solomon's flying carpets and multiple mythological creatures and fallen gods. *Two Years* also depicts a host of magical creatures especially *jinns* and *jinnias* in the Peristan, the Fairyland, which directly resemble the magic land Qaf in Hamza tales. Madhumita Roy and Anjali Gera Roy succinctly voice that "the world of *dastan* is an integral part of Rashid's imagination and is 'the most exciting of all' storyworlds as Luka observes" (Roy, 2014, 177).

In *Haroun*, the elements of *bazm* or courtly splendour can be found in the description of King Chatterjee's court and palace. While Luka does not contain an elaborate descriptions of courtly life, it is populated by three Aalim, the ultimate guardians of time appropriately named Jo-Hua (What Was), Jo-Hai (What Is), Jo-Aiga (What Will Come) and several mighty kings in the forms of fallen gods. The young protagonist's crushes on Blabbermouth, the sprightly page in *Haroun*, and the liking for Queen Soraya, the Insultana of Ott in *Luka* fulfil the criteria of *husnoishq* or the trope of beautiful women. The components of 'enchantment', 'trickery', and 'magic' also fully abound in these three novels. The Fairy Queen Soraya, who remains a sky-bound creature in *Luka*, literally embodies the Asman Peri or sky fairy of Hamza tales. Soraya (*Haroun*), Blabbermouth (*Luka*) and Dunia's (*Two Years*) feisty temper can be compared to the aggressive Asman Peri in the first half of *Dastan-e-Amir Hamza*. In true *dastan* tradition, *tilism* is represented as a space of enchantment and illusion in *Dastan-e-Amir Hamza*. However, a long sequence of *dastan* has been built up around the central symbol of *tilism*. What is more, the *dastan*-tellers or *dastan*-writers belonging to Lucknow and Rampur also singled out various peripheral stories from these *dastan* and attempted to retell them in their own style or to create further *tilisms* along similar lines. So the huge cycles of these tilismic *dastans* are part of our literary history. The beguiling *tilism*, designed by the Khattam-Shud in *Haroun* is an elaborate shadowy realm in which his shadowy self plots various ways of destroying the Wellspring of the Sea of Stories, and threatens the existence of both the stories and the storytellers.

M.A. Farooqi, while discussing some essential features of *dastans*, refers to the term "idle tales" that "underscores that from the start the *dastan* followed a certain ideal in its narrative, which aimed at escaping reality" (Farooqi, 2000, 123). The tales of Amir Hamza also provides this 'escapist' virtue of *dastan*. The escapist elements were significant factors for the popularity of *dastan* and the world of *dastan* was a 'world of dream that shut out all troubles' (Farooqi 124). These escapists elements abound in plenty in the three novels under discussion; in fact, the central stories are performed by Haroun, Luka and Dunia only to transcend us into some certain colourful, magical and make-believe worlds. Another striking feature of dastangoi is *dastan rokna* or 'stalling the dastan'. According to M.A. Farooqi:

> The clue to understanding the function of the *dastan* is found in the term *dastan rokna* used by the *dastangos*. Literally the term means "to stop the *dastan*," and it conjures up the image that narration has stopped. However, that is not the case. In instances where the term was used, the narration continued with great gusto. Only "action" came to a standstill. Therefore we translate the term as *dastan rokna* "stalling the dastan" (Farooqi, 2000, 131).

The elements of *dastan-rokna* can be found in Luka's first conversation with the beautiful queen Soraya, and in the action involving the warfare between Respecto-Rats and the Otters froze (Rushdie, 2010, 14-87) in Dunia's meeting with Geronimo after so many years (ages).

In *Two Years*, in the kingdom of Qaf, in Fairyland or Peristan where the jinns live, the Lightning Princess opens a Chinese box of stories that has poisoned her father, the king. As the incomplete stories—of 'strangenesses' taking place in the city of B. or the village of I.—pour out, one interrupting the other before it can come to a satisfactory end, Princess Dunia and the half-human Geronimo Manezes, her great-grandson find their own way into these stories, latching on to resemblances with stories that make up their own lives. The narrators of the story of those eventful two years, eight months and twenty-eight nights that changed human life heavily depend on their age-old memory and try to preserve the memory so that they may not forget where they came from and why they live as they do. Rushdie warns against the dangers of forgetting in these three novels where we encounter multiple levels of lost epistemologies such as the ancient Islamic philosophy of rationalism, knowledge of magic, sorcery and the ancient Hindu philosophy of reincarnation. Rushdie's return to post-lives of some dead characters through the lens of memory and magic not only allows him to restore the alternative world of magic and trickery, but also helps him to revive the forgotten art of *dastan*. Hence, these three novels can be called the literary afterlives of *dastango*. As the *dastan* was chiefly an oral art form, the *dastangos*, while performing before the audience, solely depend on their memories. Rushdie's protagonists in all these three novels also solely depend on their memory in their respective quests. In the essay 'Thesis on the Philosophy of History' Walter Benjamin addresses the relation of our utopian imagination to the redemptive aspect of memory:

> ...our image of happiness is indissolubly bound up with the image of redemption.... The past carries with it a temporal index by which it is referred to as redemption. There is a secret agreement between past generations and the present one. Our coming was expected on the earth. Like every generation that preceded us, we have been endowed with a *weak* Messianic power, a power to which the past has a claim (Benjamin, 2007, 154)

In *Haroun*, *Luka* and *Two Years* we encounter Rushdie as a historian, or rather as Walter Benjamin's privileged historian, who, while "articulat(e)ing the past historicality" seizes "hold of a memory as it flashes up in a moment of danger" (Benjamin, 2007, 125). Benjamin goes on to say that the "image of the past... unexpectedly appears to man singled out by history at a moment of danger. The danger affects both the content of the tradition and its receivers" (Benjamin, 2007, 255). Being Benjaminian story-tellers, a continual yearning runs through the retelling of the past in the 'possibility of reproducing the story' but in a sort of creative tension between 'memory and hope', between "nostalgia and utopianism" (Benjamin, 2007, 97).

Memory, Story, and Afterlives of *Dastan*

The *Dasten-e Amir Hamza* was an oral narrative cultivated by the imagination of successive generations of storytellers. It existed not in a handful of manuscripts, but in the memories of an unknown number of men. Each narrator made his own choices in the narration, as the "recitals of the *DAH* did not have to start at the beginning, but could begin from any point in the narrative, and end likewise. Again, since the whole *dastan* remained in the memory, it could be accessed at any time from any point—a principle known to the CD-ROM user" (Farooqi, 2000, 134). Like Haroun's adventure, Luka's journey is driven by the memories of his father Rashid's stories. In his almost impossible task of stealing the 'fire of life', Luka depends heavily upon the knowledge of mythical creatures like Bear the dog, and Dog the bear, Elephant Birds, and the wisdom of Queen Soraya with her "thousands of years old" magic carpet (Rushdie, 2010, 82), Coyote and the legendary Titan Prometheus, the first thief of fire. Luka is able to defeat every deadly peril not because of his gaming skills but by recalling the knowledge and wisdom contained in his father's stories. When Luka faces the 'Old Man of the River' with his 'Terminator in his hand' he 'did his best to summon back the memory of what else the Shah of Blah had told him about this malevolent river-demon' (Rushdie, 2010, 51-52) in order to get rid of him. Nobodaddy stresses the significance of memory to invoke our past: "And if you want to travel up the River, Memory is the fuel you need" (Rushdie, 2010, 66).On his 'Path to the Three Fiery Doughnuts' (Rushdie, 2010, 93) he again has to 'rely on the Memory of the Elephant Birds for fuel' (Rushdie, 2010 97). Whenever he faces difficulties, he recalls his father's stories for the necessary knowledge because 'all the places he knew so well from his father's tale' (Rushdie, 2010, 16).

The stories of *Haroun*, *Luka* and *Two Years* are warnings against forgetting. We are living in such an age with high technology and 'High Definitions' (Rushdie, 2010, 115) that we do not even bother to hear the age-old stories, to think about magic or dream-world. Queen Soraya in *Luka* laments that, "Magic is fading from the universe... We aren't needed anymore... One of these days you'll find out what it's like to live without even the idea of Magic" (Rushdie, 2010, 130). Luka is at a loss when he faces almighty Aalim and then he recalls what his father Rashid told him one night, "Dreams are Aalim's enemies, because in dreams the Laws of Time disappear... The time of our feeling is not as the time of the clock" (Rushdie, 2010, 157). Rashid challenges the prevalent notion of reality by arguing that, "Our dreams are the real truths—our fancies, the knowledge of our hearts... I've spent my life telling people that this is the truth about Time, and that Aalim's clocks tell lies" (Rushdie, 2010, 158). In his adventure to the sea of stories

Haroun also observes that, "...the real world was full of magic, so magical worlds could easily be real" (*HSS* 50). *Dastans* also mainly deal with worlds of dream, magic and enchantment, and the *dastan* "does not necessarily follow the cause-and-effect principle" (Farooqi 164). Rushdie's stories in these three novels also do not follow any cause and effect principle; rather the stories are full of dreams, magic and fictional worlds of gods, *jinns* and *perries*. In *Luka*, the Heart of Rashid's dream world is populated by 'badly behaved' discarded gods—including 'the ancient gods of North, the gods of Greece and Rome, the South American gods, and gods of Sumeria and Egypt' (Rushdie, 2010, 127)—in whom 'nobody believed any longer, except as stories that people once liked to tell' (Rushdie, 2010, 127). These gods, powerless in the real world, still retain their 'superpower' in the Heart of Magic. This implies that if the storyteller dies, the gods, who have already lost their divinity but still survive majestically as fallible heroes in the colourful stories of Rashid Khalifa, would also be lost forever.

As in *Haroun*, in the court of King Chatterjee, young Haroun impresses everyone by his speech and as a result he is chosen for the adventure to the land of Chup. Here in *Luka* also, Luka in 'the greatest speech of his life as a performer' (Rushdie, 2010, 183) shows his skill as a storyteller. Luka truly grows beyond his father's own authority as the storyteller when in the final battle for the 'Fire of Life' Luka impresses all ex-gods by saying that, "this world of magic...is my father's world" (Rushdie, 2010, 180) and then, "listen to me; it's only through Stories that you can get out into the Real World and have some sort of power again. When your story is well told, people believe in you" (Rushdie, 2010, 182). Towards the end of *Luka*, Ratatat tells Luka that, "you've certainly got their attention now" (Rushdie, 2010, 182). Hence, Haroun and Luka become storytellers at the end and they symbolically become parts of the ongoing lives/after-lives of *dastans*. Hence, whereas Khattam-Shud, Al Ghazali and Aalim represent the totalised account of experience that must suppress differences to maintain the illusion of its own totality. The story sea in *Haroun*, the story world in *Luka* and the *jinn* world in *Two years* on the other hand, represent a riot of diverse narratives that resist the drive toward assimilation and incorporation. Here Rushdie's aim is to imagine a form for the nation as a fluid, provisional entity defined by its capacity to incorporate difference and variation. In this respect, Rushdie's Ocean of Story (*Haroun*), Parisatan, the Fairyland (*Two Years*), and the Magic Land of Story (*Luka*) can be described with more accuracy as an attempt to give shape to the Lyotardian ideal. In Rushdie's vision of a plethora of 'small' stories, set in opposition to the 'grand mythology' promoted by Khattam-Shud and Aalim, there is an echo of Lyotard's famous distinction between *petites recits* and metanarratives, as defined in his book *The Postmodern Condition: A Report on Knowledge* (Lyotard 82). Whereas Lyotard's vision of competing narratives remains at the level of metaphysical generality, Rushdie's allegorical revision of Lyotard's attack on the Platonic tradition has a more specific focus. Rushdie's aim is to reimagine a form of social and communal interaction, as it was prevalent during the time of *dastangoi*.

Shamsur Rahman Faruqi in his interview with Mohmood Farooqui, already quoted earlier, nicely posits that 'The story actually is the whole reason of life. Our story makes sense of us, our story makes sense of the world, our story tells us that there are things which can happen or do happen or may happen, and they can happen right in this world' (Faruqi, 2014, in interview with Mahmood Farooqui). The old stories or *dastans* of Rashid Khalipha, in real as well as fantastical sense, are 'the whole reason of life' in the lives of two child heroes; the stories of Haroun, Luka and Dunia in these three novels too 'make sense of the world(s)' that are lost and forgotten (Faruqi, 2014, in interview with Mahmood Farooqui). Both Haroun and Luka make their journeys respectively to save the story water and the story world. In their mission to restore the storytelling gift and the life of their father, they become the storytellers as they show their skills to pursue and impress even the strangers in their adventures. The reason for this, I think, is their extraordinary gift of recalling and repeating the stories, what their father had told them. In this process they also become successful *dastangoi* or storytellers, for 'storytelling is always the art of repeating stories' (Benjamin, 2007, 91). That is why they are swift enough to handle the difficulties in the sea of story as well as in the heart of magic land. Both the child heroes grow in knowledge and wisdom as they respectively learn the laws and inner workings of a story, which symbolically refer to the secret artistry of the age-old *dastan* tradition. Time can nourish and sustain age-old stories by reminiscence and remembrance of the past events. Stories can resist the homogeneous concept of time by making us think *backwards*; the characters of the story-world continue to live in our mind. In these novels, Rushdie makes an earnest and sincere plea not to forget our roots as in *Haroun* the water Genie Iff laments: "We lost touch with our beginnings, with our roots, our Wellspring, our source" (*HSS* 146). And significantly at the end of *Luka*, the child-hero says, "that wasn't the end of the story" (Rushdie, 2010, 211).

Now, here is a question. Who are Luka, Haroun and Dunia? Are they kinds of saviours of the community, like a modern Prometheus? They undertake their imaginary journeys not only to restore and preserve the lives and afterlives of their family, but also many lives of the community. The story water, the story-world and the magical world are saved in the ends of these select novels. The multiple lives of fairy and magical creatures and characters (like Water Genie, Iff, fallen gods, *jinns*) are saved. To my mind, they are nothing but *dastango* or storytellers who love listening to stories and love telling stories; love recalling old stories and love repeating them, even to the characters of the stories; they are always on imaginary journeys because they are not only onlookers but also participants in their stories.

Conclusion

Here in these three novels, age-old stories are 'perpetually actual phenomena' and always in the process of 'permanent evolution' (Nora, 1989, 8); and a part of 'an undifferentiated eternal present'.[1] Rushdie's characters, here in this novel, fall in an eternal tension between rediscovery and reinvention of stories in remaking new tales or *dastans*; the lives and afterlives of these stories, rest, to my mind, in the apt phrase of the eminent subaltern historian Ranajit Guha—"borne again in repetition" (Guha, 2002, 70) or in living/after(-)living in the age 'coming-after'[2] (Rushdie, 2015, 157). The 'afterlives project', in these above-mentioned novels, unites together the past, present and future; they not only successfully deal with the afterlives of magical creatures of multiple storyworlds and magical worlds, but also revive and revise the oral art forms of storytelling, namely *dastangoi*. Hence, these three novels can be viewed as Rushdie's 'afterlives projects' of *dastan* tradition on the cultural, social and literary planes.

The *dastan*is strengthened themselves as a genre through the medium of orality. Since the whole narrative is stored in the memory, it could be accessed from any point. Sometimes this exercise creates an overlap of the realities of the narrator, the character and the reader, which sustains the enchantment, e.g., the case of the character regarding our world in his crystal ball. In their journeys both Haroun and Luka use their memories, full of the *stream-water*, and the *magic-land* of the story worlds, invented by their father; and their journeys too are remembered by their father. Both Haroun and Luka begin their journeys with an eye to save the source of story-water from pollution (*Haroun*) and to save the characters of the story-world from destruction (*Luka*); interestingly and significantly enough they become the source as well as the character of their father's stories at the end. It is significant because, it is not from their father's story that we come to know the stories of Haroun and Luka. Rather the journeys that they undertake tell us the stories of their father, the story of Kahani and stories of other people. It is the story of Haroun and Luka, not Rashid's. At the end of *Two Years Eight Months and Twenty Eight Nights* Rushdie laments that:

> We read of you in ancient books, O dreams, but the dreams factories are closed... One thousand and one nights may pass, but they pass in silence, like the army of ghosts, their footfalls motionless, marching invisibly through darkness, unheard, unseen, as we live and grow older and die... But Sometimes we wish for the dreams to return (Rushdie, 2015, 286).

We also have been waiting for the *dastans* or the magical worlds or *tilisms* to return. At the end of *Haroun*, Rashid Khalifa tells the story named 'Haroun and the sea of stories' by 'recalling' his 'dream' (204), and in *Luka*, Rashid does the same thing by 'remembering' 'the strangest dream' about Luka's 'adventure in the world of Magic' (Rushdie, 2010, 210); in both cases, the *dastans*, that Rashid Khalifa was going to tell the audience, were performed by the characters before us. We might take these stories just as 'written oralities', as proposed by Brenan, or, for these three stories, we may propose a term— 'audio novel(s)', that are intended to be heard than read, or we may look at these stories as *dastans* that are narrated or recited to us by a generation storytellers or *dastangoes* (Haroun, Luka and Dunia), before Rashid Khalifa, the age-old *dastango*, performed them to the audience.

REFERENCES

1. Gyanendra Pandey in *Memory, History and the Question of Violence*, quotes this phrase from David Lowenthal's work *The Past is a foreign Country*. *The Past is a Foreign Country*, Cambridge UP, 1985.
2. I have used the term in slight alteration of the words '*came after*', as used by Rushdie. To describe the love between Gerenimo and Dunia Rushdie writes the line—'their post-love that *came after...*' Rushdie, 2015, 157. See Works Cited.

BIBLIOGRAPHY

Assmann, J. (1995). 'Collective Memory and Cultural Identity.' *New German Critique*, Vol. 65. pp. 125-33.

Bakhtin, M. (1981). *The Dialogic Imagination: Four essays*. (Trans.) Emerson, C. & Holquist, M. (Ed.) Holquist, M. Austin: University of Texas Press.

Bandyopadhyay, S. (2013). 'Myth O Itihas'. *Gopal-Rakhal Dvandva Samas: Upanibeshbad O*

Bangla Shishusahitya. Kolkata: Karigar.

Benjamin, W. (2007). *Illuminations: Essays and Reflections*. (Ed.) Hannah Arendt. (Trans.) Harry Zohn. New York: Schocken Books.

Brenan, T. (1989). *Salman Rushdie and the Third World: Myths of the Nation*. New York: St. Martin's.

Farooqi, M.A. (2000). 'The Simurge-Feather Guide to the Poetics of Amir Hamza Sahibqiran'. *Annual of Urdu Studies*, Vol. 15. pp. 118-87. Retrieved from www.urdustudies.com/pdf/15/11farooqim.pdf on 30 June 2016.

Faruqi, S.R. 'Performing Arts: *Dastangoi*.' Interviewed by Mahmood Farooqui. Retrieved from *Youtube*, uploaded by Sahapedia online, https://www.youtube.com/watch?v=Pux5mqbZbeg&index on 15 June 2014,

Farooqi, M.A. (2009). 'Introduction' in Jah, M. H., et al. (2009), *Hoshruba: The Land of Tilism*. (Trans.) Musharraf Ali Farooqi. Noida: Random House India.

Guha, R. (2002). *History at the Limit of World History*. New York: Columbia UP.

Jah, M.H., et al. (2009). *Hoshruba: The Land of Tilism*. (Trans.) Musharraf Ali.

Farooqi. Noida: Random House India.

Khan, S.A. (2000). *The Symbolic Aspects of Tilism*. *Annual of Urdu Studies* Vol. 15. pp. 71-78. Retrieved from www. urdustudies. com/pdf/15/11farooqim.pdf on 30 June 2016.

Lakhnavi, G. & Abdulla Bilgrami (2008). *The Adventures of Amir Hamza*. (Trans.) Musharraf Ali Farooqi. (Intro.) Hamid Dabashi. Noida: Random House India.

Lowenthal, D. (1997). 'History and Memory.' *The Public Historian*, Vol. 19. No. 2. pp. 30-39.

Lyotard, J. F. (1984). *The Postmodern Condition: A Report on Knowledge*. (Trans.) Geoff Bennington & Brian Massumi. Manchester: Manchester UP.

Mukherjee, M. (2013). *The Perishable Empire: Essays on Indian Writing in English*. New Delhi: OUP.

Nora, P. (1989). 'Between Memory and History: Les Lieux De Mémoire.' *Representations*, No. 26. pp. 7–24.

Pandey, G. (1999).*Memory, History and the Question of Violence*. Kolkata: Kolkata: Centre for Studies in Social Sciences.

Pritchett, F. (1992). 'The romance tradition in Urdu: Adventure from the *Dastan-e-Amir Hamzah*.' *India International Centre Quarterly*. Vol. 19, No. 3. pp 27-47.

Roy, M. & Roy, A. G. (2014). '*Haroun* and *Luka*: A study of Salamn Rushdie's talismanic stories'. *The Journal of Commonwealth Literature*. Vol. 49, No. 2, 2014, pp. 173-87. Retrieved from journals.sagepub.com/doi/pdf/10.1177/0021989414525182 on 27 Oct. 2015.

Rushdie, S. (1990). *Haroun and the Sea of Stories*. New Delhi: Penguin-Granta Books.

Rushdie, S. (2010). *Imaginary Homelands: Essays and Criticism 1981-1991*. London: Vintage Books.

Rushdie, S. (2010). *Luka and the Fire of Life*. London: Jonathan Cape.

Rushdie, S. (2015). *Two Years Eight Months and Twenty-Eight Nights*. London: Penguin Books.

CHAPTER 10

The Painted Story of *Chandimangal*: Images and Songs

Reeti Basu

Chandimangal Kavya is one of the poems of the *Mangal Kavya* genre. The poem recounts the story of Chandi, the goddess and her desire to establish her glory among the human race. This article will explore the appropriation of this poem into the tradition of painted scrolls which is popularly known as *patachitra*. *Patachitra* or *patashilpa* is a form of scroll painting. The *Patuas*, or *Chitrakars* of West Bengal, have been making *patachitra* or *patashilpa* for centuries. They paint their stories on long scrolls and sing them, as the scroll is unrolled frame by frame. This essay would particularly focus at the Chandi *pat* tradition carried on by the *patuas* of Naya village, located in the western part of Medinipur, West Bengal, India. The community of *patuas* is spread over many districts of pre-partition Bengal: Murshidabad, Bankura, South Twenty-four-Parganas etc., and parts of the present-day Bangladesh.

Mangal Kavyas are a collection of several medieval Bengali poems. These poems were composed during the period between fifteenth to eighteenth centuries (Curley, 2008, 10). These poems were based on different Hindu gods and goddesses and stories of their worship. Historian Kumkum Chatterjee defines it as, 'The corpus of narrative and performative poetry...emphasised the involvement of various gods and goddesses in the lives of human beings and thereby made them more familiar and accessible.' (Chatterjee, 2013, 9). David

Curley points out that these *Kavyas* were subjects of performance for audiences in social or religious gatherings (Curley's preface). Within the *Chandimangal Kavyas* there are poems written by different poets. The poems tells the story of goddess Chandi and her desire to establish her glory among human race. There is more than one version of the poem and it is difficult to locate which version of the poem has been adapted by the *patuas*. Among all the versions of *Chandimangal Kavya*, Mukundaram Chakrabarty's late sixteenth century/early seventeenth century *Chandimangal* is the most famous. So it is an assumption that *patuas* followed Mukundaram's version of the poem.

Mukundaram's *Chandimangal* has mainly three sections *or Khandas*, the *Debata Khanda* section is devoted to the gods; the next two sections address the world of humans the *Akkhettik Khanda* or the *Byadh Khanda* (the hunter section) and the *Banik Khanda* (the merchant section).[1] These stories are found in other versions as well but with different details. *Akkhetik Khanda* is the tale of a hunter named Kalketu and his wife Phullora/Fullora. In this section of the poem, Chandi appears as a forest goddess. In the course of events the animals of the forest complain to Chandi about the hunting by Kalketu. Chandi decides to teach him a listen. So Chandi resorts to illusion and hides all the animals of the forest. Kalketu could not hunt any game for three days. At the end of the third day, he catches a golden coloured lizard and brings it home. This lizard then takes the shape of a beautiful woman and Kalketu threatens to kill that woman. Then the woman reveals her identity of Chandi and gives the couple a ring and caches of gold and gems. With that wealth Kalketu builds the city of Gujurat (not the present day Western Indian state of Gujarat) after depleting the forest. At this point of time, a cunning newcomer comes to the kingdom of Gujurat, Bhanu Dutta, who instigates a war between Kalketu and the King of Kalinga. The King of Kalinga defeats Kalketu and imprisons him. During captivity, Kalketu starts praying to Chandi and the goddess comes to his rescue at the last moment. Threatening the King of Kalinga she asks him for Kalketu's release and to return his kingdom. The King sets Kalketu free and builds a huge temple for worship of Chandi. (Chakravarty, 1921, 45-115) (Sen, 1956, 38-105). (Yazijian, 2007, 148-286)

Banik Khanda is about goddess Chandi's treatment of Dhanapati, the merchant, his two wives Khullona and Lahana, and Khullona's son Srimonto or Sripoti. In Mukundaram's version of the poem, *Banik Khanda* goes like this: Dhanapati Saodagarh is a rich merchant of Ujani Nagar. His two wives are Lahana and Khullona. Lahana is a good woman but is influenced by her evil maid Durbala. Taking advice from Durbala, Lahana sends Khullona to tend the goats as a punishment. One day, one goat was lost by Khullona and seeing her in distress Chandi sends her eight heavenly attendants. They instruct Khullona to worship Chandi. As a result of her worship, Khullona gets back her missing goat. In the meantime, Dhanapati returns home. On the night before Dhanapati's trading trip to Sinhala, he finds Khullona worshipping the goddess for his safe return. Being a worshipper of God Shiva, Dhanapati becomes angry and kicks the sacred water pot and sets out for his voyage. Chandi takes revenge for her being insulted and as a result Dhanapatis's six boats sink into the sea. On his way to Sinhala (Sri Lanka), Chandi shows her *Kamale Kamini* image i.e. a lady swallowing and belching up an elephant, to Dhanapati. Dhanapati repeats this story to the King of Sinhala, but fails to make the King believe it. Then the King challenges Dhanapati to show him the image, failing which he would be imprisoned and ultimately it happens that he was taken captive by the King. While Dhanapati was away, Khullona gives birth to a boy and names him Srimonto. One day, his teacher calls the twelve year old Srimonto a 'bastard' and being angry Srimonto decides to go in search of his father. On his way Srimonto sees the same vision that his father had seen years ago. When he narrates the scene to the King, like what happened with his father he also could not show the image of the lady to the King. He was condemned to death. At the time of execution, Chandi appeared in the disguise of an old Brahmin lady and appealed to the King to spare the boy. (Chakravarty, 1921, 116-305) (Sen, 1956, 108-297) (Yazijian, 2007, 287-666)

David Curley, a scholar on the *Kavyas*, writes that on several occasions when the *Mangal Kavyas* were adapted by other performative traditions, they changed their course. . In some cases, a particular plot became more important than the whole storyline (Curley, 2008, Preface). In the case of Chandi *pat* also we will see how the poem has been recreated by the *patuas*. The reason for choosing this particular poem is to see, how two different sections of the poem have been adapted and interpreted by the *patuas*. Quite interestingly, the Chandi *pat* largely focuses on the excerpts of the *Banik Khanda*, based on the voyage of Srimonto and his confrontation with the King of Salban, also known as Shalibahan or King of Simhala. The story of Kalketu and Fullora/Phullora was depicted sketchily in the *patachitra* tradition. It had been described as, being pleased, goddess Chandi gifted Kalketu some treasure. By this given wealth Kalketu built a city called *Gujurat* or *Gujarat*. As mentioned in Mukundaram's poem, the story does not only tell Srimonto's voyage, but also it focuses on Dhanapati Saodagarh's life (Chakravarty, 1921, 116-212). The relation between *Chandimangal Kavya* and Chandi *pat* is a journey from a written object to visual imagery and oral narration. The *pats* are not only painted, but also have been sung. Hence, it would be interesting to explore the relation between the text, *Chandimangal* and its performance in *patachitras*. The songs or narrations of the *pats* are in Bengali. In the late twentieth century, two scholars named David McCutchion and Suhrid Bhoumik first collected a traditional Chandi song and translated it into English, and called it 'Srimanta Masan' or 'Srimanta in place of Slaughter' (McCutchion and Bhowmik). However, they did not record the name of the author or the place from where they collected the song. In the recent past, Wesleyan University has devised a project to collect commentaries of different kinds of scrolls from the village Naya ('Singing Painters of Naya', learningobjects.wesleyan.edu). I have also interacted with the *patuas* of Naya to explore their understanding of the poem. The purpose of this essay is to understand how the tradition of Chandi *patachitra, both* the songs and the paintings evolved over time.

This article is divided into four sections. The first section of the paper, 'Evolution of a Tradition: The Journey of the Poem to Songs' will deal with the similarities and discrepancies between the poem and the songs or stories narrated by the *patuas* over time. The second section 'Representation of Chandi as Goddess Durga: Weapons and No Weapons' will explore the image of Chandi represented in the oral narratives and also in the painted version of the scroll. The third section is on 'The Art Market and the Changing

Nature of the Performance', will examine, how, to cater to the commercial market. Present *patuas* have changed the style of the narrative which automatically changes the theme of the main story. The last part of the article 'Memory and Imagination: Recreation of a Narrative' deals with the fact that seeming repetitions of old narratives produce new ones and in doing so, how the effort to continue with a tradition creates a new tradition.

Evolution of a Tradition: The Journey of the Poem to Songs

This section of the essay would see how the oral narrative of the poem has changed over time. By comparing it with the present Chandi *patachitra* tradition of Naya and also with the late twentieth century song, I would like to explore how it evolved. It is necessary to look into the old narrative or the song of the Chandi scroll, which is the first recorded source available, to explore the similarities and deviations from the original text.

In the Chandi song of late twentieth century, the demarcation between the two sections of the poem is very clear. The characters of the song have been introduced very strategically to show the break up between the two sections of the original poem.[2] However, unlike the poem it did not mention the economic or social 'class', the characters belonged to. For example, in the original poem, the poet explicitly mentions that Kalketu is a hunter and Dhanapati or Srimonto belongs to the merchant class. The economic background of the characters is very clear in the poem. Here, it is necessary to understand that it is not possible for a performer to follow all details. According to the need of those entertained they have portrayed certain parts of the poem, but each and every ingredient of the poem is touched upon by the narrator.

In the present tradition of Chandi *pat* in Naya, some of the elements of the old narration have remained the same and they have changed at places. For instance, certain geographical locations remain alike in both the present and old traditions and also in the poem. The name of the city (*Gujurat*) built by Kalketu and the name of the place called *Ratnamala Ghat,* where Srimonto landed at the kingdom of the Salban King both remain unchanged. In

McCutchion's collection of the song, the reference to *Ratnamala Ghat* appears as: 'And (Srimonto) reached the *Ratnamala* Ghat' (McCutchion and Bhowmik 55). In both the older and the newer versions of the songs the *patuas* say that following the instruction of Chandi after cutting down a forest he established a city called Gujurat. For instance, the previous adaptation says: 'Then he (Kalketu) cut down the forests of Gujurat and established a town' (McCutchion and Bhowmik, 1999, 54-57). In the later version by Hazra Chitrakar it goes like this, 'Digging out the treasure Kalketu established a city in Gujurat' (Hazra Chitrakar, '*Chandi Mangal*', learningobjects.wesleyan.edu).

The lake where *Kamale Kamini* is seen referred to as *Sakha Jala Lake* in the old tradition of the *patuas* song (McCutchion and Bhowmik).Through this line the *patua* depicts how Srimonto brings the King to the above-mentioned place to show *Kamale Kamini.* However in one of the present *chandi songs by* a *patua* named Mina Chitrakar, the name of the same place is Kalidaha—'Having made that promise, King Shalibahan came to *Kalidaha* to see *Kamala Kamini*' (Mina Chitrakar, 'Chandi Mangal', learningobjects.wesleyan.edu). Another *patua* song by another *patua* Hazra Chitrakar, also refers to the above-mentioned place as Kalidaha—'Srimanta took him to Kalidaha but the goddess didn't show up. So he was handed over to the city keeper and sent to prison.' (Hazra Chitrakar, '*Chandi Mangal*', learningobjects.wesleyan.edu).[3] It is difficult to determine why the name of the place so drastically changes over time. The name of two places do not even slightly resemble each other. Although as the geographic references of the both the places are not quite clear in the original poem, there is a possibility that both Kalidaha and Sakha Jala Lake are the two names of only one place.

Representation of Chandi as Durga: Weapons and No Weapons

In the *patachitra* tradition, Chandi is perceived more as Durga, with ten, sixteen or eighteen hands, in accordance with its painting part in the *patachitra* of both old (Fig. 1) and the recent ones (see Fig. 2 and 3). Chandi has always been described as the mother of her four children. To the *patuas*, goddess Chandi as Durga is more acceptable than Chandi as a forest goddess. However in *Chandimangal Kavya*, Chandi's image is binary. One is that of a forest goddess who is worshipped by the animals and eventually by the hunter and the other is worshipped primarily by merchants. Although this image of goddess Durga is not completely imaginary as Mukundudaram himself refers to the goddess as Chandika, who appears before Kalketu in her Mahishasurmardini form, which is a female figure with ten armed hands, killing Mahishasur or demon with her spear and is surrounded by her children Kartika, Saraswati, Lakshmi and Ganesha (Chatterjee, 2013, 8).

Fig. 1: Chandi as Durga in Chandi Scroll. Time period: Nineteenth Century. Provenance: Midnapore. Source: Gurusaday Museum

(Fig. 2)

(Fig. 3)

Fig. 2: Chandi as Durga. Time period: Twentieth Century. Provenance: Naya, Medinipur. Source: Personal Collection. **Fig. 3** Chandi as Durga in a Chandi Scroll. Time period: 2010. Provenance: Naya, Medinipur. Source: Personal Collection

Tithi Bhattachaya argues that in the ancient texts, Durga does not appear as a mother goddess. It is only from the time of *Mangal Kavya* genre more specifically first in *Chandimanagal*, the image of familial Durga appears (Bhattacharya, 2007, 919-962). Ashish Nandy has suggested that the concept of 'mother goddess' as a protector emerged only in nineteenth century Bengal. About Durga he writes:

> Durga became a more benevolent incarnation of Chandi and gradually emerged as the most important deity in Bengal. The changing cartography of Gods and Goddesses, who can be benevolent but are also associated with extra-social, the amoral and the criminal, gives an altogether different set of insights into cultural changes. It profiles the anxieties, fears and hopes of a society that is neither a desiccated, formal study of theology and high culture yield nor any study of the more formal, better known deities (Nandy, 2001, 134).

Supporting Nandy's view Radha Kumar writes as well that the image of Chandi appears in the nineteenth century in two ways, one is the 'demon-slaying mother Durga' and other is the 'punitive and unpredictable Kali' (Kumar, 1997, 45). In their portrayal of Durga, the *patuas* were thus confronting a tradition that had consolidated by the twentieth century. Chandi had become either Kali or Durga.

It is true that in both the old and new paintings, Chandi has been portrayed as Durga but all the features of Durga or the characters surrounding her are not the same. There is, for instance, one striking difference. In most of the old Chandi *pats*, Durga is not carrying any weapon (Fig. 1). However, in the twentieth century and also in recent *pats* drawn by the *patuas* of Naya, Durga is seen carrying a weapon in her hands (Fig. 2). Pika Ghosh, a scholar on the *patachitra* tradition of Bengal observes that the figure of Durga in the nineteenth-century Ramayana *pats* also does not have any kind of weapons (Ghosh 848-849). The description provided by Ghosh, confirms that both the images of Durga in Ramayana and Chandi *pats* are quite similar to each other.

The Art Market and the Changing Nature of the Performance

In discussing different traditions of Ramayana, Philip Lutgendorf also observes, that depending on the time limit, the nature of retelling changes. He writes:

> The Ramlila of Ramnagar, which tells roughly the same story, averages three hours per night for 31 nights, and has been playing to enraptured audiences for more than a century. And an oral expounder like Ramnarayan Shukla, who proceeds through the epic in daily installments at the Sankat Mochan Temple in Banaras, may take more than 700 hours, spanning two years or more, to complete a single "telling"... (Lutgendorf , 1990, 142).

Not only Ramayana, but any repetition of even an ordinary story also leads to change. Depending on the character of the audiences it changes its form. In this case also we will see, how the global art market changes the nature of the story line. Contrary to the older version of the song, the present oral narration combines the two sections by omitting some of the incidents or characters. For example, in the old song, Phullora is referred along with Kalketu. Although she is not mentioned as his wife, Khullona, the second female character is mentioned as the mother of Dhanapati's son Srimonto (the same as in the original poem). But in the present narration, both these two female characters have been portrayed as Khullona, the wife of Kalketu.

The lines in the sons have been written in such a way, as if Kalketu was imprisoned and during this period, Srimonto his son was born to Khullona. However, the narrator mentions the word 'Sadhu' which according to Mukundaram's poem was Dhanapati, but the narrative style of the patua song does not reflect that. Mina Chitrakar of Naya sings, 'Kalketu got the jewels from under the *dalim* tree and established a city, cutting down the Gujurat jungle / Sadhu was imprisoned for 14 years. Srimanta was born in Khullana's womb' (Mina Chitrakar, '*Chandi Mangal*', learningobjects. wesleyan.edu). Also in the case of another contemporary Chandi song by Hazra Chitrakar, Khullona is mentioned along with Kalketu. Dhanapati's name is not found mentioned anywhere. The line goes like this, 'Digging out the treasure Kalketu established a city in Gujurat/He took all the riches home to show it to Khullana who was waiting at the door of their hut'. (Hazra Chitrakar, '*Chandi Mangal*', learningobjects.wesleyan.edu)

To see how a new story is emerging from the original poem, one needs to look into the nuances within the poem and within the oral tradition of the *patachitra*. As earlier shown, in Mukunduram's original poem, Kalketu, the protagonist of the hunter section and Srimonto, the hero of the later section belong to two different classes. When the stories got merged, it appears that the class division got erased. It is difficult to know whether it is a conscious effort of the *patuas* or just an unconscious adaptation of the story.

One of the reasons behind this is the nature of the art market. Most of the old *patuas* of Naya felt that due to the needs of the commercial market these oral narrations have lost their importance. The *patua* community has lost its role as performers. They now concentrate only on artistic production. One of the *patuas* is the seventy years old, Shyamsundar Chitrakar who said: 'As the commercial market is emerging now people do not have time to listen to the songs, they only want to buy a beautiful *pat*.' (Shyamsundar Chitrakar, Naya, Pingla, West Medinipur, March, 2014)

Dukhusyam Chitrakar, one of the oldest *patuas* of Naya complained: 'Most of the young *patuas* are not into writing songs. For that I have to train them. The beauty of the performance is missing.' (Dukhusyam Chitrakar, Naya, Pingla, West Medinipur, March, 2015) Most importantly, people are not interested in mythical songs or stories; rather the interest of the audiences lies in the representations of the paintings. Naturally, the accuracy of the storyline is not that important and that is how a mythical story becomes a source of entertainment.[4]

In earlier times the purpose of the poem was to convey the importance of Goddess Chandi, and more importantly to revitalise Hinduism. Curley writes that in the eighteenth century a change took place in the whole genre of *Mangal Kavya*. During this period the writers of the poems tried to balance the 'didactic and ritual' nature of the poem with the 'performative pleasures' (Curley, 2008, 27). In case of *Chandimangal* also there is a possibility that initially, the utility of these mythological scrolls was simultaneously for rituals and entertainment. To some extent, the purpose was to convey a moral and spiritual awareness to the villagers. It is a possibility that this culture continued till the twentieth century. Folklorist Beatrix Hauser writes that in the twentieth century when at a very slow pace *pats* were becoming famous within the Bengali middle class along with the earlier village audiences, spectators were still interested in the performances (Hauser). However at present there is a decline of the practice of singing the *Chandimangal* while displaying the scrolls. However in some special cases patrons from different places arrange *patua* performances for entertainment purposes. These *pats* have already bridged the gap between the local and global market. On an annual basis Naya organises a fair where not only Indians, but also foreigners come from abroad. Obviously these foreign clients are not looking for the authentic storylines; rather they are more interested in the oriental form of the art.

One of the reasons behind the alteration of the story from the poem to the present tradition is also the time constrains of the performance. As the *patuas* have to complete a performance within a particular time period they automatically take the freedom to improvise the story. In case of the *patuas* of Naya also the specific song which is generally performed by the *patua* depends on the interest of the audiences. Beatrix Hauser, a folklorist, writes, 'The picture showman's (*Patua's*) emphasis was less on the actual process of narrating and illustrating a story (i.e., entertainment) than on the display of his scrolls as a means to attract his customers. His performance became a part of selling his art; hence the customer/patron was given the right to listen the song to match 'his' scroll. The song or performance itself was not paid for. Instead, one bargained on the price of the painting.'(Hauser, 2002, 115). Naturally, the *patuas* would spend less and less time to sing the narrative and would skip many stanzas. As a patua named Yakub said: 'In case of *choukopat* (square small *pat*) we generally sing only the *Kamale Kamini* episode. How Srimonto seeing Chandi tells the king that he has seen a lady swallowing an elephant...' (Yakub Chitrakar, Naya, Pingla, West Medinipur, March, 2014).

In the recent past, the *patuas* of Naya have also started making Chandi scrolls. Their chronology of events or the visual presentation is however different. To cater to the commercial market, the *patuas* paint not only on scrolls but also on small *pats* (*chauko pat*) and on cloth the image of Chandi. That is, the narrative dimension is eliminated. What we have is a frozen image. The movement within the story gives way to a static picture.

Thus, with the expansion of the market, we see distinct changes in the tradition of *pat* painting. First, there is a change in the consumers. Before the boom in the market, the Chandimangal *patachitras* were sold to villagers in and around the places the *patuas* lived. Most sales were through direct exchanges with the villagers. Some of the *pats* were hawked around in other villages by the *patuas*. With their base in one village, they would go to other villages to sell their *patachitras*. With the boom in the market the consumers are often in distant places. Most often there is no direct face-to-face link between the consumers and producers. Sale is through intermediaries, shops, and NGOs. Second: this change in the market has meant a change in the nature of the product sold and the function of the *pats*. Earlier the *pats* visualised a narrative that was sung. The *patuas* went around the households singing the *kavyas* and the songs, and the *pats* were traded in exchange for money or grain. The visual and the narrative had an intimate and inseparable connection. Visualisation of the narrative went along with the composition of the narratives, drawing upon traditional myths and *kavyas*, but changing them around. Now there is the disruption of this link. The *pats* have become disembodied images. They circulate without being connected to any recitation of the story. Third, this means that the *pats* have become mere images, pure visuals. Those who buy them do so to decorate their homes with them; they do not hear the narrative being sung. Earlier the *pats* were embodied narratives. Now they are not. Finally: earlier, there was a sacred and ritual function of the *patachitras*. The narratives had a live presence within the lives of the people who heard the songs being sung. Now the images have an ambiguous presence. Some buy them as sacred visuals. Others see them only as aesthetic images, forms of traditional art that decorate wall spaces.

Memory and Imagination: Recreation of a Narrative

As these stories have been learnt by the *patuas* from their ancestors, the nature of the stories also changes with each generation. There is no codified written text of the stories which they follow; they only use their memory to remember these songs. They hear the story from their ancestors or fellow *patuas* who learned it from their ancestors. So it is very common to omit some of the characters or incidents, and the interesting thing is how from that a new tradition emerges. These ambiguities in the stories confirm the fact that the nature of the narration has been altered by the *patuas*, as they make it a part of an artistic culture.

It is clear from *patua* testimonies of Naya that they are aware that they are deviating from the original poem. As a *patua* named Malek Chitrakar said: 'I learned the story of Chandimangal and Manasamangal from my wife: Khullona is the wife of Kalketu. He (Kalketu) got gifts from Chandi and then made a city. But he was imprisoned by the king. Later his son Srimonto went to find him and saw *Kamale Kamini*. This is how the *Kamale Kamini* story circulates.' (Malek Chitrakar, Naya, Pingla, West Medinipur, April, 2013). Another *patua* Sumon Chitrakar said: 'Kalketu and Dhanapati, both are the same. Khullona is the name of his (Kalketu) wife and Srimonto is their son.' (Sumon Chitrakar, Naya, Pingla, West Medinipur, April, 2013) And naturally the colour of their memory always reflects on the narration.

Their imagination of the story and the influence of the commercial nature of the market also gave birth to new forms of *pat* art. For instance, a remarkable development in recent years is the importance of Santhal art forms called, *Jadupats*, among the *patuas* of Naya. It (implicitly) conceives of Chandi as a tribal figure through the image of *Kamale Kamini*. The original *Jadu patuas* or *Jadupatias* (magic painters) normally make smaller scroll paintings compared to the long scrolls of Midnapore *patuas*. Their pictures are mainly shown to the Santhals of Western Bengal and the Bediyas of Eastern Bengal (Mookerjee, 1939, 16-18).[5]

In this style of *pat* that adapt Santhal iconography, only the face of Chandi is seen clearly and her figure is surrounded by leaves, in a way that suggests the deity is in the midst of a forest. By contrast, in the 'traditional' *patua*'s version, Chandi is surrounded by petals of lotus. In the *pats* influenced by Santhal imageries, Chandi is not accompanied by Ganesha. Instead we see a tribal boy sitting on a boat (see Fig. 4 (A)). Srimonto is thus tribalised. It refers back to the episode on the boat when Srimonto first saw Chandi in *Kamale Kamini* image. It is not the second one when he was with the king because this picture only depicts figures of Chandi and Srimonto on a boat. The boat itself is very much similar to a Santhal type of *dingi* (see Fig. 4 (A)). Here Chandi does not conform to the image of Durga, but she looks like a tribal woman (Fig. 4 (A)). Even the dress worn by Srimonto, seems tribal in character (see Fig. 4 (A)). The background colour of this *pat* is not as bright as is found in the *patachitras* of Midnapore; it is in fact painted with earth colour.

A B

Fig. 4: A. *Kamale Kamini in Chouko pat.* Painter: Moyna Chitrakar, Provenance: Naya, West Medinipur, Time Period: c.2011, Source: Personal collection. 4B. *Jadu pat* or Santhal *pat,* Provenance: Midnapore, Time period: Nineteenth Century. Source: Gurusaday Museum.)

Conclusion

The focal point of this article is the nature of performance. It is quite interesting, how without reading any text, and only by listening to their ancestors, these *patuas* remember the story, which is reflected both in their paintings and narrations. In doing so, the listener becomes the teller. To interpret these, one needs to understand the mechanism of the painter's imagination. Deviations from and similarities between the poem and the oral narrative of painting and the painting itself, are all parts of the performer-craftsman's perception of the poem.

Also over time, the commercial nature of the market changes the taste of the audience and that compels the artists to alter the storyline. Commercialisation and globalisation have, however marginally interacted with the local economy of Naya... Especially the presence of Chandi in tribal art reveals a sub-conscious adoption of the art form into a subaltern location. It not only changes the course of the older narrative, but is also leading to the extinction of the older tradition with the coming of the small *pats*. Even the re-representation of Durga with weapons confirms that there is no specific code to follow. It is the demand of the market which controls the form of the paintings. So in closing, one can see that how a story has transformed over the time. With the infusion of imagination and memory, a new type of narrative has taken birth within this. An important point to note is that, it is not necessary that the person who paints does always write the song. As a cultural product the *patachitra* and the song are collectively created. So sometimes it is also the reflection of collective imagination.

Note: Oral accounts of *patuas* or Chitrakars of Naya were collected over the period from March 2013 to 2015. Among the accounts used here are those of the Dukhushyam Chitrakar, Malek Chitarkar, Shyamsundar Chitrakar, Suman Chitrakar and Yakub Chitrakar. *Patua* Songs/poems of both Mina Chitrakar and Hazra Chitrakar were collected from the online collection of Wesleyan University website. The collection is called 'Singing Painters of Naya'. URL: http://learningobjects.wesleyan.edu/naya/intro.html

Acknowledgement: I am indebted to the Gurusaday Museum, Kolkata authorities for permitting me to use the images from their collection for this article. The permission was granted via an email on 13 March 2018. Furthermore, the photographs reproduced in the article have also been personally taken by me.

REFERENCES

1. The main storyline of the poem was drawn largely from two books Mukundaram Chakravarty's *Kabikankan Chandi* published in 1921from Allahabad (Chakravarty, 1921) and Sukumar Sen's the *Kavikankan Mukunda* printed by the Sahitya Akademi in 1989 (Sen, 1985). For the translation of the poem in English Edward Yazijan's doctoral thesis from Chicago University on *Chandimangal* is relevant (Yazijian, 2007, 71-666). A very small section of this text was translated into English verse by the former president of Calcutta's Presidency College E. B. Cowell in 1902 from Calcutta (Cowell, 1902).

2. However it is difficult to determine which version of the *Chandi Mangal* is 'original' as there is more than one version.
3. Within the present tradition also the *patuas* have different versions of the narration. Regarding the Laden *patas* (based on 9/11 incident) sociologist Roma Chatterji also observed that there are variations in the scrolls following the same theme but '...they reveal a common episodic structure' (Chatterji, 2012, 64). For example, in Hazra Chitrakar's Chandi song, the chronology of the events remains same but the style of depiction is different from Mina Chitrakar's narration of the same song.
4. It is not unique to *patua* art. Studies have also shown how the adaptation of Ramayana in new tradition have changed the colour of a myth. Example Paula Richman edited, *Many Ramayanas: The Diversity of Ramayana Tradition in South Asia*, University of California Press, 1991.
5. The chief characteristic of these scroll paintings is that they contain all the qualities of mural painting. Whenever a person died in a family *Jadu patuas* used to go to that village and show a painting of the dead person from their own imagination to the family of the dead person. Mookherjee writes, '*Jadu Patua* presents the picture completely drawn in colour with one omission only, viz., the iris of the eye. He shows the picture to the relatives and tells them that the deceased is wandering about blindly in the other world and will continue to do so until they send gifts or money or some other articles through him, viz., (*Jadu Patua* himself), so that he can perform the act of *Chakshudan* or bestowal of eye-sight. So the relatives make presents of money or some other articles of domestic use to the *Jadu Patua* for transmission to the deceased and the *Jadu Patua* then gives the finishing touch to the picture by performing the act of Chakshudan or supplying the iris of the eye to the picture.'(Mookerjee, 1939, 16) Scholars assume that because of this type of magical activities they were called *Jadu Patuas* or Magic Painters.

BIBLIOGRAPHY

Bhattacharya, T. (2007). 'Tracking the Goddess: Religion, Community, and Identity in the Durga Puja Ceremonies of Nineteenth-Century Calcutta'. *The Journal of Asian Studies.* Vol. 66, Issue 4. pp. 919-962.

Chakravarty, M. (19210. *Kabikankan Chandi.* Allahabad: Indian Press.

Chatterjee, K. (2013). 'Goddess Encounters: Mughals, Monsters and the Goddess in Bengal'. *Modern Asian Studies*. Vol. 47, Issue 5. pp. 1435-1487.

Chatterji, R. (2012). *Speaking with Pictures: Folk Art and the Narrative Tradition in India.* New Delhi: Routledge.

Cowell, E.B. (1902). *Three Episodes From the Old Bengali Poem 'Chandi'.* Calcutta: The Asiatic Society of Bengal.

Curley, D.L. (2008). *Poetry and History: Bengali Mangal-kabya and Social Change in Pre-Colonial Bengal.* New Delhi: Chronicles Books.

Ghosh, P. (2003). 'Unrolling a Narrative Scroll: Artistsic Practice and Identity in Late-Nineteenth Century'. *The Journal of Asian Studies.* Vol. 62, Issue 3. pp. 835-871.

Hauser, B. (2002). 'From Oral Tradition to 'Folk Art': Reevaluating Bengali Scroll Paintings'. *Asian Folklore Studies.* Vol. 61, Issue 1. pp. 105-122.

Jain, J. (1998). *Picture Showmen: Insights into the Narrative Tradition in Indian Art.* Mumbai: Marg.

Kumar, R. (1997). *The History of Doing: An Illustrated Account of Movements for Women's Rights and Feminism in India 1800-1990.* New Delhi: Zuban.

Lutgendorf, P. (1990). 'Ramayan: The Video.' *The Drama Review.* (1988-) Vol. 34, Issue 2. pp. 127-176.

McCutchion, D. and Bhowmik, S. (1999). *Patuas and Patua Art in Bengal.* Calcutta: KLM Private Ltd.

Mookerjee, A. (1939). *The Folk Art of Bengal.* Calcutta: The University of Calcutta Press.

Nandy, Ashis. 'A Report on the Present State of Health of the Gods and Goddesses in South Asia.' *Postcolonial Studies* 4: 2 (2001): 125-141.

Sen, Sukumar. *Kavikankan Mukunda.* Calcutta: Sahitya Academy: 1956.

Yazijian, *Edward. From Performance to Literature: The Chandimangal of Kabikankan Mukundaram Chakravarty*, PhD Thesis. Chicago: University of Chicago, Dept. of South Asian Languages and Civilizations, 2007.

CHAPTER 11

Trajectories of the *Qissas* of Akbar and Birbal

Anindita Ghosh

Ethnography of the *Qissas* of Akbar and Birbal

Conceptually, the *qissas*[1], the folklores and the legends are part of the literary and non-real world. They are known to be part of the world of poesy and imagination with distant associations with the real world[2]. As an element of the popular tradition, they serve not just fantasy but also reality and history. This co-existence of reality and fantasy make these genres an interesting study. The tales of Akbar and Birbal can be seen within the popular traditions of folklore, legends or *qissas*. An attempt to locate them completely within one of these genres may not be possible, but one can see heavy influences of all the three genres. These tales bear varying aspects of reality if we look at them through these genres.

The above-mentioned three genres of storytelling are commonly grouped according to their relationship to social reality. In what ways and to what extent are the tales of Akbar and Birbal connected to the social reality can be judged if we undertake a detailed study of the prime features of the genres and perform a genre test of the tales. This essay deals with the conventional understanding and evolution of these three genres and how well the tales fit into them, each one of them, how the tales move out in varied directions out of these genres and what specificities have been added to the tales by the genres.

Ethnography of storytelling places the tales of Akbar and Birbal within the genres of folklores and legends. At a superficial level, folklores are more imagination-based and legends are inclined towards historical veracity.[3] If we categorise the tales of Akbar and Birbal as folklores, we have to grant them the space for imaginative fluidity where layers of fantastical elements will pour in to make the tales more flexible for the purposes of humour. Old narratives will be remoulded to be presented for newer and more humorous stories. However, if these tales are seen as legends, they could be more restrictive as humorous anecdotes but closer to the historical reality.

Legends are understood as closer to belief and coincide well with the existing knowledge around a theme. Based on the narrative functions of the narrator, in a legend, the narrator experiences a compulsion of telling the truth to his readers/audience. He reports the story, but with scarce report details of the event. Rohrich explains that the narrators of such reports very often confess to tampering with the details or forgetting them altogether. Their inclination to historical truth earns them faith but lowers the possibility of critical engagement and entertainment for the audience/readers. The narrator in the folklore, on the other hand, consciously uses fantasy to substitute the details that have been lost or forgotten. The narrator will pursue imagination to give flesh to his story instead of using tedious details. That does not imply that the audience/readers will not invest critical engagement or derive no entertainment out of it. As folklore is formulaically designed to fortify credibility, it hardly relies on details but on storytelling.

For a better understanding of the dilemma faced in locating the tales of Akbar and Birbal within the genre of folktales or legends, a tale told by Narayan Das, a teacher at the Shahpur School, Etah District, Uttar Pradesh and recorded by Sadhana Naithani is reproduced for analysis:

> When Birbal was appointed to be the Prime minister of Akbar, many persons, and particularly Muhammadans, were jealous of him. One day a Muhammadan came to the court and endeavoured to supplant him by a show of superior wisdom. Akbar asked him first—"Which is the best of flowers?" He replies "the genda" or the marigold, which is used in daily Hindu worship. Next, he was

asked—"Whose son earns most?" His answer was "the baniya." Then he was asked—'Who is a great man?" He replied, "The king," and to the last question: "Which is the sweetest thing in the world?" He said; "Nothing is sweeter than sugar cane."

When the daughter of Birbal heard of the contest of wisdom, she instructed her father on how he should answer. When he came to the court and was asked what was the best flower, He answered: "The cotton flower. The son who earns most is that of the cow. The virtuous are the great". "The sweetest thing in the world is one's own interest".

The Muhammadan's rage was fierce and he left the court in disgrace. (Naithani, 2005, 256)[4]

The narrative by Das sounds both believable and not believable. If we consider it to be a folktale, we have to recognise that these tales conveniently neglect the historical details yet they are believable as legends. As legends, these tales work within a historical knowledge widely available on Birbal in popular books of history. Birbal is known for his witty encounters but no historical evidence is available except a few witty couplets on his name.[5] In most of these tales, the narrator presents a balanced concoction of fantasy and substituting details with a vivid historical consideration of the Mughal royal court and culture during Akbar's reign.

To justify the tales of Akbar and Birbal as legends, we have to start by considering these tales as historical legends. Though they offer ample proof of their closeness to the historical reality, their believability lies on various factors like the subjectivity of characters, the ease of acceptance by the audience/readers, the possibility of rejection by the same as impossible, the time and space in which the narrator and the tales are located etc. Usually, legends of historical figures like Akbar and Birbal would rely on outrageous outlaws or wonders to create the required impact. They spread roots by locating themselves in a specific historical time and place in the narrative with references to specific people. The tales gain a background where the historical past is fictionalised only to the extent of localisation and mixed chronology. Every tale has its own unique subject matter with overt plays on time and place. The larger catchment area is the modern Northern India in the medieval age. To define these tales as legends will not be a complete misnomer, yet one has to consider them as folktales too.

An alternative study of the tales of Akbar and Birbal as folktales will highlight several newer aspects. Far from rational and subjective reality, these tales are often not set in the real world of the Mughal royal court where Akbar and Birbal would have encountered or interacted with each other and definitely not in the described fashion. The details provided in them are very generic and local in nature. They never lay stress on specific empirical or historical evidence available of the Mughal age. Instead, they fictionalise the Mughal past as a historical and beyond time. The tales of Akbar and Birbal have been generating themselves as folktales since very long, but away from history and reality. The larger formula for a folktale is that it begins with an unresolved chaos and the narrative by the narrator is a journey of conflict, overcoming the chaos and restoration of order. The given tale narrated by Narayan Das also follows the same trajectory. A Mohammadan outsider comes to the court of Akbar where he is entertained and questioned. On replying well to the question that has been asked, the visitor creates an imbalance in the court by challenging Birbal. Birbal is instructed by his daughter to deliver a certain answers which are better than those of the visitor and he wins the challenge.[6] Unlike a legend which may end in dissonance, this tale like many others mitigates the chaos. Always, Birbal has the ultimate word and Akbar applauds him for resolving the deadlock. Following the formula of generic folktales, it is easy to categorise these tales as a folktale, but an overlapping study of a legend and a folktale would yield different results.

Folktales and legends share several commonalities. Though legends maintain better connections with reality and folktales are more dream-like. They frequently break down the fine dichotomy of the former as more believable and the latter as only a disbelief.[7] The tales of Akbar and Birbal keep vacillating over the line between real and unreal that shifts over time, space and is highly relative in nature. Considering this collapse in the generic division, we may assume that these tales are midway between legends and folktales. When recounted by a narrator, the generic rules are not followed as closely as they are defined textually. Within oral tradition or documentation of oral tradition, every period and set of tales produces its own peculiar prescription to entice the audience and the readers. Even the experience of reality is different in these tales from time to time immaterial of their categorisation as legends or folktales. Often, a historically validated anecdote too passes down a few generations as a legend and a folktale with ever-increasing distance from reality and history. As I make an inquiry into the generic positioning of these tales within one of the two genres, I would wish to consider the possibility of an inquiry into the history of the narrative formation of these tales and not just the generic position. However, in this essay I will not be pursuing that line of inquiry.

To be precise, the tales of Akbar and Birbal can be categorised as jestful folk narratives. Such folktales of farce and jest are of localised origins. If we look at the inception of these tales, the narrators invent these tales from the bare bone versions available in history or the simpler versions in circulation. By supplying jestful layers to the existing versions, these tales become closer to reality and history as compared to their fantastical counterpart. Yet they do not lose their critical engagement or entertainment value. The audience and the readers along with the narrator tip-toe through an imagined world of jest drawn from reality. With regional and individual variants, this sub-genre ranges from humorous anecdotes of real events to newly invented stories based on older ones which in all ways define the nature of the tales of Akbar and Birbal. We cannot arrive at a generalised opinion of what a jestful folk narrative should be, but we can safely theorise our concerned tales as part of that broad category. As these tales are free from the fantastical element, with higher entertainment values and their popularity they are wider than the rest. Rooted in reasoning and logic, jest thrives and colludes with almost all the genres to create new sub-genres with different dynamics with reality, fantasy and history. In fact, the element of jest can be introduced into every kind of folk narratives. We can have jestful legends as well as jestful folktales. But all these jestful folk narrative forms may never claim complete secularity as after all they remain fantastical tales. Here, the fantastical element has been changed from the conventional element of magic to something of an almost magical quality, Birbal's wit. This ultra-natural element exists in this world as a miraculous solution to chaos, thereby fitting into the formulaic structure for folk narratives. The fantastic ability of the protagonist, Birbal is not just his wit but also his eccentricity. The misfit narrators exaggerate the ultra-natural quality of these jestful characters to a humorous extent. These jestful figures are audacious for they mix rebellion with jest, blasphemy with religion and teach us a continuing lesson in social survival.

The tales of Akbar and Birbal, instead of being categorised as either legends or folktales, fit better in the category of jestful folk narratives. Secular in content, these tales are far more connected to reality than folktales or legends are. Birbal's ultra-natural wit is appreciated and glorified thoroughly. The onus of entertainment through these tales falls primarily on the witty twist that accompanies Birbal's presence in these tales.

The *Qissas* of Akbar and Birbal as Jestful Folk Narratives

The tales of Akbar and Birbal flourish as jestful folk narratives with heavy local colouring. Local colouring is important as it allows us to create indices for tales of similar origins. The jest and wit are local in nature. Certain irony, sarcasm and arguments in these tales can only be understood within a particular cultural and regional setting. A lot is revealed about the reality, history and location through the narrator's way of creating the landscape and ambience for the tales. These decorative elements, though subsidiary to the tales provide input about the spatial location of the tales. Known for expressing the regional, historical and political realities, such elements are vital for our study. Here, I will again use a tale from Sadhana Naithani's anthology for my analysis. This tale is by Shyam Lal, an elderly from the district of Etah, Uttar Pradesh;

> Akbar once asked Birbal: 'What is your opinion of me?" Birbal, replied: 'I have the same opinion of you which you have of me; because hearts read hearts.' Akbar said: 'This is impossible.' But Birbal said, 'Come for a walk in the city and I will prove it to you.' As they were going along they saw a miserable old woman begging. Akbar said; 'I do pity this poor creature. Cannot you, in so great a kingdom as this, make some provision for her by which she may pass her last days in comfort?' Birbal asked Akbar

> to stop, and going up to the old woman said: 'Old woman, do you not know that Akbar Badshah is dead?' When she heard this, she began to weep and said: 'Alas! Alas! How shall I now pass my days? It was by his virtue that I gained my daily bread, and now that he is gone, I must starve.' Birbal came back to Akbar and said; 'Now your Majesty sees that the old woman loves you because you feel for her.' They went on a little further in the bazaar and saw a Sewara faqir begging, and as he beats on his stick, he was abusing a banker and extorting alms. When Akbar saw him, he said: 'Birbal, these wretched are the curse of the land. Why do you not make a law to repress them?' Birbal asked Akbar to stop, and going up to the faqir said: 'O Baba! Do you not know that Akbar Badshah is dead?' The Faqir cursed him and said: 'May his soul rest in the lowest hell! Did he ever give me a pice?' Now said Birbal, 'Your Majesty sees that this man hates you because you do not feel for him. Do not hearts read hearts?' Akbar said: 'I am convinced. (Naithani, 2005, 229)[8]

This tale of Akbar and Birbal narrated by Shyam Lal is an apt example to show how the narrator's perception of the real world percolates into his narrative. The narrator always uses his own surroundings as a stencil to fill in the details in the narrative. If we are careful, we can notice the narrator has transferred his reality in subtle bits to his audience and readers. We see Akbar and Birbal out on a walk into an unnamed Northern Indian city where they encounter an old beggar. I have selected this tale from the anthology by Sadhana Naithani, as it brings the local flavour in the narrative. Shyam Lal, an elderly person from Etah has made special reference to the Sewara Faqirs who are to be seen only in this specific region of North India where they encounter an old beggar. Historically, it was implausible for Akbar to have gone out as described. If not in disguise, such an adventure by the duo can only be seen as Shyam Lal's distorted understanding of a King and his courtier's conduct in public. The old beggar earns alms by singing praises of Akbar and the Sewara Faqir earns alms by abusing a banker. For Shyam Lal, a resident of Etah district in Uttar Pradesh, witnessing these two begging for alms were very likely part of his conventional reality. As he weaves his story, these realities seep into his narrative. Thus, while reading these tales we need to be alert about the personal and the local inflections.

The local inflections become more prominent if we locate these tales within the *qissa* narrative tradition. These tales have gained popularity beyond the folk realm only through the secular forms of *qissas* in the print edition. Now will be a good time to understand the *qissa* tradition and its evolution and effect on the tales of Akbar and Birbal.

The Cultural History of the *Qissas* of Akbar and Birbal

One of the most prominent categorisations of the tales of Akbar and Birbal has been the '*qissas*'. The term originates from the Persian literary tradition and has been accepted globally as it moved around. The few scholars who have studied this genre in detail, consider it to be primarily an oral folk narration technique with middle-eastern and nomadic origins. Known for its crispness and brevity, *qissa* literally means a short narrative or an anecdote. With that literal definition, a wide variety of narratives can be clubbed under this genre. Any oral folk romance that is generated, explained and arrived at by professional narrators will be called a *qissa*.[9]

The *qissa* genre has a high universal appeal, and it was easily accepted and promoted in Persian royal courts and in the folk realm. These *qissas* carried history with them. The Persian nomadic narrators of medieval ages who travelled across deserts and from one royal court to another accompanied the Persian-speaking rulers who invaded the northern part of the Indian subcontinent. The former brought the genre of *qissa* to the subcontinent. The professional *qissa* narrators practised this art at several royal courts. The Mughal Court too provided patronage to several such professional *qissa* tellers. Initially, these *qissas* were narratives of mythical heroes and their magical quests in the world of the unknown. The hero undertook an adventure to find the answer to an enigma, to kill an evil creature plaguing innocent people or to procure a magical object or spell. The most common quest of the hero was to rescue or unite with his beloved after a magical pursuit. Induced with *jadui* and *tilismi,* these narratives were far from being secular narrations.

Gradually the themes of these *qissas* changed. More secular and realist elements trickled into the narrative tradition. In the

Indian subcontinent, these tales were changed from the narratives of marvellous encounters to narratives of historical or social encounters. With the coming of the print culture in the twentieth century, secular narratives became more popular than the magical ones. Of the many pioneering secular *qissa* narratives, the *qissas* of Akbar and Birbal were listed widely.

The *qissas* tradition as a print culture and genre flourishes and developed in the latter-half of the twentieth century in the mainland of the Indian subcontinent. The colonial era facilitated the beginning of an easy and cheap print culture in India. By the late twentieth century an indigenous printing industry registered its presence. The print editions of these *qissas* were not in Persian any more. The popular languages for reproducing these *qissas* in print form are Hindi and Urdu. A chart on the number of *qissas* being published in North India shows a rise in the *qissas* print culture even over the Hindi novel culture. According to the study, 259 novels are published against the ever-increasing 254 *qissas*. And if we dilute the term *qissas* and accommodate all the Hindi terms that translate as short stories, the numbers will be even higher.[10]

The Print History of the *Qissas* of Akbar and Birbal

The *qissa* print industry in India is an ephemeral industry of transient texts which are printed cheaply and circulated widely. Most of these texts have anonymous authors and the publishers control the conceptualisation. Plagiarism, overlaps, translation, reprinting and transliteration are common occurrences in the formulation of these texts. Only those *qissas* that sell well are reprinted. The *qissas* of Akbar and Birbal have survived due to the various survival strategies the publishers undertook for them to thrive. These *qissas* are a major component of the fluid and ever-evolving printing industry. In the latter half of the nineteenth century, several popular *qissas* of Akbar and Birbal were chosen by the publishing market. Most of these texts bear *qissas* as titles. Arrived at by a consensus within the then contemporary publishing industry, the generic term '*qissa*' was widely used as the titles of these texts, these narratives replicated the essential narrative techniques of the traditional *qissas*. These fluid texts rarely have a single origin indicating an easy mutability as they grow. However, there remains a core plot and formulaic development central to all these *qissas* of Akbar and Birbal. On the contrary, one may claim that it is only through these texts that these *qissas* can arrive at a synchronic and diachronic balance. But how often does that happen is a potent question. With multiplicity in versions, no copyright laws, these *qissas* can hardly gain any stability in their form and content.

As evident, the *qissa* as an oral narrative tradition and the *qissas* of Akbar and Birbal have suffered in spite of their success in the print industry. Referring to the survey by Pritchett, the varied collections of the *qissas* of Akbar and Birbal are printed as mere assorted collections of jestful and comic anecdotes with no loyalty to the genre. They lack the basic structural integrity where a literary piece, even if it begins in media res has a beginning and an ending. However, these texts also remind us that genres and their defined characters are ever-changing. They exist to help us simplify classification. But, if a literary tradition does not fall within a genre completely, there is no reason to remove it altogether. *Qissa* as a traditional genre will expand into newer and more secular forms. Eventually, any secular prose narrative will qualify to be called a *qissa*. It can become an umbrella term to cater to any compilation of closely related short texts.

Keeping the episodic form in sight, the *qissas* of Akbar and Birbal have become ephemeral in existence. The ephemerality becomes so profound that it seeps into the form and structure of these *qissas* too. If we look at the structural formation of these *qissas*, the sentences begin with more temporal notes. There is a sense of 'occurrenceness', as claimed by Frances Pritchett, in these short narratives. (Pritchett, 1985, 148) Though in translation the impact will be low, one can hardly ignore the temporary nature evident in the syntax and paragraphing. The speakers are changed explicitly without coherence as they occur in oral narratives. Important emotions are reduced to a few words and vital turns in the text are left half-explained. We can notice that a lot is left to the imagination of the readers and the audience. Primarily a part of oral tradition, printing and cataloguing these *qissas* have brought about a lot of changes in the tradition.

Conclusion

To conclude, the short narratives of Akbar and Birbal have evolved a lot from their origins in the realm of folklore. They have nourished the narrative tradition in a sustained manner as folklores, legends and *qissas*. By maintaining the right balance between humour and narrative tradition, these tales have become an important part of the popular culture. According to the above -mentioned survey by Pritchett, these tales are commonly published in Mathura, Hathras, Delhi, Agra, Kanpur and Banaras by the local press and narrated in the North Indian region. With this huge catchment area, the genre, form, content and narrative techniques are bound to change depending on the background of the audience/the readers, the narrator and the location.

REFERENCES

1. I am loosely using the term *qissas* for the anecdotes of Akbar and Birbal by drawing my understanding of how they were shaped in the second half of the eighteenth century in Northern India. My knowledge of the *Qissa* publishing industry and its growth is derived from my reading of Francis W. Pritchett's thesis, '*Marvelous Encounters: Folk Romance in Urdu and Hindi*' (1985). In her thesis she has given historical accounts of the transition of the *qissas* tradition from the marvelous-folk to secular-folk. By charting the local publishing industry of Northern India, she has given consolidated statistics of the transition and evolution of the tradition.
2. Lutz Rohrich in his book, '*Folktales and Reality*' claims that folklores are essentially fantasy and imagination. He calls them 'fabula incredibilis' whereas he claims that legends are 'more historical'. Though they both are beyond objective reality, the latter requires some amount of subjective reality to foreground itself.
3. As I intend to bridge the distance between folktales, legends and reality, I will use my study of Lutz Rohrich's theorisation of the folktales and legends with regard to reality in his work, '*Folktales and Reality*' (1991)
4. Taken from the book '*Folktales from Northern India*', The tales of Akbar and Birbal in this book are part of the colonial project

by William Crooke, a prominent anthropologist and British civil servant and his Indian subordinate, Pandit Ram Gharib Choubey. This anthology of varied folktales from North India is a compact collection of recordings across class, religion, caste and gender. Sadhana Naithani has supplied ample citations and theorisation to locate the evolution and existence of the tales.

5. In fact, Birbal has authored a few witty couplets. They are called *Samasyapurtis*. Eg.

   "*Randhi to galti nahi bin randhey gal jahi*
   Kahi paheli birbal suniye Akbar sahi.

   (What is that which left uncooked quickly decays, but when burnt lasts longer?—brick)" (Sinha, 1980, 141)

6. Birbal's daughter deserves a special mention as we talk about the tales of Akbar and Birbal. She features in quite a few of these tales and serves as a wit. Her presence is registered not in the Mughal court but within the ambit of these tales. Popularly known as Birbali, she is a constant accomplice to her father in his mischiefs. At times she surpasses her father in display of wit as she helps him in solving challenges. Younger and smarter, she is one of the few female representations of wit within the Indian folk tradition. In fact, the present tale by Narayan Das shows her as the one with all the answers and not Birbal.

7. This is explained in details in Lutz Rohrich's '*Folktales and Reality*'.

8. I have selected this tale from the anthology by Sadhana Naithani, as it brings the local flavour in the narrative. Shyam Lal, an elderly person from Etah has made a special reference to the Sewara Faqirs who are to be seen only in this specific region of Northern India.

9. In her book, '*Marvelous Encounters: Folk Romance in Urdu and Hindi*', Frances W. Pritchett (1985) has opened up the meaning of Romance which in turn changes the meaning of qissa in its newer versions.

   'Romance, then is a narrative liberated both from the imitative constrains of realistic fiction, and from the intellectual constraint of allegory: narrative controlled by the uninhibited artistic imagination. Its content includes visions shaped by dream and nightmare, and fantasies of achieved perfection—often of perfect love and perfectly accomplished adventure. Except for an authoritative, detached, but partisan narrator, highly stylised characterisation, and a 'happy ending' (for the audience, if not for the characters), the term 'romance' implies a few structural conventions.' (Pritchett, 1985, 164)

10. The survey list has been shared by Frances W. Pritchett in her book *'Marvelous Encounters: Folk romances in Urdu and Hindi'* (1985, 171)

    This is from a chart derived from the survey by Pritchett. The catalogue consists of these publishing houses across Northern India

    "Dehātī Pustak Bhañdār, Pustak sūchī (Delhi: Dehātī Pustak Bhañdār, 1977, Hindi); N.S. Sharmā Gaur. Book Depot, Grahakānā sūchīpatra (Hathras: N.S. Sharmā Gaur. Book Depot, 1977, Hindi); Ratan and Co., Nayā sūchī patra (Delhi: Ratan and Co., [1977], Hindi); Shrī Loknāth Pustakālay, Navīn Sūchī-Patra (Calcutta: Shrī Loknāth Pustakālay, 1977, Hindi); Shyāmkāshī Press, Pustakoñ kā Navīn Parichay (Mathura: Shyāmkāshī Press, 1977, Hindi); 'Hākurprasād and Sons, Sūchīpatra (Banaras: Hākurprasād and Sons, 1977, Hindi).' (Pritchett, 1985, 170)

BIBLIOGRAPHY

Bhatnagar, P. (1645). *Sachitra Birbal. Vol. 2.* Lucknow: Educational Publishing Company.

Moosvi, S. (1994). *Episodes in the Life of Akbar: Contemporary Records and Reminiscences.* (Ed.) Shireen Moosvi. (Trans.) Shireen Moosvi. New Delhi: National Book Trust.

Naithani, S. (2005). *Folktales from Northern India: William Crooke and Pandit Ram Gharib Choubey*. Gurgaon: Shubhi Publications.

Pritchett, F.W. (1985). *Marvelous Encounters: Folk Romances in Urdu and Hindi.* Retrieved from http://www.columbia.edu/itc/mealac/pritchett/00litlinks/marv_qissa/index.html on (30 January, 2015)

Rohrich, L. (1992). *Folktales and Reality*. (Trans.) Peter Tokofsky. Stuttgart: Indian University Press.

Sinha, P.P. (1980). *Raja Birbal: Life and Times.* Patna: Janaki Prakashan.

Unpublished. None, n.d. Private email. 22 January 2015. Retrieved from http://www.columbia.edu/itc/mealac/pritchett/00urduhindilinks/txt_akbar_birbal.html on (22nd January, 2015)

PART V

The Gender and the Popular

CHAPTER 12

Undoing Queer: Privatising the Political through Popular Advertisements

Saheli Biswas

The neoliberal policies of reform instituted in the post-90s, India intensified India's encounter with global capital. The state, various organisations in civil society, the media, and representatives of domestic and global capital functioned as flashpoints that brought together a series of different actors. These actors changed the sites and the manner in which globalising India represented both an opportunity and a threat to the State. The resultant loss of sovereignty did reflect in displacement of control onto national culture and identities which manifested themselves by fortifying rigid gender and sexual identities. These reify that national and gender identities are not simply orchestrated by a hegemonic state apparatus pitted against civil society. Rather, different actors (by different actors, I here refer to Arjun Appadurai's theorisation of 'five global cultural flows)' remapped India in unprecedented ways. He writes:

> An elementary framework for exploring such disjunctures is to look at the relationship among five dimensions of global cultural flows that can be termed (a) ethnoscapes, (b) mediascapes, (c) technoscapes, (d) financescapes, and (e) ideoscapes. The suffix -scape allows us to point to the fluid, irregular shapes of these landscapes, shapes that characterise international capital as deeply as they do international clothing styles. These terms with the common suffix '–scape' also

> indicate that these are not objectively given relations that look the same from every angle of vision but, rather, that they are deeply perspectival constructs, inflected by the historical, linguistic, and political situated-ness of different sorts of actors: nation-states, multinationals, diasporic communities, as well as subnational groupings and movements. (Appadurai, 1996, 33).

These five cultural components participate in promoting particular normativity even when certain actors pretend to act as pro-movement and then manoeuvre the movement in their desired direction.

A large part of the recent flourish in gender consciousness in India has more recently manifested itself in the idioms of safety conversation. In December 2012 the heinous rape and murder of Jyoti Singh, aka *Nirbhaya* brought different kinds of people onto the streets, not just in Delhi but in other cities as well. This was an unprecedented scenario which was considered to be a watershed moment in Indian gender studies. More and more students as well as activists, enthusiastically got involved in feminist studies. This sudden surge of interest in gender studies has necessarily spilled over to mainstream media (social network, popular advertisements, soap operas etc.). What followed is the rise of pop feminism—a partially flawed idea of feminism that played around certain keywords but was miles away from theories, histories of activism or lived realities of queer lives in India. In this paper, I will mainly focus on recent popular advertisements that have targeted the queer movements and utilised the opportunity to find new markets.

Privatising the Political

A recent popular advertisement for Ebay.in with the tagline 'Things don't judge' (which is basically a montage of different social situations), showcases one such scenario where a man is proposing to his partner. The ad was lauded all over the social media for being inclusive of these sensitive issues. Yet, what was carefully swept under the carpet was how blatantly it propagated homonormativity. In another advertisement for Anouk (with the tagline—'Bold is Beautiful' wherein this particular segment is called 'The Visit') portrays an anxious lesbian couple because one of their parents is coming to visit them for the first time, and their entire relationship/partnership will be sanctioned by said visit. What these advertisements actually do, is much more significant than they appear at the first glance. These advertisements are an exercise in appropriation of queer politics, commodification of lives and desires, and branding a certain privileged existence as distinctly desirable. They propagate homonormativity through the represented culmination in marriages. Even though same sex marriage is a significant agenda of the queer movement, these essentialised representations of queer lives repeatedly reduce the multiple possibilities to one outcome, catering to the sensibilities of the mainstream media. They are essentially directed towards an ever-growing market— the marriage market, objectified glamour market and so on. Indeed an ad is supposed to sell a product, but we are yet to witness a queer person appear in a condom ad, which is to be noted as absolutely necessary for sexual health awareness, irrespective of an individual's orientation and preference. These characters as represented in these advertisements dress up in the requisite manner as they belong to a certain class. Perhaps, they do not need the space offered by queer movements to flaunt their 'boldness' in a market-friendly way, unlike certain other queer people who do not have a privileged position facilitated by class and caste. The Anouk ad was applauded because the lesbian individuals did not adhere to the butch-femme heteronormative binary. Yet, there were some questions regarding why one of the girls flaunts a bob cut, which perhaps exhibits assimilationist tendencies.

The Idea of Homonormativity

The culture in the context that I speak of is primarily heteronormative. But as queer experiences and rights have become more visible and accepted to certain degrees, proclivities of policing of sexual and gender expressions within LGBTQ spaces are also mounting. This is precisely, what can be termed as 'homonormativity'. Homonormativity is an idea that addresses the problems of privilege one comes across in the queer community within the current context, as they intersect with White privilege, capitalism, sexism, transmisogyny and cissexism. These tendencies exclude a multitude of people out of the movement that is supposedly aimed at greater sexual freedom and equality. Homonormativity has been widely discursified. It is an idea which advocates the assumption and promotion that heterosexuality is the only 'normal', 'natural', and 'acceptable' orientation out there. Naturally, it privileges those who fit the norm, marking anyone outside of these boundaries as abnormal and a misfit.

It is also based on the assumption that queer people want to be part of the dominant, mainstream, and heterosexual culture and the way in which our society reward those who fit into the norm, identifying them as most worthy and deserving of visibility and rights. All the representations of queer lives that have been done through television or magazine or fashion advertisements are more than likely to be of the cisgender, gender-normative, middle class, strictly gay or lesbian-labelled characters. The voices that are given, along with the space and visibility, tend to be from a particular class, of a particular gender expression, body type, and age. When it comes to the representation of gender fluidity in fashion or beauty market(like in a recent advertisement for Jabong), one constantly comes across cisgender men or women trying to fetishise gender fluidity, adorning one's sexual identity as a fashion statement. Yet what blatantly stands apart in these advertisements, is the lack of trans-visibility.

The kind of queer relationships we see represented in the media are also reductive as they tend to mimic heteronormative binary gender expressions. Earlier when I mentioned the lack of queer representation in a condom ad, I wanted to draw attention to how these social actors routinely deny sexually active queer people the things they need—intelligible information, support and respect, condoms—to protect themselves from venereal diseases. The systematic separation of people from queer adults causes an organised sequestration from the knowledge and lived realities of queer lives. Seemingly, this socio-cultural context wants its people to remain ignorant. It demands its queer citizens to conform, and wants them to not know about the rights.

Fighting for sexual liberation and equality is so much more than fighting for the right to marry. But the positioning of marriage equality becomes a trope for promoting homonormativity at the hands of these operators. Marriage as an issue sets up the requirement that all relationships should mimic the heteronormative standard of sexuality and family structure. It is defined by the bundling of various privileges and standings as a single, strait-jacketed, lucrative package. The argument for gay marriage might appeal to many people because it is a shortcut to equalising these practical social advantages. Inspiring gay couples into the legal sorting machine that is marriage, would not confirm the relevance of spousal status. Instead it would leave unmarried queers looking more deviant before the legal system that could claim broader legitimacy. The queer subject itself is discursively produced by the law and is interpellated in structures of legality through the registers of trauma/pain/abuse. Whether unmarried or married, any kind of official legality of relationships brings it into the direct radar of institutionalised administration. The main force that drives this tendency is the claim that sexuality needs to be organised by the service of reproductive relations. It promotes the idea that all people want to emulate straight, monogamous couples. When we focus only on this particular issue, we exclude polyamorous and other non-normative relationship structures from the scope of acceptability, including those who simply don't desire to get married. Even as marriage becomes inclusive of a particular kind of queer relationship, it perpetuates a policing of other manners of relationships, maintaining the borderline of what is an 'acceptable queer relationship'. The focus on marriage challenges very little, and it prioritises the legal sanctioning of one's relationships over relational and societal transformation.

'Queer' is a notoriously slippery term that resists precise definitions. There are, nonetheless, a number of core values that are shared in different combinations, and with different emphases by queer political movements. From the beginning, queer political activism developed in dialogue with the queer theorising, which emerged in parallel to it in the late 1980s. It adopted queer theory's post-modern, post-structuralist and social constructionist approaches to sexual and gender identity and attempted to operationalise these in political praxis. On the one hand, queer movement is a sense of enormous possibility of a new social world coming into being. On the other hand, there is a sense of closure of potentials seemingly realizes, and of questions now answered.

Queer activism requires sociality, but that sociality takes the form of a commons in which the radical, creative possibilities that the commons enables must also to some extent, be enclosed within itself in order for those possibilities to thrive. In this context, the use of the term 'commons' denotes the people from the queer community who have formed a public space. Sometimes marginal, it bears the possibility of challenging the status-quo. Thus it always ends up reproducing certain disciplinary apparatuses which were to be refuted in the preliminary stage. This is one of many tensions between the ethics of de-normalisation and some sort of recourse to norms.

How these Advertisements are Failing the Queer Politics?

These popular advertisements aided by the corporate sectors continue to dismantle collective politics, and privatise the political element today. They promote a class of politics that does not contest dominant heteronormative assumptions and institutions such as marriage and its call for monogamy and reproduction. But it upholds and sustains them while promising the possibility of a demobilised gay constituency and a privatised, depoliticised gay culture anchored in domesticity and consumption. Since the late 1970s, a variant of conservative politics that can be termed as the 'New Right' burst onto the western political scene. Closely related to neoliberalism, the New Right contained a number of disparate conservative currents. The New Right was active on a number of political fronts, some of which went beyond the concerns of neoliberalism. The term is borrowed from the essay 'Neoliberalism, the New Right and Sexual Politics' by Lesley Hoggart in *Neoliberalism: Critical Reader* (2005, 149-156). The New Right adherents were economic liberals but defenders of the traditional family. If I take the liberty of superimposing this idea to post-1990s India, then the State allied corporate sector with its monolithic national identity seems to have tried to bind people of varying sexualities by heterosexual ideals.

Every social practice can be termed as a junction where political, cultural and economic processes intersect. Social democratic movements have always played into the hands of corporate sectors that reaped the benefits out of the situation for profit. Similarly, queer rights are being co-opted and used by these privatising sectors initially to showcase their pretense to be a part of feminist movements as a tokenist form of social welfare. But deep down, it bears the threat of homonationalism. The term is a coinage by Professor Jasbir K. Puar that reflects on the intersection of gay identity and nationalist ideology. In a more specific definition of 'homonationalism,' Puar contends that this "brand of homosexuality operates as a regulatory script not only of normative gayness, queerness, or homosexuality, but also of the racial and national norms that reinforce these sexual subjects" (Puar 2). Now the term homonationalism became pertinent in the aftermath of the legalisation of same-sex marriage in June 2015 in America. These victories have created space for the homonationalist queer who abandons intersectional activism and advocates racist, xenophobic, capitalistic self-interest.

Homonationalism involves conceptually realigning the ideas invested within the realm of LGBT activism to fit the goals and ideologies of neoliberalism and the far-right. But in India, the benevolent players like different corporate sectors in the garb of social welfare attempt to realign socially privileged queer people within the nation-state, through patriotism, nationalism and support for a nation's military and other forms of state violence. Ultimately, it all boils down to the nation's grip over people's varying sexualities .Through the dangling hope of visibility and acceptance, the progress has been used to nullify intersectionality.

It is however under this useful concept of homonormativity that we can examine how each issue is tied to the next so that we can begin the work of challenging them from this larger connected framework of understanding. In order to challenge the homonormative structures stacked up against us, we must work from a place that supports inclusivity, grassroots organising, coalition building, a global queer solidarity, and a consistent intersectional analysis and it is important for us to remember history: The queer rights movement's beginnings were based on radical politics that consistently challenged corporate capitalism, the military, and the heteronormative structure of marriage. It is by honouring this legacy of radical politics and prioritising the needs and voices of those most marginalised that we can truly work toward greater sexual and gender liberation and equality.

Having said what I have, I must conclude on the note that there are few advertisements that represent the open-endedness of queer lives. In one Fastback ad bearing the tagline 'Move on', we see two girls literally coming out of the closet and they go their own ways. It is important to note that popular culture through social media and independent journalistic pieces are also in a way facilitating the course of queer movement. They have the potential to gain visibility, like several interviews of Pakistani trans model Kami Sid where she has talked about her politics. These videos are hugely shared on social media and bear the potential to form a mass movement in a short span of time or attempt to resist certain homophobic practices. Social media has proved to be a powerful vehicle for bringing feminist issues to the attention of a wider public, galvanising action on the streets of cities around the world and encouraging policy makers to step up commitments to gender equality. Beyond its use as a social networking tool, social media allows for the first time any individual to share narratives and opinions with a global audience, bypassing traditional media or other modes of information transmission. But queer spaces, including online space(s), need to be continually interrogated and challenged — especially if these spaces reproduce homonormative ideals. Gay and lesbian media continue to contribute to the production of a homonormative and homonationalist entity, allowing for the reproduction and exclusion of 'the other', the invisible, of the 'bad' queer subject who is neither respected, nor represented as a legitimate subject of the nation.

BIBLIOGRAPHY

Appadurai, A. (1996). *Modernity at Large: Cultural Dimensions of Globalization.* Minneapolis, MN: University of Minnesota Press.

Dave, N. N. (2012). *Queer Activism in India: A Story in the Anthropology of Ethics.* Durham: Duke University Press.

Ebaydotin. (2016). 'eBay India-Things don't judge'. Retrieved from <https://www.youtube.com/watch?v=_ZOW6W4DK-M> on 14 December 2016.

Jabong. (2016). 'Be You: Discover All Things Fashion-TVC' Retrieved from https://www.youtube.com/watch?v=9h5BFXMz_XU&t=12s on 7 January 2016.

Myntra. (2015). Anouk, Bold is Beautiful—A Wonderful Video Titled 'The Visit'. Retrieved from https://www.youtube.com/watch?v=Ef27m5ocK6Q on 28 December 2016.

Oza, R. (2006). *The Making of Neoliberal India: Nationalism, Gender, and the Paradoxes of Globalization*. New York: Routledge.

Puar, J.K. (2007). *Terrorist Assemblages: Homonationalism in Queer Times*. Duke University Press.

Fastrack. 'Fastrack—The Closet'. 4 April 2013. Web. 23 December 2016. <https://www.youtube.com/watch?v=fmk9D53G6F8>

Hoggart, L. (2005). 'Neoliberalism, the New Right and Sexual Politics'. *Neoliberalism: A Critical Reader.* (Eds.) A. Saad-Filho & D. Johnston. London: Pluto Press.

Imtiaz, S. (2017). 'Pakistan's first trans model: 'People think we're sex workers but we can be doctors'. Retrieved from < https://www.theguardian.com/lifeandstyle/2017/may/01/pakistans-first-trans-model-people-think-were-sex-workers-or-beggars-but-we-can-be-doctors-or-engineers> on 6 June 2017.

CHAPTER 13

Masculinity in the Bengali Comic Strips of the 1960s

Sourav Chatterjee

'Might will be right, and shame will cease to be': The 'Bengali effete' and the Comic Strips

The representation of masculinity, one might observe, in the Bengali comic strips of the mid-twentieth century was a direct revolt against the colonial constructions of 'the Bengali effete', the insult which held sway from the late eighteenth century to the early twentieth century. This contempt was inchoate around the 1770s when the British historian Robert Orme in the *History of the Military Transactions of the British Nation in Indostan* (1861-62) thought all Indians showed 'effeminacy of character' but that Bengalis were 'still of weaker frame, and more enervated disposition than the rest' (Rosselli, 1980, 123). This insult became a common trend by the time T.B. Macaulay wrote in his essay 'Warren Hastings' (1843) that:

> [t]he physical organization of the Bengali is feeble even to effeminacy. He lives in a constant vapour bath. His pursuits are sedentary, his limbs delicate, his movements languid. During many ages, he has been trampled upon by men of bolder and more hardy breeds. Courage, independence, veracity, are qualities to which his constitution and his situation are equally unfavourable. (Rosselli, 1980, 122)

The British conservative newspaper *Spectator* on 9 May 1868 published an article entitled 'Hindoo 'Civilians' and their Value', which mentioned that by this period members of the Bengali elite society were aware that the British had certified them as unmilitary and cowardly, in a word, effete: 'soft-bodied little people', who could none the less compete with Englishmen in civil service examinations (Rosselli, 1980, 122). The Tagore family as well as other Bengali intellectuals and social leaders by the 1860s and 1870s appropriated the stereotype (Rosselli, 1980, 123). Thus began the internalisation of this insult, as these early English educated elites were convinced of their own effeteness and finally admitted that they were "lilliputian in size and weak in constitution", "physically about the weakest people in India", "in mere physique and courage ... inferior to Englishmen" (Rosselli, 1980, 123).

Rajnarayan Basu, the intellectual of the Bengal Renaissance in his *Ékāl ār Sékāl* [*This Time and That Time*] in 1874 wrote that the symptoms of physical degeneration accompanied varied complaints about young people who had strayed from conventional norms of manners and morals, and a result of which they became less happy in their family lives, lost the capacity to laugh and "lost their politeness" (Rosselli, 1980, 124). The English educated elites often thought that for physical downfall, environment was to be blamed: either the climate (Macaulay's "vapour bath") or the fertility of the soil, which made it unnecessary to exert oneself, or both. Diet of the educated Bengalis was equally to be blamed as they either ate too much or too little. Above all, educated Bengalis had concentrated to excess on their studies: from where all types of ills, from indigestion and brain fever to 'the feeble development of muscles' emerged (Fig. 1) (Rosselli, 1980, 124).

Fig. 1: Kafi Khan's Khooro depicts the workout of the Bengali *babu* in the *akhra* who simultaneously struggles to overcome his revolting corpulence. *Kafi Khan Samagra* (2012), Lalmati Prakashan, p. 298.

The system of English education, thus Rajnarayan Basu concluded, was "a machine for killing human beings" (Rosselli, 1980, 124). The hypermasculinity promoted by the imperialist ideology made the figure of the weak and effeminate *babu* a special target of contempt and ridicule. The colonised literati internalised this insult and inflicted upon itself a fierce barrage of self-ridicule through their literary publications. Bankim Chandra Chatterjee, the celebrated nineteenth century Bengali author, wrote in his essay 'Anukaran' ('Imitation') that the creator devised the extraordinary character of the modern Bengali by taking the grains of bestiality from all animals, slyness from the fox, sycophancy and supplication from the dog, cowardliness from sheep, imitativeness from the ape and volubility from the ass, and by a combination of all these, the Modern Bengali shines in the firmament of the society.' (Chatterjee, 1997, 61-62).

In 1905, Sir James Dunlop Smith, the private secretary to the Viceroy Lord Minto, wrote that the Bengalis were a 'low lying people in a low-lying land...with the intellect of a Greek and the grit of a rabbit' (Rosselli, 1980, 121). The stereotype of the Bengali effete was prevalent throughout the British rule. From the mid-nineteenth century to the 1930s, Bengalis strove to ameliorate this detrimental notion of their supposed degeneracy through the pursuit of physical culture. And in order to overcome the undesirable state of their humiliation they sought to remedy in physical culture and martial arts.

It so happened that the members of the Tagore family and their allies in the Adi (Original) Brahmo Samaj were the ones who launched the first response to the stereotype of effeteness. In 1866, Rajnarayan Basu's prospectus of a *Nationality Promotion Society* put revival of 'the national gymnastic exercises' first among the society's tasks, followed by the publication of tracts in Bengali giving instances of 'the military prowess of the ancient Bengalis' (Rosselli, 1980, 127), and the reform of the Bengali diet. In the following year (1867), members of the Tagore clan launched the Hindu Mela (Fair), an annual festival in Calcutta which combined displays of handicrafts as well as cultural and sporting events. It was termed as the 'National Gathering' by its promoters. From the start, the Hindu Mela under its chief organizer Nabagopal Mitra made much of gymnastics, wrestling and other traditional sports. In 1868, Nabagopal set up a gymnastics school from which there later developed a well-known though short-lived National School. Within a few years, he trained and sent out several physical education teachers and founded a number of *akharas*. In 1876, Bipin Chandra Pal founded a secret society with the intentions to develop physical culture and train all adults in handling weapons (Rosselli, 1980, 127). Shib Chunder Bose 'The Hindoos as they are' (Calcutta, 1881) predicts that a society,

> ... whose constitution is folded in diplomacy cannot be a fit subject to be congratulated upon, its sight makes us sick, and the heart in despair seeks for the more bracing atmosphere of reality elsewhere. Our role is patience, and our faith rests upon a future not yet seen. The young man of the future, our heart tells us, will be very different (Rosselli, 1980, 126).

It was only in the wake of the 1965 Indo-Pak War that the 'young men of the future' were conceived of in the form of Bengali comic strips as evident in the first publication of *Bñãtul the Great* in the May-June, 1965 edition of the *Shuktara* magazine. Jeffrey A. Brown explicates that comic book masculinity has been strongly elevated in superhero comics to the sphere of the exclusively hypermasculine. The descriptions of comic book masculinity are perhaps 'the quintessential expression of our cultural beliefs about what it means to be a man' (Brown, 2001, 168). He also writes that the male identity in the twentieth century 'is perceived in extremes: man or mouse, he-man or a ninety-eight-pound weakling. At one end is the hypermasculine ideal with muscles, sex appeal, and social competence; at the other end is the skinny and socially inept failure' (Brown, 2001, 167). Here, masculinity is not defined relatively, by how it is not feminine, but by its entire associated traits of being hard, strong, reserved and active (Brown, 2001, 168) (Fig 2):

Fig. 2: Taming a wild elephant? Not one of the greatest tests of masculinity for Bñātul. Bñātul Samagra (2014), Den Sahitya Kutir, p. 626.

Susan Bordo noted that a masculine body often operates as a symbol for coding the 'naturalness of sexual difference' (Brown, 2001, 169). Hence, over the ages, the muscular body is read as signs of male superiority and masculine power while women who develop noticeable muscularity are often accused of transgressing gender roles, and are designated as too 'manly' (Brown, 2001, 169). The body of Bñātul is then an important object of sociological study (Fig. 3). His hard male body armoured with muscles and a forty-inch chest has the status and power of a superhero. This idealised masculinity in the superhero myth is caused due to the split between the 'soft other' and the 'hard male', and it is hard to overlook the obvious homophobic and misogynistic view of this status (Brown, 2001, 169).

Fig. 3: Bñātul in the Indo-Pak War of 1965. Aug-Sep 1966, Shuktara. Narayan Debnath Comics Samagra, Vol. 1 (2013), Lalmati Prakashan, p. 25.

Masculinity also plays a very special role in the theme of comic-book retributivism. It can be differentiated from normal defensive aggression in two ways—first, it occurs after the damage has been done, and hence it is not a defence against a threat, but of a much greater intensity; and second, it is often cruel, lustful and insatiable. The problem of vengeance and retribution is thus a social problem, which arises from an elementary sense of injustice that must be resolved in the complex interaction between the victim, the perpetrator, and the social group (Fromm, 1974, 271).

The Roaring Sixties: Comic Strips Production in West Bengal

Alan Moore writes: 'Some people thought it was war and others thought that it was flying saucers, but those things weren't really bearing down upon us. What was really bearing down upon us was the 1960s'. (*Watchmen* #3, 1986, 32). In West Bengal, 1965 to 2015 turned out to be the epoch of Narayan Debnath. He single-handedly ruled these fifty years and has dwarfed all his contemporary comics illustrators like Mayukh Chowdhury, Soilo Chakraborty, Goutam Karmakar and others with the range and ever-expanding nature of his corpus. Narayan Debnath is the illustrator of the celebrated comic strips and graphic narratives *like Nanṭē ār Phōnṭē, Hṃādā Bhṃōdā*, *Patalcṃād* the Magician (Fig. 4), *Bāhādur Bēḍāl, Śṃutki ār Mutki, Pētuk Māstār Bṃātuklāl* (Fig. 5), *Ḍānpitē Khādu ār tār Chemical Dādu* (Fig. 6), *Indrajīt Rāy ō Black Diamond, Detective Kauśik Rāy, Citrē Durgēśnandinī, Rabi-chabi, Chabitē Bibēkānanda* and *Bñātul the Great.*[1] Debnath's interest in the style, form and medium of the comic strips was an eclectic one. His illustrations were influenced by the comic art of Wilhelm Busch, Dudley W. Watkins, James Crighton, Norman Rockwell, Alex Raymond, and John Prentice.

The times of living dangerously demanded a resurrection and a simultaneous exploration of the figure of the Bengali superhero, Bñātul the Great. Bñātul's protean nature makes him more than just a superhero—he is 'one of us'. He is the representation of the working class heroes, of the supermen and superwomen of everyday life. Bñātul among all his contemporary comic characters emerges to be the most absurd, real, altruistic and ideologically driven.

Scott Bukatman and Frederic Wertham come across as two most important scholars in the domain of superhero studies whose influence is insurmountable. Bukatman and Wertham deal with the politics of the superhero at a very basic level. The universal paradigms of the figure of the superhero propounded by Bukatman and Wertham have fostered analyses of the characteristics of various Bengali comic-strip superheroes in the context of post-colonial West Bengal. Scott Bukatman wrote that superheroes 'embody social anxiety' and reflect the 'ambivalent and shifting attitudes towards flesh, self, and society' (Hatfield, Heer, and Worcester, 2013, xiii). Bukatman also observed that the superhero is 'a figure of great independence who chooses to serve the laws and moral values of our society' (Bukatman, 2013, 171). Bñãtul's independence lies not only in serving the laws and moral codes of the society but also in serving his personal self. The occasional retreat into the self from the society as depicted in the illustrations where he is either dozing off, relaxing or out on an angling trip are symbolic of his free will. Moreover, Frederic Wertham's attack on the comic book superheroes and their inherent fascism in his 1954 book, *Seduction of the Innocent,* remain one of the seminal texts which reveal the negative influences and the malignant nature of this superhero genre. Bukatman and Wertham are two sides of a coin. Bukatman's optimism and Wertham's cynicism seem to locate the figure of the superheroes in a dialectical space that explores the grand paradoxes of their existence. The extensive repository of Bengali comic strips, cartoons and graphic narratives from 1950 to the present can be employed to examine the periods of social reconstruction in post-Independence (1947) West Bengal. The critical capabilities of the genre of Bengali comics have long been neglected in Indian literary history. The engagement of the comics of this period with political history is likewise under-researched.

The above-named comic-strip superheroes entered the literary scene in a time that was marked by a number of critical events in a momentous period of post-Independence West Bengal: the roaring forties, the decadent fifties, the Sino-Indian War (1962), the birth of Left Politics in Bengal (1964), the death of Jawaharlal Nehru, India's first Prime Minister (1964), the Indo-Pak War (1965), the Naxalbari

Uprising (1967), the Bangladesh War of Liberation (1971), and the Emergency (1975-77). These events had several prodigious impacts on the five decades of production and dissemination of the comic strips. Moreover, the 1960s were the cradle of comics culture in West Bengal that witnessed a massive rise in readership following the publication of Narayan Debnath's *Hṃādā Bhṃōdā* in 1962. The monthly and weekly periodicals like *Shuktara*, *Nobokollol*, *Sandesh*, *Anandamela*, and *Kishore Bharati* where these comics were published are now preserved by Dr. Abhijit Gupta (Professor of English, Jadavpur University) under the 'The Comic Book Project' of The School of Cultural Texts and Records (SCTR) at Jadavpur University.

The graphic texts cited above are a vessel, a viaticum and a simulacrum of West Bengal's past, and a close reading of those texts is expected to show how they were able to penetrate, portray, caricature and critique some of the turbulent phases of West Bengal's history. Bengali comics and graphic narratives never came under the radar of critical inquiry for cultural critics. Ritu G. Khanduri's book, *Caricaturing Culture in India: Cartoons and History in the Modern World* (2014) which apparently traces the history of cartooning in India has no mention of Kafi Khan—the creator of the first comic book in colonial Bengal—nor of any other Bengali cartoonist or comic strip illustrator. Other comic book theorists like Pramod K. Nayar and Karline McLain who claim authority on Indian comics but dabble solely in *Diamond Comics* (1960), *Indrajal Comics* (1964) and *Amar Chitra Katha* series (1967) have constantly neglected the idiosyncratic nature of contemporary comics in West Bengal.

'And Never the Twain Shall Meet': On the Medium of Bengali Comics

The realistic nature of the comics of Narayan Debnath, Mayukh Chowdhury and others is derived from its simplified illustrations (Fig. 7, Fig. 8, and Fig. 9). Scott McCloud said that cartooning is a form of 'amplification through simplification' (McCloud, 1994, 30). When an image is stripped to its essential meaning that meaning is amplified better than any realistic art. Here, before we proceed any further, it is necessary to outline the basic differences between cartoons and comics. Observations on the form of comics are varied, eclectic and contestable[2] and for a better understanding, this thesis resorted to the most widely circulated and readily comprehensible ideas regarding the medium. Scott McCloud's analysis of the form of comics[3] in *Understanding Comics: The Invisible Art*, is considered to be essentially broad, yet provisional for critics and practitioners.

Figs. 4 & 5: John Prentice's Rip Kirby[4], and Narayan Debnath's Kauśik Rāy in *Sarpōrājēr Dvipē*, Narayan Debnath Comics Samagra, Vol. 1 (2013), Lalmati Prakashan, p. 402).

McCloud defined comics as: '[j]uxtaposed pictorial and other images in deliberate sequence, intended to convey information and/or produce an aesthetic response in the viewer' (McCloud, 1994, 9). The cartoon form here differs from the comics form in a way that cartoons have single-panel images, while comics unfold over multiple frames and deviate from the regular interval of space (Chute, 2008, 454).[5] Moreover, the gutter—the blank space between the panels of illustration—that 'plays host to much of the magic and mystery' (McCloud, 1994, 66) at the heart of the comics is the only element of comics that remains unduplicated in any other medium. The 'closure' or our mental process that bridges the spatio-temporal incompleteness of the diegesis in the 'gutter' allows readers to participate in the completion of the narrative. Scott McCloud describes 'closure' as the everyday process of 'observing the parts but perceiving the whole' (McCloud, 1994, 63). He argues, '[i]f visual iconography is the vocabulary of comics, closure is its grammar. And since our definition of comics hinges on the arrangement of elements, then, in a very real sense, comics is closure' (McCloud, 1994, 67).[6] Moreover, this 'hybrid word-and-image' comics form does not coalesce the visual and the verbal, neither does it use one to illustrate the other, it rather presents the two 'nonsynchronously' (Chute, 2008, 452).

Comic strips, according to Noël Carroll are a mass art, whose mass scale production and distribution in the twentieth century have expanded massively due to the invention of information technologies (Carroll, 1998, 1-2). But the culture of mass art, as Umberto Eco writes, was also a move toward an 'anti-culture' or rather anti-high culture, since it arrives when the presence of masses in the realm of the society becomes the most fascinating phenomenon of the age (Eco, 1994, 21). Literary critics like Harold Bloom and Jeffrey Hart have censured the study of comics in colleges and scholarship as irrelevant and facetious. They also argued that comic books are too playful to address the pressing issues of any time (DiPaolo, 2011. 6). However, it seems, Debnath and his fellow illustrators believed that the best way to redress and strengthen societal norms was through the dissemination of morally informed art to the masses that would propagate the terms of dominant civic morality and act as instruments to pacify the mobile population.

Illustrators and editors of comic books in Bengal have defined comics and graphic narratives as stories in picture and picture stories respectively (Gangopadhyay, 2015, 3). In the light of the extremely fecund comics scholarship in the Western academia, this minimalist definition of Bengali comics is inadequate for a critical venture. The delineations of Bengali comics are embedded in a completely different cultural matrix. South Asian comic book theorists are insouciant to consider Indian comics as anything but 'variations on the master narrative' from the West, which as a result, further relegates this genre to a position of marginality in West Bengal (Chakrabarty, 2000. 27). To analyse the form of comics for a postcolonial critic in total ignorance of the Western theoretical frameworks and their conceptual paradigms, is to provide an incomplete and an 'outdated' project, which would further smear the credibility of the work (Chakrabarty, 2000. 28). The time has not yet come to 'return the gaze' (Chakrabarty, 2000. 29), so this thesis must endure the rites of passage and contend itself with the borrowed theories from the Western comics historiography. The form of the Bengali comics cannot define themselves; they must be defined. And in the quest for a definition, one is compelled to go back to its Western precedents.

Fredric Wertham, a New York psychiatrist in his book, *Seduction of the Innocent,* published in 1954, anticipated the negative influences of comic books on children. Wertham in his book unabashedly castigated the entire enterprise of comic strips and comic books for their publication for mass consumption where *Superman* and *Donald Duck* were no less than 'adult-oriented horror and crime comic books' (Gordon, 1998, 2). Wertham's virulence toward the medium of comics was apprehended as a threatened reaction to a new form of mass culture that was beyond the jurisdiction of the cultural elites (Gordon, 1998, 2). In the United States, the academic reciprocation towards the comics culture was a hostile one, while in West Bengal it was that of indifference. Bengali comics of the second half of the twentieth century, according to the masses, politicians or intellectuals, did not even possess a destabilising potential toward the socio-political motor. Bengali comics posed no threats and had no status except light-hearted entertainment. This is one of the major reasons why comics scholarship in West Bengal after fifty years of production and circulation of Bengali comics is still suffering from a dearth of serious academic research.

With the publication of the first critical book on the great comic book heroes in the 1960s (Jules Feiffer's *The Great Comic Book Heroes*, 1965), along with other secondary materials, there emerged a widespread minimalist notion of the superhero comics as necessarily 'formulaic, masculinist, melodramatic, and morally reductive' (Hatfield, Heer, and Worcester, 2013, xiii). The celebration of the imagery of the American superhero, rather than its analysis, became a major drawback for the magical yet marginal position of the superhero comics in contemporary popular culture.

Figs. 6 & 7: L-John Buscema's *Hercules* #1006[7], July 1959 and R-Mayukh Chowdhury's *Ẏatrī*, Mayukh Chowdhury Comics Samagra (2016), Lalmati Prakashan, p. 167)

It is beyond doubt that Narayan Debnath and Mayukh Chowdhury were equally influenced by the Golden (1930-1950), Silver (1956-70) and Bronze Age of American Comic Books (1970-85). They strongly inculcated, appropriated and modified these formulae to forge their narratives and characters. Mayukh Chowdhury's list of influential comics is mentioned in his 1996 article, "কমকিস যখন গল্প বলে!" (When Comics Tell Stories!), which includes Alex Raymond and John Prentice's *Rip Kirby,* Alex Raymond's *Flash Gordon*, Neal Adams' *Green Lantern*, John Buscema's *Conan the Barbarian* and

Hercules, Lee Falk's *The Phantom* and *Tarzan* by Burne Hogarth (the person whom he hailed as the "Michelangelo of the comic world") (Maji and Ghosh, 2016, x)

Narayan Debnath and Mayukh Chowdhury were aware of the dismissive tags that were attached to the medium, but they threw down their gauntlets to define the purpose, idiosyncrasy and objective of action, and adventure comics in West Bengal. Narayan Debnath through his *Bñãtul*, *Indrajīt Rāy* and *Kauśik Rāy*, and Mayukh Chowdhury through his *Robinhood* series, *Agantuk*, *Andha Mākōḍs*ā and *Rāmdhanur Sandhānē* (Fig. 11) retaliated against the monolithic ideas of the superhero comics genre as 'an adolescent male power fantasy' (Maji and Ghosh, 2016, x) that were considered incapable of expressing thought-provoking visions and accused of being conformist and juvenile.

Conclusion

'Bengali comics' under the broader topic of 'Indian comics' was not established as a separate genre until the *Amar Chitra Katha* series/'Immortal Pictorial Tales' (henceforth ACKs) was introduced by Anant Pai in 1967 (Mathur, 2010, 176). Suchitra Mathur observed that ACKs were a deliberate nationalistic enterprise, which involved a retelling of Indian myths, legends, and history in the form of graphic narratives to 'create a visually coherent 'Indian' cultural tradition' (Mathur, 2010, 176). These comics intentionally set themselves apart from the Anglo-American comic tradition in both style and form. The larger-than-life heroes were easily recognised, as they belonged to specific socio-cultural contexts. In the 1960s along with ACKs, the establishment of the two comic book publishers in India—Diamond Comics (1960) and Indrajal Comics (1964)—resurrected the figure of the superhero in the Indian comics tradition with the initial publications of American superhero comics like *Mandrake*, *Spiderman*, *Superman* and *Phantom* in Hindi translations (Mathur, 2010, 176). It was only with the publication of *Bñãtul* that India received its first strange, distinct, and hypermasculine superheroes who created a new kind of verbal-visual literacy for the masses.

REFERENCES

1. All transliterations throughout this thesis follow the National Library at Kolkata Transliteration Scheme with the sole exception of the nasal *candrabindu* in *Bñātul* (*ñ* instead of ṃ).
2. For the various definitions of the comics form, see: Will Eisner, *Comics & Sequential Art* (Florida: Poorhouse Press, 1985), 8; Thierry Groensteen, *The System of COMICS* (Mississippi : University Press of Mississippi, 2007), 21-22; Ian Gordon, *Comic Strips and Consumer Culture: 1890-1945* (Washington: Smithsonian Institution Press, 1998), 7-11; Greg Hayman and Henry John Pratt's pictorial narrative in 'What Are Comics?' in *Aesthetics: A Reader in Philosophy of the Arts* (Second Edition), eds. Lee B. Brown and David Goldblatt (New Jersey: Pearson Prentice Hall, 2005), 423; Aaron Meskin, 'Defining Comics?' *The Journal of Aesthetics and Art Criticism* 65, no. 4 (Autumn, 2007), 369-379; Hillary Chute, 'Comics as Literature? Reading Graphic Narrative,' *PMLA*, 123, no. 2 (Mar., 2008), 452; Henry John Pratt, 'Narrative in Comics,' *The Journal of Aesthetics and Art Criticism* 67, no. 1, Special Issue: The Poetics, Aesthetics, and Philosophy of Narrative (Winter, 2009): 107-117; Roy T. Cook's mereological pictoral thesis in 'Do Comics Require Pictures? Or Why Batman #663 Is a Comic,' *The Journal of Aesthetics and Art Criticism* 69, no. 3 (SUMMER 2011), 285-296.
3. McCloud writes that comics is 'plural in form, used with a singular verb', *Understanding Comics*, 9.
4. http://davekarlenoriginalartblog.blogspot.in/2008/11/national-cartoonist-society-profile.html.
5. Kafi Khan (1900-75) was the master of drawing gag cartoons that were heavily influenced by the political cartoons and caricatures of the cartoonist David Low. Gag cartoons are single-panel drawings with verbal captions beneath. Biswadeb Gangopadhyay, 'Introduction', *Kafi Khan Samagra*, eds. Biswadeb Gangopadhyay and Pradip Gorai (Lalmati: Kolkata, 2012), 7.
6. Henry John Pratt says Scott McCloud's choice of the word 'closure' is 'unfortunate', as the term has been used to refer to the resolution of narrative tension for a long time besides its usage in epistemology. Pratt is not involving in a semasiological study of the term, but is rather delineating that other words like

'suture' from film theory (to sew a film together from various elements) can also be used to understand this concept. Pratt coins the terms 'soldering' and 'bridging', but decides not to use in the light of the prominence of McCloud's 'closure'. See: "Narrative in Comics", 111.

7. https://beachbumcomics.blogspot.in/2015/10/the-strongest-man-in-world-hercules.html?m=1.

BIBLIOGRAPHY

Brown, J.A. (2001). *Black Superheroes, Milestone Comics, and Their Fans.* Mississippi: Mississippi University Press.

Bukatman, S. (2013). A Song of the Urban Superhero. In J.H. Charles Hatfield (Ed.), *The Superhero Reader* (pp. 170-198). Mississippi: Mississippi University Press.

Carroll, N. (1998). *A Philosophy of Mass Art.* New York: Oxford University Press.

Chakrabarty, D. (2000). Postcoloniality and the Artifice of History. In *Provincializing Europe: Postcolonial Thought and Historical Difference* (pp. 27-46). Princeton: Princeton University Press.

Chatterjee, P. (1997). A Religion of Urban Domesticity: Sri Ramakrishna and the Calcutta Middle Class. In P.C. Pandey (Ed.), *Subaltern Studies VII* (pp. 40-68). Delhi: OUP.

Chowdhury, M. (2016). 'কমকিস যখন গল্প বলে' ['When Comics Tell Stories']. In T.M. Ghosh (Ed.), *Mayukh Chowdhury Comics Samagra* (Vol. 2, pp. vii-xii). Kolkata: Lalmati.

Chute, H. (Mar., 2008). Comics as Literature? Reading Graphic Narrative. *PMLA, 123*(2), 452-465. doi:http://www.jstor.org/stable/25501865.

Debnath, N. (2014). *Bantul Samagra.* Kolkata: Deb Sahitya Kutir.

DiPaolo, M. (2011). *WAR, POLITICS AND SUPERHERO: Ethics and Propaganda in Comics and Film.* North Carolina: McFarland & Company.

Eco, U. (1994). Apocalyptic and Integrated Intellectuals: Mass Communications and Theories of Mass Culture. In R. Lumley (Ed.), *Apocalypse Postponed.* Indiana: Indiana University Press.

Fromm, E. (1974). *The Anatomy of Human Destructiveness.* USA: Holt, Rinehart and Winston.

Gangopadhyay, B. (Ed.). (2015.). *Comics-o-Graphics: Chobite Golpo, Golper Chobi [Comics and Graphics: Stories in Pictures, Pictures Stories]* (Vol. 1). Kolkata: Book Farm .

Ghosh, C.L. (Ed.). (2013). *Narayan Debnath Comics Samagra* (5 Vols.). Kolkata: Lalmati.

Ghosh, T.M. (Ed.). (2013). *Mayukh Chowdhury Comics Samagra* (Vols. 2 and 3). Kolkata: Lalmati.

Gordon, I. (1998). *Comic Strips and Consumer Culture: 1890-1945.* Washington: Smithsonian Institution Press.

Introduction. (2013). In J.H. Charles Hatfield (Ed.), *The Superhero Reader* (pp. xi-xxii). Mississippi: Mississippi University Press.

Khan, K. (2008). *Kafi Khan Samagra.* Kolkata: Lalmati.

Mathur, S. (2010). From Capes to Snakes: The Indianization of the AmericanSuperhero edited by. In J.A. Mark Berninger (Ed.), *Comics as a Nexus of Cultures: Essays on the Interplay of Media, Disciplines and International Perspectives* (pp. 175-186). Jefferson: McFarland.

McCloud, S. (1994). *Understanding Comics: The Invisible Art.* New York: Harper.

Moore, A. (1986). *Watchmen.* NY: DC Comics.

Pratt, H.J. (Winter, 2009). Narrative in Comics. *The Journal of Aesthetics and Art Criticism, 67* (1, Special Issue: The Poetics, Aesthetics, and Philosophy of Narrative), 107-117. doi: http://www.jstor.org/stable/40206394.

Rosselli, J. (Feb. 1980). The Self-Image of Effeteness: Physical Education and Nationalism in Nineteenth-Century Bengal. *Past & Present* (86), 121-148. doi:http://www.jstor.org/stable/650742.

PART VI

The Popular and the Digital Media

CHAPTER 14

Popularising the Myths: Auteurism in Recent Web-Films

Sayanty Chatterjee

Mythology in the Realm of the Popular

A story, a legend passed down over time from one generation to the other, first in the oral form and gradually in the written format, is what we conventionally perceive as a myth. With time, myths become an inevitable part of the social system, rites and customs and invariably get assimilated into religion and ceremonies. In his life-long endeavour of incorporating myths in contemporary literary and social ambit, Claude Lévi-Strauss has remarked that myths 'get thought in man unbeknownst to him', that it describes 'a lived experience' (Lévi-Strauss, 1978, 3). Mythology, thus evokes several thoughts in man with each passing generation. The regenerative effect of mythology has resulted in the various experimentations with them throughout all the ages. It resurfaces in each age in renewed shapes and forms. The exemplary incident of the most popular rendition of the epic, *Mahabharata* took place in Indian television from 1988 to 1990 produced by B.R. Chopra. That particular representation of the grand epic received almost a cult status because of its grandiloquence and its socio-political situation. It was aired at a socio-political juncture when the production of this show had a specific politically motivated agenda, i.e., the propagation of a unitary Hindutva ideology. As one of the earliest trysts of popular media with mythology in globalised times, the show marked the advent of globalised economy in Indian popular media. It is to be noted here that cinema's preoccupation with the portrayal of mythological figures is a well-known phenomenon since its inception. We have several examples like *Raja Harishchandra* (1913), *Sant Tukaram* (1936) and so on. However, only recently we witnessed the ubiquitous influence of the myth in the realm of the other popular cultural mediums as well. In this article, the endeavour is to discuss one of such mediums, web-mediated short films based on mythology as a part of the project undertaken by popular new media. The article would focus on two specific short films, *Ahalya* (2015) directed by Sujoy Ghosh and *Mama's Boys* (2016) by Akshat Verma to understand the underlying enthusiasm with regard to the re-exploration of mythological figures in popular culture. While the first film, *Ahalya* is a crime thriller, *Mama's Boys* is a comical approach to a very famous event from the mythological epic of *Mahabharata.* But incidentally, both these short films centre around the figures marginally represented in the otherwise grand scope of the epics. The effort seems to be almost a postmodernist one, in Lyotard's term, positing 'metanarratives' to challenge the grand narrative structure (Lyotard, 1984, p. xxiv). Since the primary medium to be dealt with in this paper is film, the argument would be informed by a theory of film studies, popularly known as Auteur theory.

Auteur Theory and Popular Digital Media

Arising in France in the late 1940s, the auteur theory was largely derived from Alexandre Astruc's ideation of the concept of caméra-stylo («camera-pen»). The term, however, was later coined by the American film critic, Andrew Sarris. The theory considers that the director, who supervises all audio and visual elements of the motion picture, is more to be perceived as the 'author' of the movie. The 'authorial' influences of the director get more importance than the plot-line or the narrative. The intent was to safeguard the artistic and creative freedom of the director in the face of market and production economy. The origins of auteur theory lies in the critical output of the magazine, *Cahiers du Cinema*, largely associated with French New Wave. Applying this method to the short films to be discussed, the 'texts' in hand can be argued as creations of their respective directors than mere retellings of the same narrative. In that scenario, the director becomes a viewer as well as a critic whose socio-cultural background plays a significant role in 'interpreting' the text and in this case, coming up with an alternative rendition. In this context we can cite Rachel Weissbrod who remarked upon the adaptation on Shakespearean plays thus:

> Every performance, theatrical or cinematic, implies an interpretation of the play. The very fact that the living actors read the dialogue, using intonation and body language, involves interpretation-theirs or the director's-even if the script used is very close to the original play. (Weissbrod, 2006, 44)

The engagement of the popular culture with mythology is nothing new. But with the technological advancement and with the rise in digital and self-publishing, more and more voices from the periphery are emerging, often with an agenda of empowering the reimagined version of the mythological figures. Similar attempts have been made by Pratibha Ray in her *Yagnaseni: the Story of Draupadi* (1995) and by Chitra Banerjee Divakaruni in *The Palace of Illusions* (2008). Although both are retellings of the hyper-masculine epic from Draupadi's point of view, there is a stark shift in the telling from the 'other' to the self. Where Ray painted Draupadi as a woman who took pride in being the perfectly devoted wife, Divakaruni's heroine unabashedly craves for the love of two more extraordinary men—Karna and Krishna. (Chanda-Vaz, 2017) Another author famous for her feminist revisionist mythological stories is Kavita Kané. Her first novel was titled *Karna's Wife: The Outcast's Queen* (2014), which narrated the story of Karna from the perspective of his (fictional) wife, Uruvi. It is interesting that Kané chose to introduce an entirely new character to tell Karna's story in the space of mythological fiction. Her later publications like *Sita's Sister* (2014), and *Menaka's Choice* (2015) trace the untold journeys of these two female figures to empower them with agency. Her latest book *Lanka's Princess* imagines Surpanakha more than just a lustful demoness whose nose was cut off by Lakshman. Amish Tripathi's *Shiva Trilogy* (2010-2013) opens up new horizons for distribution and new marketing strategies, making these renditions of the myths popular but also commercially successful. The nuances attributed to the otherwise marginal stories of the epic are undoubtedly due to the intervention of the popular media into the collective consciousness of the mythologies. The particular case of web-mediated short films is even more intriguing considering their wide accessibility and even wider scope of consumption. These web-films not only popularise the mythological characters but also make us rethink about the very premise of the popular and the blurring line between high and low cultural products.

The Transgression in *Ahalya*: The Myth vs. the Modern

The new take on the Ahalya myth, Sujoy Ghosh's *Ahalya* (2015) is complex, layered and captivating. The short film throws fresh light on the discourse of sexuality and infidelity in the known story of Ahalya. In its limited time-span, the film succeeds to reveal a dark, much more nuanced side to the character of Ahalya. In an aesthetically decorated, beautiful old Kolkata house which is the abode of our modern-day Ahalya, she is no longer a victim of sexual deceit. Rather from the very beginning, she is portrayed as a seductress. The way she opens the door to the police officer, Indra Sen who came to investigate the famous artist Gautam Sadhu, Ahalya's husband for an alleged abduction and missing person case determines the mood of the film. The camera captures her sensual movements as she invites Indra Sen to their drawing room and glides through their house. The settings, the mise-en-scène of the room in terms of the curious placement of an apparently magic stone which can turn anybody into any form capture the tone of the short film quite aptly. Even more intriguing is the presence of the miniature statues of real people, which we would later realise are cast in the images of men who were trapped through clandestine treachery by Gautam Sadhu with the help of none other than his wife, Ahalya. In fact, in the film we hear Gautam attributing all of his creations to Ahalya. "All of my creations are because of her. Every inch of her inspires me." All of these collectively build the suspense and the storyline. Unlike the mythic Ahalya, her transgression is wilful and does not bear any stigma of shame.

There are at least five different versions of Ahalya, Gautam and Indra's sex triangle available in Hindu mythology. The most popular version is mediated from the *Ramayana*, but all of them have the same plotline. Ahalya is the beautiful, young wife of the old sage Gautam. Indra, the god of gods becomes captivated with lust upon seeing the beauty of Ahalya. In Gautam's absence, Indra appears at their home disguised as Gautam and engages in love-making with Ahalya. After the return of the real Gautam, Ahalya realises that she has been deceived by the fake Gautam who is still in her bed. Infuriated at the deceit, Gautam curses both Ahalya and Indra (who has, for some ineffable reason, turned into a cat by then). Indra (by now, de-felined) becomes *sahasrabhagavat* — or one with thousand vulvas although this curse eventually turned out to be more useful for Indra. The vulvas turn into eyes allowing him to literally keep an eye on everything. In an astoundingly prescient transition that is richly prophetic, Indra goes from 'sex-obsessed to a potentially creepy voyeur'. (Pal, 2017) In spite of Ahalya's incessant pleading, Gautam could not accept the gullibility and treachery of Ahalya. Consequently, she was cursed by him to be a stone for many years until Ram rescues her, in the *Ramayana* version. In another rendering, she was reduced to a skeletal hag and one of the earliest retellings claims that Ahalya was turned into a dried-up river. (Pal, 2017).

In this cinematic edition, Ahalya does not get retribution for her infidelity; rather Indra gets trapped into a miniature statue curated by Gautam Sadhu. The myth of Ahalya gets redefined and rewritten as Gautam Sadhu becomes an equally responsible accomplice in the act of crime. Interestingly, transgression and seduction is a common thematic streak that runs through the short film, *Mama's Boys* as well. Transgression takes place primarily in the context of the mainstream, or the norm, and its boundaries. Michel Foucault claims in his essay, 'A Preface to Transgression':

> Transgression is an action which involves the limit, that narrow zone of a line where it displays the flash of its passage, perhaps also its entire trajectory, even its origin; it is likely that transgression has its entire space in the line it crosses. The play of limits and transgression seems to be regulated by a simple obstinacy: transgression incessantly crosses and re-crosses a line which closes up behind it in a wave of extremely short duration, and thus it is made to return once more right to the horizon of the uncrossable. (Foucault, 1977, 33-34)

In the book, *Against and Beyond: Subversion and Transgression in Mass Media, Popular Culture and Performance*, Magdalena Cies`lak and Agnieszka Rasmus valorised transgression as an integral concept in representation as they borrow the Foucauldian paradigm of transgression while discussing areas such as subculture, gender, identity, taboo, form, or aesthetics in various mediums of performance, television and cinema. Paradoxically, in Hindu scriptures, both Ahalya and Draupadi are considered to be one each of the 'panchayakanya' who are the archetypes of female chastity and the mere recital of their names washes away sin and impurity.

Ahalya Draupadi Kunti Tara Mandodari tatha/Panchakanya smaranityam mahapataka nashaka, roughly translated to mean that one who always remembers the five great women, Ahalya, Draupadi, Kunti, Tara, and Mandodari—is saved from all manner of sin and failure. (Pal, 2017)

Ostensibly, Ahalya's story is a covert warning to women who cross or try to cross the 'limits' of domesticity, patriarchy or sexuality. It is much like Sita's literal transgression of crossing the 'limits' of Lakshmanrekha. The exploration of uninhibited sexuality is what sets this rendition apart from the other Ahalya myths.

Mama's Boys: A Satirical Narrative of *Mahabharata*

A humourous interpretation of *Mahabharata, Mama's Boys* was written and directed by Akshat Verma from the *Delly Belly* fame and was released in 2016. The appeal of the *Mahabharata* is truly an enthralling one in popular Indian psyche. Ashis Nandy comments on the ubiquitous influence of the *Mahabharata*:

> Of the two epics (*Ramayana* and *Mahabharata*)..., the *Mahabharata* is the one that underpins the Indian consciousness. It serves as a mythography of the Indian self and, at the same time, as a record of the disowned selves within culture. (Nandy, 2001, 10)

Consequently, we can anticipate numerous renditions surrounding the epic narrative of the *Mahabharata*. However, this particular version attracted backlash from fundamental Hindutva groups on the ground of its blatant projection of sexuality and promiscuity and tampering with the original narrative of the Pandavas.

In response to the accusations, in an interview with *Hindustan Times*, Akshat Verma clearly mentions that his is not an "adult Mahabharata. I made it from the point of what went on in the minds of characters. Bhaiyo ne kya socha hoga, Draupadi ne kya socha hoga and all. (What did the brothers think, what were Draupadi's thoughts and all)." (Verma, 2016)

Mama's Boys is, in fact, a sharp satire under the garb of comedy. The story revolves around the unfortunate mistake by Kunti upon hearing that Arjun had brought 'something' followed by her command to share "it" among the brothers. That 'thing' turns out to be Draupadi whom Arjun 'conquered' from her *swayamvar* with his heroic prowess. Arjun's failed attempts at convincing his mother by proclaiming "bhaajiya nahi laya hun" (I have not brought vegetables) is a comical twist to the sad realities of the archetypal Draupadi myth. Arjun in this cinematic version, on being unable to contest his feisty mother on his own, tries to make all the other four siblings to renounce their claim on Draupadi. The question of safeguarding/asserting one's masculinity over a conquered object or in this case on a female body is an issue that the film manages to raise within its narrow scope.

The short film throws up new possibilities relating to the characters known to us since time immemorial. The youngest Pandavas, Nakul and Sahadev are projected as the probable closeted homosexuals who accuse Arjun of harbouring 'repressive view of sexuality'. While Bhim is an avid worshipper of fitness training regimes, Judhisthir is an incurable gambler, playing for money with Kauravas and Shakuni. The most interesting aspect of this short film is not projecting Draupadi as a victim *par excellence*; rather she is excited at the idea of exploring her sexuality with three different men. One can understand the problem of the conservative groups with this short film. This version gives birth to the multiplicity of meanings and the possibility of various interpretations of the epics that the fundamentalists desperately try to obliterate. This proclivity towards creating a unitary 'myth', necessarily stemming from our current political milieu, can be well understood through the official exclusion of the text of *Three Hundred Ramayanas* by A.K. Ramanujan from Delhi University graduation curriculum in 2011. Much along the lines of the film, the essay by Ramanujan talks about the multitudinous approach to the epic which debunks the entire project of unitary and linear narration. On the other hand, it is this concept of promoting plurality that had been a consistent project of the popular production.

Another exciting aspect about this representation is that, the auteur has decided to keep the entire ensemble of the royal costumes with the thrones, jewelleries and all, even in an ultra-modern adaptation of the narrative. The authorial influence of peculiarity is evident in the otherwise mythical story, which proclaims that myths can be played out in any plane, even within the parameters of the most mundane quotidian realities of life.

Conclusion

In his book, *Structural Anthropology*, Claude Lévi-Strauss has compared myth with language, "functioning on an especially high level where meaning succeeds practically at 'taking off' from the linguistic ground on which it keeps on rolling." (Lévi-Strauss, 1963, 210) Thus, meaning is mediated through these popular cultural domains, not only by language but in the context of auteurism through camera work, mise-en-scène, costumes and thought processes of the characters. As a result, these cultural products transcend the boundary of the merely mythical and become popularised versions of the mythology with streaks of evidential authorial interventions.

While reading these films, the question that invariably arises is, what is the objective of the popular? Is it the mere commodification of the existing genres? Or is it a new category in itself? Or is it an approach to subvert the very concept of categorisation itself? In conclusion, popular becomes a category that incorporates the cultural practices and our way of life in order to delineate an alternative version of the known narratives of mythology. Both the short films discussed in this article serve that purpose.

BIBLIOGRAPHY

Ahalya. (2015). Dir. Sujoy Ghosh. Boundscript Productions.

Chanda-Vaz, U. (2017). 'Indian Mythology is a New Medium of Choice for Feminist Narratives (and it's Working)'. Retrieved from *scroll.*

in on 9 February 2017. <https://scroll.in/article/828515/indian-mythology-is-a-new-medium-of-choice-for-feminist-narratives-and-its-working>

Cieslak, M. & Rasmus, A. (2012). 'Introduction'. *Against and Beyond: Subversion and Transgression in Mass Media, Popular Culture and Performance.* United Kingdom: Cambridge Scholars Publishing.

Foucault, M. (1977). 'A Preface to Transgression.' *Language, Counter-Memory, Practice.* (Ed.) Donald F. Bouchard. (Trans.) Donald F. Bouchard & Sherry Simon. New York: Cornell University Press. pp. 29-52.

Lévi-Strauss, C. (1963). *The Structural Anthropology*. (Trans.) Claire Jacobson & Brooke Grundfest Schoepf. New York: Basic Books Inc.

Lévi-Strauss, C. (1978). *Myth and Meaning*. Routledge: London.

Lyotard, Jean-François. (1984). *The Postmodern Condition: A Report on Knowledge.* (Trans.) Geoff Bennington & Brian Massumi. Minneapolis: University of Minnesota Press.

Mama's Boys. (2016). Dir. Akshat Verma. Flying Unicorn Productions.

Nandy, A. (2001). *An Ambiguous Journey to the City: The Village and the Other Odd Ruins of the Self in the Indian Imagination*. New Delhi: Oxford University Press.

Pal, D. (2015). 'Seen Sujoy Ghosh's Ahalya? Here are Myths of Sex and Infidelity that Inspired the Film'. Retrieved from *Firstpost.com* on 5 February 2017. < http://www.firstpost.com/entertainment/seen-sujoy-ghoshs-ahalya-heres-myth-sex-infidelity-inspired-film-2358486.html>

Verma, A. (2016). 'Mine is not an Adult Mahabharata, says Akshat Verma.' Interviewed by Ruchika Garg. Retrieved from *Hindustan Times* on 6 February 2017. <https://www.hindustantimes.com/bollywood/mine-is-not-an-adult-mahabharata-says-akshat-verma/story-DHSE8Cl3q5sQduYuDFW0KO.html>

Weissbrod, R. (2006). 'Inter-semiotic Translation: Shakespeare on Screen'. *Journal of Specialised Translation*. Issue 5. pp. 42-56. < http://www.jostrans.org/issue05/art_weissbrod.pdf>

CHAPTER 15

Reimagining Pride and Prejudice in the Age of Tumblr

Naomi Jose

The Novel Form and New Media

Milan Kundera in his essay 'The Depreciated Legacy of Cervantes' (Kundera, 2000, 1) connects the beginning of the Modern Era with the emergence of the novel. For Kundera, what is at the heart of a novel is the 'wisdom of uncertainty' and in a period when answers are readily and easily given, the novel has no place. The spirit of the novel, one that challenges the singular perspective, is now challenged by the process of reduction and simplification that comes with the spread of mass media.

> The novel's spirit is the spirit of continuity: each work is an answer to the preceding one, and each work contains all the previous experience of the novel. But the spirit of our time is firmly focused on a present that is expansive and profuse that it shoves the past off our horizon and reduces times to the present moment only. Within this system, the novel is no longer a work (a thing made to last, to connect the past with the future) but one current event among many, a gesture with no tomorrow. (Kundera, 2000, 18-19)

What is intriguing though about what Kundera proposes is the connection he sees between the death of the novel and the role the media plays now in disseminating information. Kundera's essay was a response to the political atmosphere of the 1960s: hence his concern about how the media was shaping opinion and not allowing space for reflection. The 'din of easy quick answers' that he talks about in the essay is perhaps louder now than it was while he was writing the essay what with the advent of the internet. In the face of new media forms like YouTube, tumblr and Twitter what happens to the novel? How does the novel respond to these new media? Is the novel form really dead? This seems an unnecessarily bleak vision of the future of the novel and perhaps Kundera is wrong. If the novel has indeed died then what has replaced it?

In order to be able to say what has replaced the novel, it would perhaps be helpful to start off by defining what exactly is being replaced in the first place. Defining the novel though is a fraught exercise as there is no one definition of the novel as is evident from the works of Henry James, Northrop Frye, Tsvetan Todorov, Mikhail Bakhtin, Ian Watt and so on and so forth. However, since the concern here is Kundera's definition of the novel and its subsequent death, the focus will be on the feature of the novel that he considers most significant—the 'wisdom of uncertainty' that the novel provides, its 'spirit of complexity.'

What Kundera identifies as key to the function of the novel is remarkably akin to Theodor Adorno's own understanding of what it is that art does. For Adorno art, is the ideal Other against which the subject understands itself as art is 'the most thoroughly subjective of objects' (Huhn, 2004, 8). Consequently it forces subjectivity to constantly project and re-project itself against it. There can be no certainty with an art object as it constantly forces the viewer to reconsider what it means. As a viewer or a reader then one cannot either subsume or be subsumed by the art object or the novel.

The materiality of the art object, of the novel gives the impression of it being a distinct object; however as Adorno points out, the art object or in this case the novel is incomplete without the reader. The novel implicitly invites the reader to complete it by reading it. The novel is an 'image of the ongoing incompleteness of subjective activity' and thus works against the reification of subjectivity. It becomes an 'occasion for subjective dissolution and reconstitution' and this is possible only because its own subjectivity is incomplete without the viewer. (Huhn, 2004, 8)

Kundera's point is not simply that the media does not allow for differing opinions, but that it insists on a certain kind of absoluteness. There may be differing voices but each of those voices is absolutely convinced that they are right and do not allow for the possibility that perhaps there is no absolute right or wrong and that things are not as simple as they may seem. There is no space to discover different segments of existence or to recognise other kinds of subjectivity. As mentioned earlier though Kundera's understanding of what it is that the media does and what it allows for is one that takes into account the older media forms. The question then that emerges is whether the new media also does not invite the discovery of alternative subjectivities.

Given what Adorno identifies about the art object and thus about the novel as allowing for the 'wisdom of uncertainty' and 'spirit of complexity' that Kundera lauds, one could say that new media is not as far off from the novel form as Kundera understands it. New media is new precisely because it offers forms of connectivity that earlier forms did not and could not, allowing for forms of interactions that could not be imagined earlier, by virtue of the speed with which connections can be made with the aid of the internet. On the surface it would appear that it would be more likely therefore to encounter the 'din of easy quick answers' in the new media rather than an object which constantly challenges one to rethink one's own subjectivity. However, the new media is not a homogenous space and different kinds of production do allow for that 'wisdom of uncertainty.'

The Lizzie Bennet Diaries (LBD), a transmedia adaptation of Jane Austen's *Pride and Prejudice* is one such example of how the novel form can become a part of the space provided by the new media. By comparing LBD with *Pride and Prejudice* one can see how it is that productions in the new media can retain certain elements of the novel forms as well as transform them. Naturally whatever points of coincidence and departure one identifies between *Pride and Prejudice* and LBD are not necessarily universal and so one cannot use this as a way to theorise in general about what happens to the novel in the hands of new media, but LBD provides a useful starting point to think about what it is that the new media allows for.

Pride and *Prejudice* in the Twenty-First Century

The advantage of using an adaptation to examine the question of how it is that a novel is transformed by these new media is that the focus is then on how the original text is adapted in order to fit the new medium—what of the form and structure is retained from the original text? How much of a difference does the change in medium make to the original text? How much is it able to borrow from the original text? What elements of the original text have to be transformed in order for it to fit the new medium? In this paper I will be examining in particular how far LBD is able to retain elements of the form and structure *Pride and Prejudice* and what elements are transformed to fit the new medium in order to see whether the new media can potentially carry on the depreciated legacy of Cervantes.

To explain what it is about LBD that makes it an interesting case study when it comes to examining how it is that the novel is transformed by the new media it would perhaps be helpful to explain what LBD is. The Elizabeth Bennet of Austen's novel is transformed into a twenty-first century American version of the character—Lizzie Bennet is a mass communication studies graduate student, struggling with student debt and living in a house that is about to be mortgaged for the second time. *The Lizzie Bennet Diaries* refers to a series of videologs or vlogs by the eponymous character narrating her life story as part of her end of term project. While Lizzie's vlogs form a bulk of the universe of LBD, LBDverse is split up across tumblr, Twitter and YouTube with interactions on Facebook and Google+ as well. Lydia, Collins, Maria and Gigi also have their own vlogs. All of the characters including Bing Lee (the LBD version of Bingley), Caroline and Darcy have Twitter accounts. These tumblr and Twitter accounts maintained by the other characters serve to supplement the gaps that would otherwise occur given the shift from an omnipresent narratorial voice to a singular first person point of view narrative. They also serve to remind the audience that Lizzie's point of view is an incomplete one and a biased one.

Financial security and ownership are issues in both LBD and *Pride and Prejudice*, but where the original focuses on marriage as the means to ensure financial security, in the adaptation, the female characters are concerned with securing their own jobs. While marriage continues to be the main concern of the Mrs Bennet in this series, for Lizzie, Charlotte and Jane in the series, the central anxiety is what kind of job they will get after they are finished with their studies Their lack of financial security does not stem from their inability to inherit or possess property but rather from heavy student loans and mortgages. In Charlotte's case, the fact that her parents have already had to sell their own house and are living in an apartment is what makes her position more precarious than Jane and Elizabeth's rather than her age as it is in the novel. The conversation between Charlotte and Elizabeth about marriage and courtship that happens in the novel is transformed into a conversation about future job prospects with Charlotte cautioning Lizzie that success is dependent on chance. Instead of a proposal of marriage, Lizzie receives a job offer from Collins which she turns down as it doesn't match her expectations of what it is she wishes to accomplish through her job. Rather than aspiring to find love in marriage as it is in the novel, Lizzie wishes to find a job that would allow her a certain degree of independence which she feels a job in Collins' company Collins and Collins would not give her and hence her disappointment in Charlotte when she chooses to take up the job offer that Lizzie had rejected. The basic trajectory of the novel in terms of the development of Darcy and Elizabeth's relationship is left untouched but a lot of issues that those of us who have studied the novel would see as central to the novel—that of marriage, social mobility, property—are removed and replaced with twenty-first century equivalents.

Restructuring Narrative Form in the Space of New Media

This transformation of a nineteenth century novel into one that is more relevant to the time in which it is being produced is not something radical amongst the many adaptations of Jane Austen's works that are available, *Clueless* being one such example that immediately comes to mind. Where LBD stands apart as an adaptation is that it does not focus on just how the story itself could be replotted to fit today's context but also picks up on narrative elements in the text and then transforms those elements to cohere with the different media that it has used. The 2011 film version of *Jane Eyre* starring Mia Wasikowska which narrated the story through a series of flashbacks from the perspective of Jane Eyre while at St. John's is another example of an adaptation which has chosen to pay attention to not only the story but also the manner in which it was first narrated. It is this ability of the adaptation to pick up narrative elements of the novel and fit it to new media that allows it to recreate the novel so closely despite having radically changed in terms of plot points in order to fit the novel to twenty-first century conditions.

It seems odd to talk about LBD carrying over the narrative structure of the original novel because perhaps the biggest point of departure is that the bulk of the narrative is carried entirely by the voice of Lizzie Bennet through her videos, moving away from the gently ironic, authoritative narrative voice that is a part of the novel. There are two major elements of the novel's narrative structure that the adaptation is able to pick up on—one, the instances of metalepsis in the original narrative and two, the connection between market, medium and audience that shapes the concerns voiced by the narrative.

Metalepsis refers to those occurrences in a text 'when an author enters or addresses the fictional world he or she has created, and when characters leave their fictional world or address their author and their readers.' (Kukkonen, 2011, 1) The very famous first sentence of Austen's novel, 'It is a truth universally acknowledged...' is an example of metalepsis—a moment where the author chooses to break the wall that exists between the reader and the text, drawing the reader into the universe of the text. Another such instance could be found in Chapter 42 of the book.

It is not the object of this work to give a description of Derbyshire, nor of any of the remarkable places through their route thither lay: Oxford, Bleinham, Warwick, Kenilworth, Birmingham, etc. are sufficiently known. A small part of Derbyshire is all the present concern. (Austen, 1999, 162)

This awareness of the reader manifesting herself/himself through metalepsis and through the conversation of the characters is something that has been elided over in adaptations of *Pride and Prejudice* such as the 1995 BBC miniseries version as well as the 2005 film version starring Keira Knightley. However, LBD manages to retain this awareness of the reader, a function largely of its transmedia format. The advantage of portraying Lizzie as a mass communication graduate student is that her consciousness of her audience or 'the Internet' as she calls them is not out of keeping with the character that she is portraying. Like the omnipresent narratorial voice, she too is aware of the medium that she is using to communicate with her viewers and the limitations of that medium. Through her conversation with characters like Collins and Darcy who are both working in the field of new media, the series takes on a fairly meta tone.

Episode 10 is one such example. The vlog entitled 'Cats and Chinchillas' is uploaded by Lizzie in order to boost the number of viewers, betraying a consciousness of what is the kind of material that could 'break' the internet and drawing attention to the fact that platforms like YouTube, Twitter and tumblr depend on the audience in order to sustain themselves. One is only as successful as the number of hits one is able to generate. Consequently, content is modified in order to ensure the maximum number of hits.

In Episode 80 entitled 'Hyper-mediation in New Media' through a conversation between Lizzie and Darcy, the series is able to explore the issues of the limits of using a form like a vlog in order to narrate a fictional story and how it is that the use of costume theatre in a vlog draws attention to how what is being presented is a construction and not reality.

Lizzie: "Look. There's this theory about levels of mediation in media that says it's possible for artificiality to both remind the audience that what they're seeing is construction while at the same time adding to their level of immersion."

Darcy: "You thought that costume theatre as ourselves would remind the audience that this isn't a conversation we would naturally have. But because of that the obviously constructed nature of the scene would by its very artificiality create its own sense of... verisimilitude." (Dunlap)

Thus while in Austen's novel it is the use of an omniscient, omnipresent narrator that allows her to introduce instances of metalepsis in the novel, in the adaptation it is again the position of the narrator in relation to the medium being used that allows for instances of metalepsis. Metalepsis performs an important function in both the novel and its adaptation in that it serves to remind the reader or viewer that it is through their participation in the narrative of the novel or the video that they take on their own meaning and that which each new subjectivity encountered that meaning shifts.

In the novel, other than these brief interventions in the text by the narratorial voice there is also a strong consciousness of the relationship between the reader and the author that marks the conversation between various characters and in some ways informs the content of the novel itself. If one considers the letters that pass between the characters and their subsequent reading by different characters lending themselves to different interpretations—such as the letter first sent by Caroline Bingley and then read by Jane and Elizabeth, both coming away with different perspectives of Caroline's character—one could interpret it as an indirect reflection on the process of reading and how contingent it is on the disposition of the reader and their manner of interpretation. In LBD, this is achieved by having different characters script certain episodes of LBD. One such significant example is Episode 15 'Lizzie Bennet is in Denial' which does not even feature Lizzie but is entirely scripted by Charlotte and Jane allowing for a new perspective on Darcy. In addition to this, the vlogs by characters like Lydia and Maria demonstrate how one-sided Lizzie's interpretation of events can be. A common refrain voiced by multiple characters through LBD is that Lizzie sees what she wants to see. Thus the viewer is reminded that what they see in LBD is determined by what they wish to see. They can choose to limit themselves to Lizzie's perspective by only following her vlog or gain a fuller understanding of the LBDverse by following the vlogs and tweets of other characters in the narrative. In both the novel as well as the adaptation, this reflection on the position of the audience in relation to the text and their manner of interpretation act to remind how incomplete any depiction or understanding of reality is as there always is some element that lies beyond what is known.

Another instance of the concerns of the author about the relationship between the reader and the author being voiced through the content of the narrative occurs in the conversation between Elizabeth and Darcy at the Netherfield Ball when she reflects that both are 'unwilling to speak' unless they 'say something that will amaze the whole room, and be handed down to posterity with all the éclat of a proverb.' While ostensibly, here Elizabeth is making an observation on Darcy's character, the conversation could also be read as a reflection on how dependent the author was on their readership in order to ensure that their work succeeds and so Elizabeth acknowledges when she says that she cannot decide on her own performance.

This awareness of the reader that the text betrays at different points is in all likelihood a product of the conditions of publishing at the time that Austen was writing. Booksellers were no longer a rag-tag bunch, but gradually becoming a publishing industry capable of transforming what had earlier been limited to the domain of the elite into a product to be devoutly consumed. By forming alliances and partnerships known as congers, book traders were able to offset the risk that had plagued the industry for so long and thus they assumed a position of authority in the market.

The advent of congers meant that booksellers increasingly became producers of literature themselves. As an association of copyright-holding publishers who both ordered works to be printed and organised the selling of the books, the conger became a kind of book selling firm empowered to tell printers, and sometimes authors too, what to produce... Moreover, they manoeuvred the courts into preserving the traditional common-law system of enduring copyright protection so that they, and they alone, had the power to issue fresh editions of old as well as new works. The bookseller became the most influential figure in publishing. (Benedict, 2004, 6)

Between the control exerted by the congers, and the different methods of publishing offered by them, the kind of subscription publishing that came into vogue was slowly diminishing any author writing during the time Austen was. The authors would have been very conscious of how dependent they were on producing texts that would be read by a large number of people in order to ensure that their texts would have a shot at being published at all.

The shift then, from the omnipresent narratorial voice to the singular perspective in the light of this outcome could be read as a function of this drastic shift in the relationship between the producer i.e. the writer and the consumer i.e. the reader that took place due to the form of the media. The kind of direct appeal that Lizzie makes to her followers to ask questions and buy merchandise is reflective of the shift in the relationship between the producer and the consumer. The internet makes possible a level of input that earlier the reader would not have been able to provide. As the series was being broadcast simultaneously, viewers could communicate with the individual characters via their Twitter or tumblr accounts. Along with the regular vlog updates about her life, there are also a series of Q and A videos with Lizzie which answer questions raised by viewers on Twitter, YouTube, Facebook and tumblr which range from questions as banal as what the books on her shelf are to questions about Charlotte's love life and whether Bing had watched the vlogs and questioning why he had not by then. LBD works as an adaptation precisely because it chooses to abandon the narratorial voice of the novel recognising that in transforming this novel into something relevant to this century and the media that belong to this century that kind of omnipresent narratorial voice is no longer imaginable. Greater leeway has to be made for possible inputs by the reader and consequently it needed to adopt the kind of narratorial voice that would allow for that kind of interaction.

Conclusion

Whether the advent of these versions of the new media mark the disappearance of the kind of omnipresent narratorial voice that is almost ubiquitous in the nineteenth century novel is yet to be seen. What LBD though does make apparent is how rooted that kind of voice is in a particular kind of dynamic between the reader and the writer. It raises the question of what are the kinds of new narratorial voices that are now available to us through the new media because of the new dynamic between the producer and the consumer.

LBD as an adaptation works primarily because it is able to successfully translate elements of the original narrative as well as the structure to the new media without compromising on what it is that the new media allows for. What it is able to demonstrate is that the new media holds within it the possibility like the novel of providing the 'wisdom of uncertainty' and possesses the same 'spirit of complexity'. Whether all productions in a transmedia format are able to do so is debatable. The Lizzie Bennet Diaries though provides hope that the novel may not have died as Kundera wrote but that its spirit now inhabits a new medium.

BIBLIOGRAPHY

Austen, Jane. (1999). *Pride and Prejudice*. Hertfordshire: Wordsworth Classics.

Benedict, Barbara M. (2004). 'Readers, Writers, Reviewers, and the Professionalization of Literature.' *The Cambridge Companion to English Literature 1740–1830*. Ed. Thomas Keymer and Jon Mee. Cambridge: Cambridge University Press. pp . 3-23.

Dunlap, Margaret. (2013). *Hyper-Mediation in New Media*. Prods. Hank Green and Bernie Su. *Youtube*, uploaded by *The Lizzie Bennet Diaries* on 17 January 2013.

Genette, Gerard. (2001). *Paratexts: Thresholds of Intepretation*. Trans. Jane E. Lewin. Cambridge: Cambridge University Press.

Hawthorn, Jeremy. (2010). *Studying the Novel*. 6th ed. Cornwall: Bloomsbury.

Huhn, Tom. (2004). 'Introduction: Thoughts Besides Themselves.' *The Cambridge Companion to Theodor Adorno*. Ed. Tom Huhn. Cambridge: Cambridge University Press.

Kukkonen, Karin and Sonja Klimek. (2011). 'Metalepsis in Popular Culture: An Introduction'. *Metalepsis in Popular Culture*. Berlin: De Grutyer.

Kundera, Milan. (2000). 'The Depreciated Legacy of Cervantes'. *The Art of the Novel*. Trans. Linda Asher. London: Faber and Faber.

Lutas, Liviu. (2016). 'Storyworlds and Paradoxical Narration: Putting Classifications to a Transmedial Text.' *Narrative Theory, Literature and New Media*. Ed. Mari Hatavara, et al. Cornwall: Routledge.

Wood, James. (2009). *How Fiction Works*. London: Vintage.

Notes on the Contributors

Ananya Saha is a doctoral researcher at Centre for English Studies, Jawaharlal Nehru University, from where she has completed her Master's degree. Her research area comprises of Japanese popular culture, with a focus on manga and globalization. Her other academic interests include Popular Culture Studies, Translation Theory, Fandom, Gender, and Performance Studies. She has presented in international conferences in India and abroad, including a paper on 'football manga' is Basel University, Switzerland and performative poetry in Tübingen University. She has been the UGC Special Assistance Programme Fellow (2016-17) at Centre for English Studies, Jawaharlal Nehru University. She has been awarded a visiting research fellowship by DAAD to Tübingen University in 2018 under the 'Literary Cultures of Global South' Project.

Anindita Ghosh is an Assistant Professor of English Literature at Maitreyi College, University of Delhi. She completed her M.Phil from the Department of English, University of Delhi. She focuses on the popular Qissa tradition of Akbar and Birbal along with similar other storytelling traditions of Medieval India. Her primary areas are—Folklore Studies, Partition and Migration Literature, Historical Studies and Dalit Literature.

Bibiana Ryntathiang is an Assistant Professor in the Department of English, St. Mary's College of Shillong. She is currently working on her doctoral thesis entitled "Understanding American Comic Strips: A Select of *Calvin* and *Hobbes*, *Peanuts* and *Dilbert*" from the Department of English, North-Eastern Hill University, Shillong.

Naomi Jose is a doctoral scholar at the Centre of English Studies, Jawaharlal Nehru University. Her research is involved with the evolution of English literature departments and pedagogic practices in the Indian university spaces.

Prerna Trehan is a doctoral scholar in the Department of Political Science, Punjab University researching on the use of music as a tool of socio-political assertion by Dalits in Punjab. Her work looks at Chamars in the Doaba belt of Punjab and their traditions of music in three key moments in the region's history, the Ravidass movement, the phase of Leftist struggle, and lastly the rise of contemporary Chamar pop. She has completed her Masters in Political Science from Centre from Political Studies, Jawaharlal Nehru University.

Reeti Basu is a Doctoral candidate at Centre for Historical Studies, Jawaharlal Nehru University, from where she has completed her M.Phil on 'Scrolls, Songs and *Kavyas*. The Making of a *Patachitra* Tradition in Naya, 1950s-2010s'. She has received her Master's degree in Modern History from Presidency University. Her present work pertains to foreign soldiers in Bengal during the Second World War ear.

Rituparna Sengupta is a PhD scholar in literature at the Department of Humanities and Social Sciences, IIT Delhi. Her doctoral dissertation is on contemporary adaptations of the Ramayana and the Mahabharata in popular fiction in English. Her academic interests lie in the realms of mythology, adaptation, fantasy literature, graphic narrative, cinema, popular culture, and gender theory. Her essays on and reviews of books and films have appeared on various online and print platforms.

Saheli Biswas is an M.Phil scholar in the Centre of English Studies in Jawaharlal Nehru University. She has done her Master's from Jadavpur University. Her research interests include gender studies, South-Asian studies et al. She is currently working on Islamic feminism and the question of sexuality in South-Asia.

Samarth Singhal teaches English Language and Literature as Assistant Professor, University of Delhi. His research interests include Media Studies, Fantasy Studies, Children's Fiction, Art History, World Literature, and Detective Fiction. His M.Phil thesis titled "Indian Fantasy: Text and Image" attempted to think about the novel, the picturebook, and the graphic novel as manipulated national concerns. He has published on Manjit Bawa, Vikram Seth, Ravi Shankar, Aubtey Collette, and Agatha Christie.

Sanchita Khurana is a doctoral researcher in Visual Studies at the School of Arts and Aesthetics, JNU. Her interests revolve around Popular Cultures, Urban Space, Street/Community Art and Visual Culture. She works as Assistant Professor (ad hoc) in English at Indraprastha College for Women of the University of Delhi and is currently writing her thesis on the political economy of urban art practice in Delhi.

Sayanty Chatterjee has completed Masters in English from Lady Shri Ram College, University of Delhi, and M. Phil from University of Hyderabad. Her dissertation was entitled "Translating Shakespeare in Indian Cinema: An Analyses of *Maqbool*, *Omkara* and *Haider*". Presently, she is enrolled in PhD programme at the Department of Humanities and Social Sciences in IIT Madras, Chennai. She is working on the representation of small-town spaces in contemporary popular Hindi films.

Shreya Sangai has completed her Masters in literature from Ambedkar University, Delhi. Her Masters' thesis was on understanding conceptual frameworks of time within the Bhil worldview. She is interested in studying changes in the culture of the tribal communities. She is working in a full-time fellowship under a UGC major project titled "Narrative, Public Culture, and Visuality in Indian Comic strips and Graphic Novels in English, Hindi, Bangla and Malayalam (1947-present)".

Soumava Maiti PhD scholar in English Literature at the University of Delhi. He has completed his M.Phil in English from Visva-Bharati University on Memory and Storytelling in select novels of Salman Rushdie. He has also published articles numerous reputed journals.

Sourav Chatterjee is a PhD candidates in the Middle Eastern, South Asian and African Studies Department (MESAAS), Columbia University. His current research interest lies in the Bengali comics, graphic narratives and cartoons of the 1960s. He is also interested in questions of the literary comic tradition and masculinities in colonial Bengal and postcolonial West Bengal.

Vandana has completed her Master's and M.Phil degree in English from the University of Delhi. Her M.Phil dissertation was titled "The Politics of Literary Historiography and a Case for a Historiography of Dalit Literature". She currently works as an Assistant Professor of English in Daulat Ram College, University of Delhi. Her research areas comprise of Autobiographies and Life narratives, Dalit Aesthetics, the Progressive Literary Movement, South Asian Literary Historiography, and Indian Literature.